Professional Plone Development

Building robust, content-centric web applications with
Plone 3, an open source Content Management System

Martin Aspeli

PUBLISHING

BIRMINGHAM - MUMBAI

Professional Plone Development

First published: September 2007

Production Reference: 1190907

Published by Packt Publishing Ltd.
32 Lincoln Road
Olton
Birmingham, B27 6PA, UK.

ISBN 978-1-847191-98-4

www.packtpub.com

Cover Image by Vinayak Chittar (vinayak.chittar@gmail.com)

Credits

Author

Martin Aspeli

Reviewers

Andrew Burkhalter

Jon Stahl

Marco De Vitis

Wichert Akkerman

Acquisition Editor

Nanda Padmanabhan

Development Editor

Rashmi Phadnis

Technical Editor

Kushal Sharma

Editorial Manager

Dipali Chittar

Project Manager

Abhijeet Deobhakta

Project Coordinator

Sagara Naik

Indexer

Bhushan Pangaonkar

Proofreader

Chris Smith

Production Coordinator

Shantanu Zagade

Cover Designer

Shantanu Zagade

Foreword

by Alexander Limi, co-founder of Plone

It's always fascinating how life throws you a loop now and then that changes your future in a profound way—and you don't realize it at the time. As I sit here almost six years after the Plone project started, it seems like a good time to reflect on how the last years changed everything, and some of the background of why you are holding this book in your hands—because the story about the Plone community is at least as remarkable as the software itself.

It all started out in a very classic way—I had just discovered Zope and Python, and wanted to build a simple web application to teach myself how they worked. This was back in 1999, when Zope was still a new, unproven technology, and had more than a few rough spots. I have never been a programmer, but Python made it all seem so simple that I couldn't resist trying to build a simple web application with it.

After reading what I could find of documentation at the time, I couldn't quite figure it out—so I ended up in the online Zope chat rooms to see if I could get any help with building my web application.

Little did I know that what happened that evening would change my life in a significant way. I met Alan Runyan online, and after trying to assist me, we ended up talking about music instead. We also reached the conclusion that I should focus on what I was passionate about—instead of coding, I wanted to build great user interfaces and make things easy to use. Alan wanted to provide the plumbing to make the system work.

For some reason, it just clicked at that point, and we collaborated online and obsessed over the details of the system for months. External factors were probably decisive here too: I was without a job, and my girlfriend had left me a few months prior; Alan had just given up his job as a Java programmer at a failed dot-com company and decided to start his own company doing Python instead—so we both ended up pouring every living hour into the project, and moving at a break-neck pace towards getting the initial version out.

We ended up getting a release ready just before the EuroPython Conference in 2002, and this was actually the first time I met Alan in person. We had been working on Plone for the past year just using email and IRC chat—two technologies that are still cornerstones of Plone project communication. I still remember the delight in discovering that we had excellent communication in person as well.

What happened next was somewhat surreal for people new to this whole thing: we were sitting in the audience in the "State of Zope" talk held by Paul Everitt. He got to the part of his talk where he called attention to people and projects that he was especially impressed with.

When he called out our names and talked about how much he liked Plone—which at this point was still mostly the effort of a handful of people—it made us feel like we were really onto something. This was our defining moment.

For those of you who don't know Paul, he is one of the founders of Zope Corporation, and would go on to become our most tireless and hard-working supporter. He got involved in all the important steps that would follow—he put a solid legal and marketing story in place and helped create the Plone Foundation—and did some great storytelling along the way.

There is no way to properly express how much Paul has meant to us personally—and to Plone—five years later. His role was crucial in the story of Plone's success, and the project would not be where it is now without him.

Looking back, it sounds a bit like the classic romanticized start-up stories of Silicon Valley, except that we didn't start a company together. We chose to start two separate companies—in hindsight a very good decision. It never ceases to amaze me how much of an impact the project has had since.

We are now an open-source community of hundreds of companies doing Plone development, training, and support. In just the past month, large companies like Novell and Akamai—as well as government agencies like the CIA, and NGOs like Oxfam—have revealed that they are using Plone for their web content management, and more will follow. The Plone Network site, plone.net, lists over 150 companies that offer Plone services, and the entire ecosystem is estimated to have revenues in the hundreds of millions of US dollars annually. This year's Plone Conference in Naples, Italy is expected to draw over 300 developers and users from around the world.

Not bad for a system that was conceived and created by a handful of people standing on the shoulders of the giants of the Zope and Python communities.

But the real story here is about an amazing community of people—individuals and organizations, large and small—all coming together to create the best content management system on the planet. We meet in the most unlikely locations—from ancient castles and mountain-tops in Austria, to the archipelagos and fjords of Norway, the sandy beaches of Brazil, and the busy corporate offices of Google in Silicon Valley. These events are at the core of the Plone experience, and developers nurture deep friendships within the community. I can say without a doubt that these are the smartest, kindest, most amazing people I have ever had the pleasure to work with.

One of those people is Martin Aspeli, whose book you are reading right now.

Even though we're originally from the same country, we didn't meet that way. Martin was at the time—and still is—living in London. He had contributed some code to one of our community projects a few months prior, and suggested that we should meet up when he was visiting his parents in Oslo, Norway. It was a cold and dark winter evening when we met at the train station—and ended up talking about how to improve Plone and the community process at a nearby café. I knew there and then that Martin would become an important part of the Plone project.

Fast-forward a few years, and Martin has risen to become one of Plone's most important and respected—not to mention prolific—developers. He has architected and built several core components of the Plone 3 release; he has been one of the leaders on the documentation team, as well as an active guide in Plone's help forums. He also manages to fit in a day job at one of the "big four" consulting companies in the world.

On top of all this, he was secretly working on a book to coincide with the Plone 3.0 release—which you are now the lucky owner of.

This brings me to why this book is so unique, and why we are lucky to have Martin as part of our community. In the fast-paced world of open-source development—and Plone in particular—we have never had the chance to have a book that was entirely up-to-date on all subjects. There have been several great books in the past, but Martin has raised the bar further—by using the writing of a book to inform the development of Plone. If something didn't make sense, or was deemed too complex for the problem it was trying to solve—he would update that part of Plone so that it could be explained in simpler terms. It made the book better, and it has certainly made Plone better.

Another thing that sets Martin's book apart is his unparalleled ability to explain advanced and powerful concepts in a very accessible way. He has years of experience developing with Plone and answering questions on the support forums, and is one of the most patient and eloquent writers around. He doesn't give up until you know exactly what's going on.

But maybe more than anything, this book is unique in its scope. Martin takes you through every step from installing Plone, through professional development practices, unit tests, how to think about your application, and even through some common, non-trivial tasks like setting up external caching proxies like Varnish and authentication mechanisms like LDAP. In sum, this book teaches you how to be an independent and skillful Plone developer, capable of running your own company — if that is your goal — or provide scalable, maintainable services for your existing organization.

Five years ago, I certainly wouldn't have imagined sitting here, jet-lagged and happy in Barcelona this Sunday morning after wrapping up a workshop to improve the multilingual components in Plone. Nor would I have expected to live halfway across the world in San Francisco and work for Google, and still have time to lead Plone into the future.

Speaking of which, how does the future of Plone look like in 2007? Web development is now in a state we could only have dreamt about five years ago — and the rise of numerous great Python web frameworks, and even non-Python solutions like Ruby on Rails has made it possible for the Plone community to focus on what it excels at: content and document management, multilingual content, and solving real problems for real companies — and having fun in the process. Before these frameworks existed, people would often try to do things with Plone that it was not built or designed to do — and we are very happy that solutions now exist that cater to these audiences, so we can focus on our core expertise. Choice is good, and you should use the right tool for the job at hand.

We are lucky to have Martin, and so are you. Enjoy the book, and I look forward to seeing you in our help forums, chat rooms, or at one of the many Plone conferences and workshops around the world.

— Alexander Limi, Barcelona, July 2007

```
http://limi.net
```

About the Author

Martin Aspeli has been active in the Plone community since 2004. He has contributed a number of new features since then, including the Plone 3 Portlets infrastructure and the Content Rule engine. He served on the Framework Team for Plone 3.0, acting as the team's spokesperson.

Outside the Plone core, Martin is responsible for popular third-party products, such as *Poi* (an issue tracker), *RichDocument* (a document type with attachments and inline images), and *b-org* (a user and group management tool). He also looks after the *PloneHelpCenter* and *PloneSoftwareCenter*, which power the Documentation and Products sections on plone.org, respectively.

A frequent attendee at conferences and sprints, Martin has presented several well-received tutorials, such as "Rich Document – Creating Content Types the Plone 2.1 Way", "b-org – Creating Content Types the Plone 2.5 Way", and the "Testing in Plone" manual. Acting as the de facto head of the Plone documentation team for well over a year, he has witnessed an explosive growth in the documentation available for Plone. He frequently answers questions from new users and developers online, and is well aware of the more common stumbling blocks for new Plone developers.

Martin gained an MSc in Analysis, Design, and Management of Information Systems at the London School of Economics in 2005. His thesis was entitled: "Plone – a model of a mature open source project".

The author would like to thank: Alexander Limi and Alan Runyan for starting such an exciting project; Jon "Active Voice" Stahl for language and grammar review; Andrew "Awesome" Burkhalter for language and technical review; Marco "The Guinea Pig" De Vitis for being a sharp critic; Wichert "LDAP" Akkerman for technical review, invaluable tips on LDAP, CacheFu, and PAS, and for being a great release manager; Balazs "KSS" Ree for review of the KSS chapter; Philipp "Zope 3" von Weitershausen for guidance and an excellent book on Zope 3; and finally, to the Plone community for playing host to so many good friends.

About the Reviewers

Andrew Burkhalter lives in beautiful Seattle, Washington, and is employed at ONE/Northwest, an environmental nonprofit that helps other organizations use new tools and strategies to engage people in protecting the environment. In just over two years, Andrew has helped launch over 100 Plone-powered websites. He also co-founded the Seattle Plone user group and assisted in the running of the 2006 Plone conference in Seattle. When not doing Plone projects, he likes to spend time with his supportive wife, Sarah. Or was that the other way around?

Jon Stahl has over ten years of experience providing online communications solutions and strategies to social change organizations. Jon works at ONE/Northwest, where he has helped build a thriving Plone consulting practice and has been an activate participant in the Plone community since 2005. Jon was also the primary organizer of the high successful 2006 Plone Conference.

Marco De Vitis lives in Rome, Italy, where he is getting a degree in Electronic Engineering while working freelance as a do-it-all computer guy. Keen on everything computer-related, with a sharp eye for detail and a passion for well-written language, he couldn't avoid falling in love with technical documentation, and has thus been translating and reviewing software localizations and manuals every now and then since 1997, often focusing on open-source projects. He enjoys listening to some good music while doing it.

Wichert Akkerman has been active in the ICT industry for over 10 years. He is well known in the open-source community where he has had roles as Debian Project Leader and Plone 3.0 release manager. Currently he works is an independent consultant, specializing in Zope and Plone.

Table of Contents

Part 2 – Customizing Plone

Part 4 – Real-world Deployments

Preface

Plone is an open-source content management framework, built on the top of the Zope application server and written in Python. As a ready-to-use Content Management System with a focus on usability, Plone makes it easy for content authors to create and edit web content.

Plone is also used by developers, as a framework for building content-centric web applications such as dynamic websites and intranets. This book focuses primarily on the developer-oriented aspect of Plone.

Throughout the chapters, there is an emphasis on demonstrating key concepts with practical examples. The reader should be able to borrow from the examples to get up and running quickly, but refer to the explanations provided to fully appreciate what is going on under the hood.

The book takes a pragmatic approach, building a realistic example application based on a case study. The code for this application is included with the book, and should serve as a useful starting point and source of examples for the reader.

What This Book Covers

Chapter 1 discusses Plone's history and community.

Chapter 2 introduces a case study, setting the scene for the rest of the book.

Chapter 3 teaches you how to set up a development environment, using zc.buildout to orchestrate various dependencies such as the Zope application server and Plone itself.

Chapter 4 looks at the various ways in which Plone can be customized and issues a few warnings about the perils of relying too much on persistent through-the-web settings that are difficult to reproduce across environments.

Chapter 5 concentrates on creating a *policy product* to manage site policy decisions and configuration settings related to the case study application. This is expanded with new policies in nearly every subsequent chapter. This chapter also emphasizes the importance of automated unit and integration tests.

Chapter 6 explores Plone's security model, and makes the case for using workflow as the primary tool for implementing a security policy by showing how to install a custom workflow using GenericSetup.

Chapter 7 demonstrates how to safely test, install, and customize Plone add-on products.

Chapter 8 deals with re-branding the growing case study application with a custom theme. It illustrates how to customize style sheets, templates, browser views, viewlets, and portlets—all without modifying the source code of Plone itself.

Chapter 9 delves deeper into the nine core concepts underpinning Zope and Plone development. Some of you may find this chapter a little fast-paced at first, and you may want to go back to it when you have had more time to see the described techniques in practice in the subsequent chapters.

Chapter 10 dives into the most important skill Plone developers need: building custom content types with the Archetypes framework. Here we will also create a custom portlet using Plone 3's new portlets infrastructure.

Chapter 11 describes forms and other types of browser views in more detail. Here we will use `zope.formlib` to generate forms with minimal configuration in Python. We will also be looking at ways of managing page flow, including the older CMFFormController product, and creating viewlets—snippets that can be *plugged in* to the standard user interface at various points.

Chapter 12 shows how to connect your application to an external relational database, using the SQLAlchemy library and a little bit of Zope glue. We will also be using some advanced features of the `zope.formlib` library to create a ticket reservations form and a Plone control panel to configure database connections.

Chapter 13 concentrates on how to manage personalized information, building a form and a portlet to track a user's *preferred* cinema.

Chapter 14 aims at improving the user experience of a few of the application's features by using KSS, the new AJAX framework adopted in Plone 3.

Chapter 15 describes ways in which the example application could be taken further and briefly covers issues of internationalization.

Chapter 16 shows how to move the example application from a development environment to a production server using ZEO (Zope Enterprise Objects) for improved scalability and resilience.

Chapter 17 describes how to configure Apache, the popular web server, and Varnish, a caching *reverse proxy*, in front of Zope, in order to improve performance, stability, and fault-tolerance.

Chapter 18 describes how to connect Plone to an LDAP repository providing authentication services and user properties.

Chapter 19 describes some tips on managing releases of a live application, and performing migrations.

Who This Book is For

This book is aimed at developers who want to build content-centric web applications leveraging Plone's proven user interface and flexible infrastructure.

Some familiarity with the Python programming language and basic web technologies such as HTML and CSS is assumed. Readers would also benefit from some prior experience with Zope or Plone, for example as site administrators or "power users".

Conventions

In this book, you will find a number of styles of text that distinguish between different kinds of information. Here are some examples of these styles, and an explanation of their meaning.

There are three styles for code. Code words in text are shown as follows: "We will assume that Python 2.4 gets invoked when you run `python` on the command line."

A block of code will be set as follows:

```
[buildout]
parts =
    plone
    zope2
    productdistros
    instance
    zopepy
```

When we wish to draw your attention to a particular part of a code block, the relevant lines or items will be made bold:

```
[buildout]
parts =
    plone
    zope2
    productdistros
    instance
    zopepy
```

Any command-line input and output is written as follows:

```
$ wget http://peak.telecommunity.com/dist/ez_setup.py
```

New terms and **important words** are introduced in a bold-type font. Words that you see on the screen, in menus or dialog boxes for example, appear in our text like this: "If you used the Windows installer, you can start and stop the instance from the **Services** control panel in **Administrative Tools**."

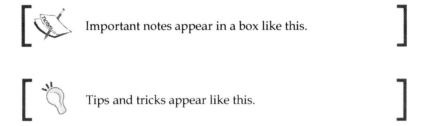

Important notes appear in a box like this.

Tips and tricks appear like this.

Reader Feedback

Feedback from our readers is always welcome. Let us know what you think about this book, what you liked or may have disliked. Reader feedback is important for us to develop titles that you really get the most out of.

To send us general feedback, simply drop an email to feedback@packtpub.com, making sure to mention the book title in the subject of your message.

If there is a book that you need and would like to see us publish, please send us a note in the **SUGGEST A TITLE** form on www.packtpub.com or email suggest@packtpub.com.

If there is a topic that you have expertise in and you are interested in either writing or contributing to a book, see our author guide on www.packtpub.com/authors.

Customer Support

Now that you are the proud owner of a Packt book, we have a number of things to help you to get the most from your purchase.

Downloading the Example Code for the Book

Visit http://www.packtpub.com/support, and select this book from the list of titles to download any example code or extra resources for this book. The files available for download will then be displayed.

The downloadable files contain instructions on how to use them.

Errata

Although we have taken every care to ensure the accuracy of our contents, mistakes do happen. If you find a mistake in one of our books—maybe a mistake in text or code—we would be grateful if you would report this to us. By doing this you can save other readers from frustration, and help to improve subsequent versions of this book. If you find any errata, report them by visiting http://www.packtpub.com/support, selecting your book, clicking on the **Submit Errata** link, and entering the details of your errata. Once your errata are verified, your submission will be accepted and the errata added to the list of existing errata. The existing errata can be viewed by selecting your title from http://www.packtpub.com/support.

Questions

You can contact us at questions@packtpub.com if you are having a problem with some aspect of the book, and we will do our best to address it.

Part 1

Getting Ready

Plone in Context

The Case Study

The Development Environment

1
Plone in Context

Over the past few years, Plone has grown from "Just another open-source Content Management System" into a platform, and from which many people make their living with hundreds of service providers worldwide. Big and small businesses, NGOs and charities, governments and individuals, are building websites, intranets, and specialized applications on top of Plone with great success.

Spurred by advances in Python and Zope, along with increased media attention and credibility, Plone has steadily improved over the past few years. Plone 2.1 (released 2005) and Plone 2.5 (released 2006) were largely focused on incremental improvements and laying the foundations for future leaps in functionality. Now, with version 3.0, Plone is once again delivering innovative and exciting new features.

In this chapter, we will place Plone in the context of modern web application development. We will consider how Plone fits in with the ongoing evolution of Zope, and how Zope 3 and newer Python technologies are changing web development practices. We will consider when Plone may be a good choice for solving your web development problems, and we will discuss why and how you may want to become part of the Plone community.

A Brief History

The history of Plone begins with Zope. Zope was, in the words of Paul Everitt, "the first open-source application server", and that is not the only way in which it was ahead of its day. Zope 2, on which Plone is built, started life as an environment in which power users could build web applications through the Web. It was at one point the *killer application* for the Python programming language, and has inspired various other applications and frameworks, as well as improvements in Python itself.

See Phillip J. Eby's foreword to Philipp von Weitershausen's excellent book *Web Component Development with Zope 3*, also available at `http://dirtsimple.org/2007/01/where-zope-leads-python-follows.html`

Zope 2 turned out to be a good platform for building content management systems, and the Content Management Framework (CMF) was born to make this easier. Eventually, CMF began to change some of the emphasis of Zope programming towards file system-based development and applications that could more easily be packaged up and re-deployed. It also brought us *tools*, *skins*, and many other concepts fundamental to Plone.

CMF ships with an example portal application called CMFDefault. It is fair to say that CMFDefault is not the prettiest of systems, and it is not widely used except as an example. Plone was born to make CMF pretty and user-friendly. It was initially a night-time collaboration between Norwegian Alexander Limi and Texan Alan Runyan, but other Zope and Python developers soon began to contribute as Plone's potential became clear.

Zope old-timers sometimes joke that Plone is "just a bunch of skins". As Plone grew in scope, however, it gained a lot more Python code. CMF components were customized and new functionality was added. Somewhere along the way, the Plone community probably lost touch a little with the CMF community and ended up inventing things that would have been better placed "further down the stack" at the CMF level, for better or for worse.

At the same time, Zope mastermind Jim Fulton and his band of renegades were creating Zope 3. The main premise of Zope 3 is that small, re-usable, easily testable, and well-documented components should be orchestrated into complete systems. It should also be possible to use them inside other Python applications. One such application is of course Zope 2. Via a piece of integration code called **Five** (Zope 2 + Zope 3 =?), it is possible to use a large number of Zope 3 components and concepts directly in Zope 2 applications such as Plone.

Zope 3 and Five revitalized the development of Zope 2. Zope 2.8 shipped with the components from Zope 3.0 as an add-on library. Zope 2.9 followed soon after, incorporating Zope 3.2; Zope 2.10, on which Plone 3 is built, contains Zope 3.3.

At the same time, more and more parts of Zope 2, CMF, and Plone were (and still are) being rewritten to make use of Zope 3 concepts and, where applicable, existing Zope 3 components. Some predict that Zope 2 and Zope 3 will eventually converge, becoming two different configurations of the same application.

If you find this confusing, you are not alone. A common misconception is that Plone 3 will run in a pure Zope 3 environment. This is not the case; doing so would most likely require re-writing Plone from scratch, and would break every third-party product and customization in use.

Zope 3 is simply not an upgrade to Zope 2, but a whole new way of building software. Whereas Zope 2 is a fairly monolithic application server, Zope 3 aims to be a collection of components and of technologies for pulling those components together. There are some who feel that the name *Zope 3* is unfortunate, and it should have been named something else altogether, so as to not imply a linear progression from Zope 2.

Although it may be confusing, the mixing of Zope 3 into Zope 2 has had a profound impact. Almost every new feature in Plone 3 relies on Zope 3 technologies in some way. Several developers report being much more productive than before, and say that Zope 3-style programming makes Plone development more fun.

Further, Zope 3 has brought the developers of Zope, CMF, and Plone closer than they ever were. The Goldegg Initiative, a sponsored effort to improve Plone's framework stack in ways that most customers would not be willing to pay for, helped set off a snowball that has seen major improvements in community relationships as well as in the code itself.

At the same time, the wider Python community, which sometimes views Zope with some suspicion, has been developing great tools of its own that the Zope community is busy adopting. The most important one is perhaps *eggs*, a way of packaging Python libraries for easier deployment and dependency management, somewhat similar to Java JAR files.

Not far behind is WSGI, the Python Web Services Gateway Interface, which defines ways in which Python web applications written in different frameworks can interoperate at the HTTP level. WSGI thus promises to let developers stitch together complete systems from multiple specialized applications. Zope 3 already supports WSGI, and various projects are under way to explore ways to integrate it better with Zope 2 and Plone.

Competition

Zope had little competition when it was first introduced in 1999. That is no longer the case. Ruby-on-Rails is probably the best known of the new breed of rapid application development frameworks, but Python has a few of its own: Django, TurboGears, and Pylons to name a few. Zope may go head to head with these through a new and exciting project called Grok, which aims to bring techniques such as convention-over-configuration to Zope developers by building a higher-level framework on top of Zope 3. Grok is not yet directly relevant to Plone development, but it is possible that Grok programming will one day be available to build Plone extensions.

The common theme running through all of these developments is greater interoperability. The Zope 2, Zope 3, CMF, and Plone communities are becoming more and more open to external influences, adopting code, standards, and tools from other projects and offering a few of their own in return. For example, the Twisted web server project uses Zope 3's `zope.interface` as its interface implementation, and Zope 3 is using Twisted's web server code to provide WSGI support.

The corresponding challenge is that there are many new tools and techniques with which Plone developers may want to be familiar. At the same time, some old tools and techniques have been superseded by new technologies. Keeping up with it all can be daunting. Hopefully, this book will help, by focusing exclusively on "new-world" techniques and current best practices.

Plone-the-Application and Plone-the-Framework

New users sometimes appear on the Plone mailing lists asking for a comparison of Plone and PHP, the popular web programming language. That is pretty crazy if you consider that PHP is a language and Plone is first and foremost a content management application. You can download Plone, put it on your server, configure a few options, perhaps install a third-party add-on product or two, and use it to solve your everyday content management needs.

Thus, *Plone-the-application* is used to power intranets, public websites, document repositories, and a host of other web-based systems. Plone successfully competes in the "upper mid-tier" CMS market, and is often chosen over commercial systems such as RedDot CMS and Microsoft SharePoint in head-to-head evaluations.

Plone is developed almost exclusively by volunteers. It is open source, which means that you can obtain and use it for free, and that you are free to modify the underlying source code. There is no commercial "high-end" version (although Enfold Systems does offer a commercial version of Plone for Windows called Enfold Server). There is no single company behind Plone selling support or certifications (although professional support is available from a multitude of smaller vendors). There is no specific hardware tie-in. So why have thousands of man-hours gone into making Plone an ever more sophisticated CMS?

The answer is two-fold. We will consider the community drivers later in this chapter, but there are strong commercial reasons as well. The majority of Plone's core contributors make their living from what is often referred to as *Plone-the-framework*. They are professional web developers who sell consulting services and support, and have found that by working off a common base platform that is as good as possible, they can offer better value to their customers. A few Plone contributors work for companies with large Plone installations that have found that paying someone to spend part of their time contributing to Plone and getting changes into the core is cheaper than buying ad hoc support and development resources.

This model is, of course, not new in open source, but it happens to fit content management systems quite well. Customers rarely need a CMS as it comes out of the box. Most will want to customize its look-and-feel, workflow, security, and site structure. Frequently, customers also need some integration with existing systems, or may wish to build a portal that includes not only web page content, but various interactive tools and mini-applications.

If a customer is going to pay for consultants or developers to create the system they need, buying an expensive software license as well seems unnecessary. At the same time, developing a complete system from scratch is normally prohibitively expensive and risky. Better then, to take a system that comes close to meeting their needs, turn off the parts that are not relevant, and add the pieces that are missing. This is where Plone comes in.

Because the people who build Plone spend the rest of their time building these more specialized systems on top of it, Plone's architecture has evolved in such a way that is easy to extend. Indeed, this kind of extensible application is how Zope 2 (the application server on which Plone runs) was originally marketed. Almost any part of Plone can be extended, changed, or modified in such a way that Plone itself can be upgraded later without needing to re-apply changes to the actual code base. That is, you should never have to fork Plone for your own needs.

Additional Considerations when Deciding on Plone

Whether Plone is a good base for your application or not will depend on how much Plone offers you out of the box, and how difficult it will be to provide the rest. (For more information, see `http://plone.org/documentation/faq/is-plone-for-me`.) Usually, this means that your requirements can be modeled in a "content-centric" way, making use of Plone's infrastructure for managing hierarchical, semi-structured content. Being able to re-use Plone's workflow-based security model, its tried-and-tested user interface, and its infrastructure for things like user management and other administration tasks also tend to be strong selling points.

At the same time, it is important to bear in mind that to get the most out of Plone, you will need to make an investment of time, money, or both. Zope and Plone are RAM hungry and run best on a modern server. Proper infrastructure is never free, and requires some planning. Similarly, if this is your first Plone project, you should bear in mind that there will be a learning curve. Hopefully, this book will prove a good investment. Various companies also offer training courses and specialized consultancy, should you need it.

Licensing

Most parts of Plone are licensed under the GNU General Public License (GPL) Version 2, with various components alternatively licensed under the Lesser General Public License (LGPL), MIT, and BSD licenses. You should seek qualified legal advice if you are concerned about the license.

In practical terms, the license means that you are free to modify and re-use parts of Plone for your own needs. However, if you build a custom application on top of Plone and you intend to distribute (e.g., sell a license for or a boxed version of) that application, you will need to distribute your source code as well. You do not need to make the source code available if you are simply deploying a solution on an internal server.

The Plone source code is legally owned by the Plone Foundation, and is protected by a contributor agreement drawn up with the aid of the Software Freedom Law Center. This "software-conservancy" model is very similar to the framework used to protect the integrity of other major open-source projects such as Apache and Mozilla. The Plone Foundation is able to negotiate alternative license arrangements in special circumstances. Please see `http://plone.org/foundation`.

The Plone Community, and Why You Belong There

The word "community" permeates any discussion on what Plone is, and where it came from. In practical terms, Plone may be a piece of software, but in the truest sense, Plone is first and foremost a community. In the words of Paul Everitt, "Plone, the software is an artifact of Plone, the community."

Almost all of Plone's core contributors are friends in real life. They arrange "sprints" — short, intense development sessions — sometimes in exotic locations like an Austrian castle, a former military base on a Norwegian island, and a cabin high up in the Alps. There is an annual conference and usually a symposium or two throughout the year. And every day, the developers meet in online chat rooms and on mailing lists.

This friendship and the mutual respect developers have for each other are important factors in Plone's success. Many of us care quite passionately about making Plone the best it can be, and happily expend both personal and professional time on Plone-related activities without direct financial reward.

The Plone community itself is larger than just the two or three dozen core developers, though. Firstly, Plone's sister communities — those of Zope3, Zope 2, CMF, and Python — overlap with the Plone community and with each other in socially complex ways. And secondly, a larger number of developers contribute third-party add-on products, answer questions from end users and other developers, and participate in discussions around the future of Plone. A larger number still are end users, reporting bugs, offering praise and criticisms, joining in the discourse. This is where we hope you will connect with the community initially, if you have not done so already!

Most open-source communities have a core of dedicated developers with some governance structure around it. In Plone's case, governance is provided by:

- The Plone Foundation, which is responsible for legal affairs and has a mission "to protect and promote Plone".

- The current Release Manager, who has final say over what goes into a particular release. A Release Manager typically serves for only one release before handing over the reins (and serving as a mentor) to the next Release Manager.

- The current Framework Team, who review contributions and make recommendations to the Release Manager during the early stages of the release cycle.

In practical terms, however, Plone's governance is extremely democratic, and there is very little conflict and very few emotional disputes.

Because of this, most people find the Plone community open and approachable. Most developers are very happy to give help to those who ask for it, and questions on the mailing lists and in the chat room (see `http://plone.org/support`) are normally answered quickly. Many developers will also actively seek to involve more peripheral members of the community in improving Plone, for example, through mentoring or invitations to sprints and other events.

One of the best qualities of Plone is its openness to new contributors and the deliberate way in which it develops new leadership from within. The users and developers who encircle the core will sometimes move closer to the core of the community through their own learning and participation. As they gain the trust and respect of other developers, they are given more decision-making powers and less supervision, and will be able to influence the future direction of Plone more directly.

Such influence is one strong benefit of actively engaging with the community, and it is not as difficult to attain as one might think. The main factor is attitude, not knowledge. For example, there are many examples of people close to the core of the project that are less technical, but who want to help where they can. Ultimately, Plone would not survive without an influx of fresh blood and new perspectives from time to time.

Even if you are not enticed by rewards of responsibility and influence, becoming a member of the Plone community, however peripheral, will almost always be beneficial. By reading the mailing lists, for example, you will pick up a lot of up-to-the-minute knowledge that may not be readily available elsewhere. When you are stuck, asking a question in the chat room or on a mailing list can sometimes get you an answer in minutes or hours. By meeting Plone users and developers in real life, especially at user group meetings, conferences, and symposia, you will find yourself with a growing network of experts to draw upon when you need it the most. Save for Alan and Alexander, who started it all, every one of us was once a Plone newbie—many of us more recently than you might think!

Contribution to the community should be fun, fit your skills and interest, and give you something back. The easiest way to make a contribution is simply to start answering questions on the mailing lists. If you have some code you want to write, ask about how it may overlap with existing projects, and how you may best contribute it to the community. If you feel there is a gap in the documentation and you would like to write a how-to or tutorial, you can do so at `http://plone.org/documentation` and submit it for review. If you would like to host a user group meeting or a sprint, get in touch! You will find that if you show a willingness to give a little, you will get a lot.

Summary

In this chapter, we have learned:

- A brief history of Zope, Zope 3, and Plone
- How Plone-the-application and Plone-the-framework are related
- Some considerations you should bear in mind when deciding to use Plone
- What the Plone community is and why you may consider knocking on its door

In the next chapter, we will introduce the example application that we will use throughout this book.

2
The Case Study

Throughout this book, we will build a semi-realistic application that demonstrates various Plone technologies and concepts. The source code for this application can be found on the book's accompanying website.

 Please see the README.txt file in the source code archive for more information on how the examples are structured and how to run them.

We will explain the various packages and modules over the next several chapters but if you are the type of reader who likes to start from the end, feel free to browse through the code now.

In this chapter, we will present the case study and our fictitious client's requirements, and do some high-level modeling of what the application may look like in Plone.

High-Level Requirements

Optilux Cinema Group is a mid-sized chain of cinemas. They currently have a limited web presence, but wish to expand it to offer movie-goers a better way to find out about the latest films and reserve tickets for screenings.

The following high-level requirements have been presented to potential vendors for the cinema's web application:

	Requirement	Importance	Chapter
1	The site should have a look and feel consistent with Optilux's corporate branding.	High	5, 8
2	The site should show information about all of Optilux's cinemas.	High	7, 10
3	Non-technical cinema staff should be able to update information about each cinema.	High	7, 10
4	The site should allow staff to highlight promotions and special events. These may apply to one or more cinemas.	High	10
5	Cinema staff should be able to publish information about new films. It should be possible to update this information after publication.	High	10
6	Customers should be able to find out at which cinemas a particular film is showing, and which films are showing at a particular cinema. Note that the scheduling of films at cinemas is managed in an existing relational database.	High	12
7	Only films that are currently showing or will be shown in the near future should be viewable.	High	10
8	Customers should be able to search and browse films by cinema, location, date/time, or film name.	High	10, 12
9	Customers should be able to reserve tickets online. Tickets will be picked up and payment taken at the cinema. Reservations must use Optilux's existing relational database-based ticketing system.	Medium	12
10	Cinema managers should be able to view reports on reservations and site usage.	Medium	11
11	Customers should not need to log in to use the site, but a username and password should be required when they wish to reserve tickets.	Medium	12, 13
12	Logged-in customers should have easy access to their preferred cinema or cinemas, e.g. those in their area.	Medium	13, 14
13	Customers should be able to email enquiries to the site manager if they have questions or feedback.	Low	11
14	Customers should be able to discuss and rate movies.	Low	11, 14
15	The site should support cinema staff in developing future programming and promotions through a private collaborative workspace.	Low	13

As you become more accustomed to Plone development, these requirements will start to ring a few bells. For example, we may identify some custom content types by finding the nouns in the requirement descriptions (e.g., #2, #3, and #5), such as *Cinema* and *Movie*. We may be able to satisfy a few requirements by using Plone's standard content types or simple extensions thereof—a *Promotion* (#4) could be an extension of an *Event* or *News Item*, for example.

It is also very likely that the various content types will require custom workflows and security (e.g., #5, #7, and #15). We can identify user roles like *Customer*, *Staff*, and *Management* from the subjects in the various requirement descriptions, and start to understand what permissions these roles may have.

For reservations and reporting, it is clear that we will need some relational database connectivity (#9). This, in turn, will probably mean developing custom forms and templates that access the information in the database.

As the system requires management of member data and preferences (e.g., #11 and #12), we may need to add additional user properties. To support collaborative workspaces (#15), we may need advanced workflow and security policies.

The terms *member* and *user* are often interchanged in the context of Plone. Registered users are often referred to as *portal members*.

Lastly, we must provide client-specific branding (#1). Plone can provide user-friendly administrative pages and content management operations. We may also want to use Plone 3's new AJAX framework, called **KSS**, to add dynamic, JavaScript-driven, user interface elements.

Modeling and Mock-Ups

As a developer you may, perhaps in conjunction with the client, decide to do some initial modeling of how the system may look. Some developers advocate very detailed modeling and strict adherence to relevant standards such as **UML** (the **Unified Modeling Language**). This depends on personal preference. In the author's opinion, the models themselves are not as important as the *act of modeling*—thinking through the client's requirements in terms of high-level components and interfaces.

Models can help structure a conversation with the client. Walking through a model often brings an abstract idea of an application to life. You may want to show screen mock-ups and design suggestions as well. These can give the client a more concrete idea of how the solution will look to end users.

For the purposes of this application, we will start by drawing a UML **Use Case Diagram**, which shows the main users of the system and the types of things they may want to do with it:

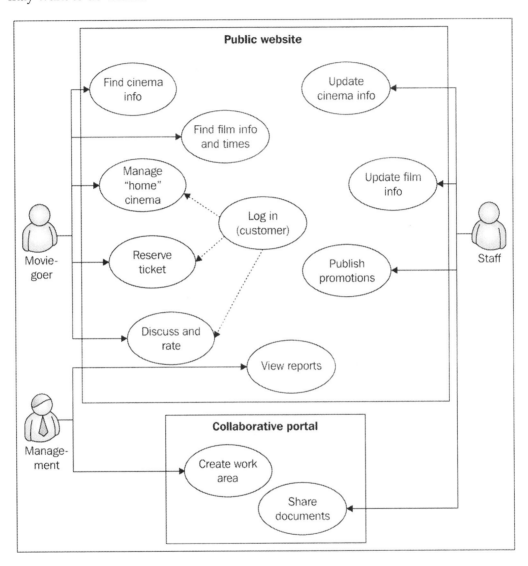

This diagram is by no means exhaustive, but it gives a quick visual representation of the kind of interactions the application will need to support.

From this, we can identify the major system components represented in a high-level **Class Diagram** as illustrated below. This also shows where external interfaces will be needed, in this case to the relational database holding movie reservations.

 This is not, strictly speaking, a correct use of the UML class diagram syntax, but it is useful nonetheless.

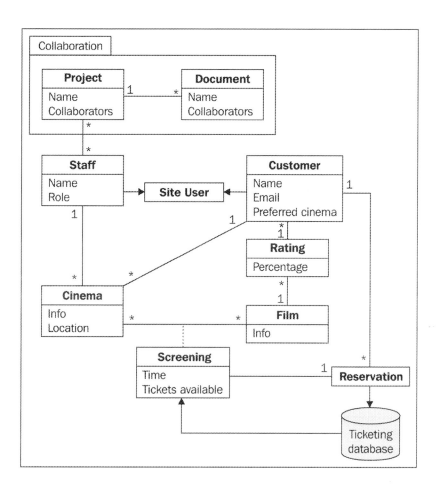

Again, this diagram is far from exhaustive, but it shows that we will need to manage **Cinema** and **Film** objects, which are related by **Screening** instances. **Customer** and **Staff** are different types of site users. A **Customer** can make a **Reservation** for particular **Screening**. A **Customer** can also add a **Rating** for a particular **Film**. In the content collaboration system, **Staff** can be members of various projects, which contain **Document** objects that staff are working on.

We will also provide some design mock-ups, drawn in a graphics program, which give an idea about the end result's look and feel:

In Chapter 8, we will see how this mock-up forms the basis of a customer site theme.

If necessary, we could do much more detailed modeling, but this is probably more than enough to have a meaningful conversation with the client. Naturally, the system will evolve from these models, and may include elements we have not captured here.

Running the Project

Project management is certainly outside the scope of this book, and every developer and organization will have different ways of managing their development projects. It is probably fair to say, however, that most Plone consultants prefer to work according to *agile* principles (see `http://agilemanifesto.org`), which typically include rapid prototyping, short development iterations, and a high degree of customer interaction throughout the design and development process.

Indeed, Python is often branded as an *agile* programming language because it is quick to write, easy to read, and lends itself well to code refactoring. Furthermore, because Plone gives us a fully featured system out of the box, you will be able to have something tangible and usable up and running almost instantly, which you can incrementally refine with input from the client.

Many developers keep a live test server for the client to play with, periodically deploying code updates to showcase new functionality. If you go down this route, you will probably want to set up an issue tracker for the client to report any problems they find. You could even do this in a Plone site (probably not the same one that the client is actively trying to destroy, though), using something like **Poi** (`http://plone.org/products/poi`). Alternatively, there are many other stand-alone solutions—**Trac** (`http://trac.edgewall.org`) being a popular and Python-based one.

Getting a draft version of the client's desired branding available for testing quickly can be very valuable, as the client may have trouble making the conceptual leap from vanilla Plone to their own requirements. Even just putting a logo and color scheme into a site otherwise using the standard Plone theme can give the client a greater sense of ownership and generate some excitement. It is normally advisable to turn off core Plone functionality that the client does not need sooner rather than later, though, to avoid confusion.

As you work with our clients, you will get a better idea about what is important to them. Giving them what they want most first, getting them involved in testing early, and being receptive to the changes in the specification is usually a very good idea.

Because of this, many Plone consultants will work on a time and expenses basis and promise frequent code releases, allowing the project to grow with the client's understanding of their needs. This is not so different from how Plone itself grows as people discover new things they would like it to do. By following good development and project management practices, and effectively leveraging Plone's base functionality, you can ensure that at any given point in time, the client has a fully functional (but partially complete) application at their disposal for testing and experimentation.

Summary

In this chapter we have been introduced to:

- A semi-realistic case study that will be used throughout this book
- High-level requirements for the example application following this case study
- Some initial models that point the way to how the application will look and work
- A few tips for running Plone development projects

In the next chapter, we will learn how to set up our development environment, before we start building the application for real.

3
The Development Environment

Before we can start building our application, we should set up a suitable development environment. This should as closely as possible mirror the final *live* server configuration, so that we can test our software locally before deploying it. The environment should also provide appropriate tools to support us during development.

In this chapter we will learn more about the elements of Zope's software stack and how they can be configured for development. We will also cover some supporting tools and technologies, such as Python *eggs* and *Paste Script*.

Prerequisites

Pre-built packages for Zope and Plone are available for many operating systems. These can be tempting, but as developers it is normally better to configure the environment ourselves, in order to fully understand and control it. During development, we need write access to the Python code and configuration files. We may also need to run different versions of Zope and Plone in parallel.

We will assume that you have at least the following as part of your regular development environment:

- **Python 2.4**. We will assume that Python 2.4 gets invoked when you run python on the command line. Unfortunately, Zope, at version 2.10, does not yet support Python 2.5. Note that many Linux distributions have two packages for Python — one containing the binaries, and one containing header files (typically called python-dev or something similar). You will need both in order to compile Zope.

- **PIL**, the **Python Imaging Library** (http://www.pythonware.com/products/pil), should be installed for this Python interpreter.

- **elementtree**, an XML processing library, is required for Plone to start up. Most operating systems have packages for this. It can also be downloaded from http://effbot.org/zone/element-index.htm.

- **A programmer's text editor**. Preferably one with Python, XML/HTML and CSS syntax highlighting. You should set up your editor so that a tab/indent is output as four spaces. This makes Python development a lot more predictable.

- **A shell**. Most examples in this book will show a Bash interpreter shell, though we will cover Windows syntax when it differs significantly. Bear in mind that path separators on Windows are backslashes (\), while other environments use forward slashes (/). Also, environment variables on Windows are referred to as %NAME%, while in most Unix shells, including Bash, variables are dereferenced with $NAME.

- **A Subversion client**. We will show the command line client syntax, but you can use a graphical client if you are more comfortable with that. Subversion can be obtained from http://subversion.tigris.org.

- **A C compiler**. You will need this to compile Zope. The venerable gcc is fine on UNIX-like systems. On Windows you probably want mingw32 (http://www.mingw.org). Alternatively, you can use a Zope Windows installer to get a binary Zope distribution.

Quick Start

Understanding your development environment is an important step in becoming a productive developer. If you need to get up and running quickly, however, and you have the prerequisites outlined above in order, here are the key steps.

We will assume you have Python 2.4 as your main Python interpreter. First download easy_install if you do not have it already, and use it to install ZopeSkel:

```
$ wget http://peak.telecommunity.com/dist/ez_setup.py
$ python ez_setup.py
$ easy_install ZopeSkel
```

If you do not have wget (e.g. because you are using Windows), you can just as easily download the ez_setup.py script using a web browser. When you run this script, it will install the easy_install binary to a directory that may not already be in your system PATH. Watch the ez_setup.py output to identify this directory. If it is not in your PATH, you should add it, allowing you to run easy_install as shown.

Then, use `paster`, which was installed as a dependency of ZopeSkel, to create a new *buildout*. This folder holds our source code and dependencies, including the Zope application server:

```
$ paster create -t plone3_buildout myproject
```

You can accept the defaults for all the questions, except for the password, which you must enter. Then, build the environment like so:

```
$ cd myproject
$ python bootstrap.py
$ ./bin/buildout
```

 If you are using Windows, be sure to read the README.txt file that is generated in the myproject directory before running the buildout command.

This last step may take some time, and you will need a live Internet connection. When it is complete, you can start Zope with:

```
$ ./bin/instance fg
```

Go to http://localhost:8080/manage and you should see the Zope Management Interface. Use the drop-down box to add a *Plone Site*. If you call this *mysite*, it will be accessible from http://localhost:8080/mysite.

Glossary

Let us now take a step back and consider our development environment in more detail.

The table below summarizes the various terms and technologies that you will encounter in this chapter. It pays to be familiar with these names, because you will find them again not only throughout this book, but also in other Plone documentation.

Term	Definition
Zope installation	Zope consists of Python code, C extensions, configuration files, documentation, scripts, and utilities. Collectively, these are known as the Zope installation.
Software home	The part of the Zope installation that contains the main Zope runtime. This is found in the lib/python directory of the Zope installation. The full path is assigned to the $SOFTWARE_HOME environment variable when Zope is run.

Term	Definition
Zope instance	The same Zope installation can be used to power multiple Zope servers, possibly running concurrently on different ports. Each instance has a directory containing a configuration file, instance-specific software components (e.g. an installation of Plone), and the local Zope database storage.
Instance home	When a Zope instance is running, the $INSTANCE_HOME environment variable refers to the directory where the instance is set up.
Package	A generic term for a distributable bundle of Python modules and supporting files.
Product	The traditional way to redistribute software for Zope 2 is in a "Product", which we will sometimes refer to as an "old-style Product". Products are placed in a special directory (Products/) and automatically discovered by Zope. The term "product" is also used more generally to refer to add-on components that extend Plone, even if they are not actually packaged as old-style Products.
Egg	A more generic and flexible alternative to products. Eggs are not specific to Zope, and Zope has only recently been made egg-aware. In addition to code, eggs contain metadata such as version, dependencies, and license information. Egg management tools can use this information to manage concurrent versions or automatically fetch dependencies, for example.
$PYTHONPATH	The $PYTHONPATH environment variable lists the directories containing Python packages that should be available at run time. It can also reference specific eggs. You should not have to set this manually.
setuptools	A Python library, which extends Python's built-in distutils package to support extended egg metadata and offers enhanced functionality when using software packaged as eggs.
The Cheese Shop	Also known as *PyPI* (Python Package Index). An online repository of Python eggs. Anyone can upload a package here. Egg-aware tools can use the Cheese Shop to locate dependencies and download them automatically when installing other eggs.
easy_install	A command-line tool, which searches the Cheese Shop for a given package, and downloads and installs it. Note that, by default, easy_install puts packages in the global site-packages folder for the Python interpreter that was used to install easy_install itself. Normally, we want our Plone packages to be local to a specific Zope instance, necessitating different tools.

Term	Definition
paster (Paste Script)	paster, part of the Python Paste package, is a command runner. The paster create command invokes Paste Script templates, which are used to create skeleton packages based on command-line options and questions.
ZopeSkel	A collection of Paste Script templates for Zope and Plone development. We will use this to create new egg-ready packages, as well as the buildout that manages our development environment.
Buildout (zc.buildout)	A "buildout", using the zc.buildout toolset, is a self-contained environment that is controlled through a single configuration file (buildout.cfg). We will use it to download, install, and configure Zope, Plone, and other dependencies. Buildouts are "repeatable", meaning that they can be used to replicate a particular setup across multiple servers or developers' machines.

Creating a Zope Instance Manually

To use Zope, we must first download and install its libraries and extensions, and then create an **instance** of the application server. The Zope instance keeps track of installed applications (such as Plone), any custom configuration settings, and the object database where all our content will live.

Later in this chapter, we will show how to automate the installation of Zope and creation of a development instance using the zc.buildout tool. Our custom *buildout* will be used to manage source code and configuration throughout the book. However, it is important to understand how to install Zope manually, not least because other documentation may assume you are using this style of installation.

First, download Zope from http://zope.org. If you are on Windows and you do not have a C compiler installed, it may be easier to use an installer. For Plone 3.0, you should use the latest version of the Zope 2.10 series, and at the very least Zope 2.10.4 (if in doubt, check the Plone release notes).

For example, let us install Zope into a folder called zope in our home directory:

```
$ mkdir ~/zope
$ cd ~/zope
$ wget http://www.zope.org/Products/Zope/2.10.4/Zope-2.10.4-final.tgz
$ tar xzf Zope-2.10.4-final.tgz
$ cd Zope-2.10.4
$ python setup.py build_ext -i
```

This will download Zope (you could of course use a web browser instead), unpack it (for which you could use a graphical tool such as WinZip if desired) and build it *in place*, including its C extensions. See the documentation that comes with Zope for information on other build options.

 With this installation, our $SOFTWARE_HOME at run time would be ~/zope/Zope-2.10.4/lib/python. You do not need to set this environment variable yourself.

Next, we will create an instance of the application server using our newly installed version of Zope:

```
$ mkdir ~/instances
$ cd ~/instances
$ ~/zope/Zope-2.10.4/utilities/mkzopeinstance.py -d testinstance
```

At this point you will be asked to specify a username and password for the default Zope user. When the script is complete, you will have a fully featured Zope instance in the testinstance directory. At run time, this directory is known as the $INSTANCE_HOME.

You may want to edit testinstance/etc/zope.conf, for example to change the default port from 8080 if you have another server running there.

 The main Zope configuration file is in $INSTANCE_HOME/etc/zope. conf. With a default installation, it contains a number of comments explaining its various options.

You can start the instance like so:

```
$ testinstance/bin/zopectl fg
```

On Windows, you will need to use:

```
> testinstance\bin\runzope.bat
```

$INSTANCE_HOME/bin contains a number of scripts, including zopectl, which can be used to start and stop Zope on UNIX-like systems, and runzope.bat, which can be used to start Zope in a terminal on Windows.

When Zope is running, you can access the Zope Management Interface (ZMI) with the username and password you provided, by opening a web browser and going to http://localhost:8080/manage.

To stop the server again, press *Ctrl+C* in the terminal window where Zope was started. If you used the Windows installer, you can start and stop the instance from the **Services** control panel in **Administrative Tools**.

To be able to use Plone, you now need to install its products and packages. Stop Zope, download the Plone tarball from http://plone.org/download, and extract it into testinstance. This should put various directories into the Products folder. For example, you should have testinstance/Products/CMFPlone and testinstance/Products/ATContentTypes among other directories.

 Zope will scan $INSTANCE_HOME/Products on startup for any *old-style* **products** to initialize and load. The products in $INSTANCE_HOME/Products are added to (and could override) those found in $SOFTWARE_HOME/Products.

Similarly, several new packages should have been extracted to testinstance/lib/python. You should have testinstance/lib/python/plone and lib/python/kss, among other packages.

 When the application server starts up, the $INSTANCE_HOME/lib/python directory is added to the $PYTHONPATH, making additional "plain Python" **packages** available to Zope. However, such packages are not automatically scanned and loaded as products in the Products folder are; they are merely available for other packages to import.

You should now be able to re-start your instance, return to the ZMI and add a **Plone Site** to the root of the object hierarchy. When you add objects in the ZMI or in Plone, they are stored in the **ZODB** — Zope's built-in object data base.

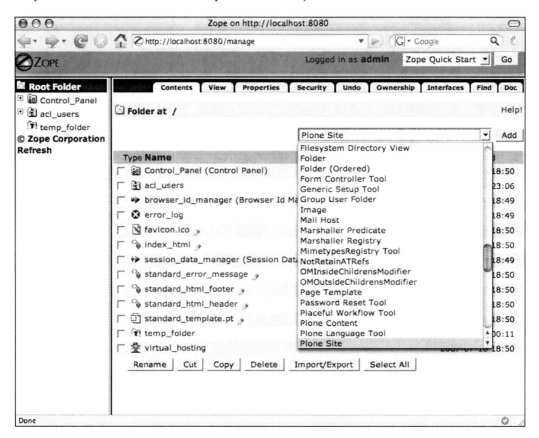

By default, the entire contents of the ZODB are stored in a single file, called Data.fs. This can be found in $INSTANCE_HOME/var. To back up your database, simply make a copy of this file. We will cover backups in more detail in Chapter 16.

If you have a problem using Zope or Plone, you may need to review the instance's log files.

> The $INSTANCE_HOME/log directory is the default location of Zope's log files. The file event.log contains most error and debugging messages. Z2.log is a low-level access log. Logging is configured from $INSTANCE_HOME/etc/zope.conf.

Understanding Eggs and Setuptools

Python **eggs** are not specific to Zope or Plone. However, since Zope has only recently become egg-aware, they are new to many developers.

Traditionally, almost all Zope add-on products, including Plone, have been distributed as Zope products. These are fairly easy to manage — you typically copy or symlink them into $INSTANCE_HOME/Products. Zope will scan this directory on startup, taking care of any product initialization and registration.

However, code inside products is nearly impossible to re-use outside Zope because Zope does magic things with the Products.* namespace. Further, the namespace quickly becomes crowded, which deters developers from breaking up functionality into smaller, more re-usable and better-isolated packages.

The Zope 3 philosophy is to be as close to "plain Python" as possible, and that means distributing code as such small packages. So long as its dependencies are in order, any package should be able to run in any environment. For example, the zope.interface package is used by the Twisted project, which is not otherwise dependent on Zope. This design goal has made it much easier to adopt Zope 3 packages in Zope 2 and Plone.

Starting with Plone 3, the Plone community has also embraced "plain Python" packages and uses them wherever possible. A number of packages, such as plone.memoize and plone.portlets are generic enough to work without any dependencies on the rest of Plone. Others are more specific to Plone and live in the plone.app namespace, such as plone.app.layout and plone.app.portlets, the latter containing Plone-centric extensions to the generic plone.portlets package.

All that is needed to use these packages is a sensible $PYTHONPATH. Thus, we can copy or link packages into $INSTANCE_HOME/lib/python/plone/memoize, lib/python/plone/portlets, lib/python/plone/app/portlets, and so forth for Zope to find them. This works, but it is pretty tedious when there are many packages, and it can become outright confusing when there are nested namespaces being used by multiple packages.

Luckily, other Python programmers have solved these problems, first creating **distutils**, then its successor **setuptools** and with setuptools, Python eggs.

 For the setuptools documentation, see
`http://peak.telecommunity.com/DevCenter/setuptools`.

Installing Eggs

When using setuptools, each project or package lives in a directory that has a top-level `setup.py` file. This contains metadata about the package itself, and declares its current version as well as any dependencies. Dependencies can be specified down to particular versions (e.g. `">=0.2,<1.0"` means "later than version 0.2 but before version 1.0"). When a package is installed, setuptools will attempt to fulfill dependencies by downloading and installing them if necessary.

If you have a setuptools-enabled package, you can use `setup.py` to install it globally, by running:

```
$ python setup.py install
```

This will copy the source code to the system-wide Python `site-packages` directory.

Having to re-run this command each time you make a change can make development a little awkward, so while you are working on a particular package, you can install a **development egg**. This is essentially a link to the package's source code that ensures it is added to the `$PYTHONPATH`. To install a development egg, run:

```
$ python setup.py develop
```

New packages can be released as binary eggs for distribution, which are just ZIP files of the package with some additional metadata. You can build an egg from within a package by running:

```
$ python setup.py bdist_egg
```

The new egg will be placed in the `dist` sub-directory, which will be created if necessary.

Eggs can be uploaded to the **Cheese Shop**, also known as **PyPI** (the **Python Package Index**). This central repository makes it easy to find packages. You can browse packages at `http://cheeseshop.python.org/pypi`. New packages can be uploaded via this website, or directly from the command line:

```
$ python setup.py egg_info -RDb "" sdist bdist_egg register upload
```

You will be asked to specify or create a Cheese Shop account if this is the first time you run this command.

A script called **easy_install** lets you search the Cheese Shop (or a similar index, if you specify a URL) for packages that it can download and install into the global Python environment. Dependencies will be included automatically. This is great for simple libraries and end-user applications, but less great when you are working on multiple Zope projects that may have different version requirements. This is why we tend to manage our eggs inside $INSTANCE_HOME or, as you will see in the next section, as part of a controlled *buildout*.

 A tool called **workingenv.py** can create a *mini-environment* where *global* commands are restricted to a particular directory. We will not cover workingenv in this book, but you can download and read more about it at http://cheeseshop.python.org/pypi/workingenv.py.

When eggs are *activated* (either explicitly, or implicitly by being unambiguously found in the $PYTHONPATH), they can be *discovered* by other packages listening for plug-ins, using a mechanism called **entry points** (see http://peak.telecommunity.com/DevCenter/setuptools#dynamic-discovery-of-services-and-plugins). Zope does not yet directly use entry points, so we will not be covering them in any detail here. However, entry points are a very powerful system, and there are proposals to let Zope's discovery of packages use entry points instead of scanning magic directories.

With eggs, we therefore have the tools to manage multiple packages, from different developers and repositories, possibly across multiple versions. By using the package management tools that the rest of the Python community employs, we also make it easier to re-use other libraries and share our own code with outside developers.

Automating the Build Process with zc.buildout

Creating a Zope instance and copying or linking packages into $INSTANCE_HOME/lib/python as we have seen earlier is not too difficult, but this approach has a few limitations.

- The process is manual and cumbersome to repeat across multiple environments.

- Multiple developers working on the same project may share the code in eggs and products by using a version control system such as Subversion. However, each developer would be responsible for setting up their development environment, and subtle differences may cause problems that are difficult to debug.

- Packages are installed manually, and so cannot benefit from setuptools' ability to manage dependencies and updates.

- Complex deployments that include other libraries, non-python code, or specific configurations will also need to be taken care of manually.

Luckily, there are tools to make deployment easier. **zc.buildout** is one such tool, written largely by Zope founder Jim Fulton at Zope Corporation. It makes heavy use of eggs and setuptools and is very flexible in supporting a wide range of deployment scenarios.

Central to a **buildout** (i.e. what zc.buildout is managing for us) is a file called buildout.cfg. This specifies various options, including a list of *parts*, which will be executed when the buildout is run. Each *part* is associated with a *recipe* — a named egg, which will be called upon to parse the options provided, and perform a particular task, such as building a Zope instance or downloading Plone.

A project-specific buildout directory can be checked into a version control system and shared among developers. It can also be used to replicate a particular environment across different servers with a high degree of predictability.

By writing custom recipes, you can make zc.buildout do almost anything. Writing a recipe is not particularly hard, and there are plenty of examples and generic solutions available. However, we will not cover creating new recipes in this book, because all the recipes we need already exist.

Installing Paste Script and ZopeSkel

To create the buildout.cfg file and some necessary boilerplate, we will make use of **Paste Script**, a tool for creating project skeletons from templates. Later, we will also use Paste Script to create new packages following standard conventions.

Paste Script is an extensible system with which other packages (or rather, eggs) can register new templates (using entry points). For Zope and Plone development, the **ZopeSkel** package provides several useful templates.

You can fetch ZopeSkel using easy_install. If you do not have easy_install, you must download it:

```
$ wget http://peak.telecommunity.com/dist/ez_setup.py
$ python ez_setup.py
```

If you do not have `wget` (e.g. you are using Windows), download the `ez_setup.py` script using a web browser instead, and run it with `python` as shown.

Keep an eye on where the script puts the `easy_install` executable. Depending on your setup, you may need to add this to your `$PATH` environment variable or reference it by an absolute directory. Adding the script's directory to your `$PATH` may be a good idea, though, since the `paster` command and other egg-installed binaries will go in the same place.

Now, simply run:

```
$ easy_install ZopeSkel
```

This will find ZopeSkel in the Cheese Shop, download it, and install it, including its dependencies.

Creating and Customizing the Buildout

Now we can create our project's buildout, using a Paste Script template from ZopeSkel:

```
$ paster create -t plone3_buildout optilux
```

If you run this command, you will be asked a series of questions, including:

- The path to an existing appropriate installation of Zope 2. You can specify an absolute path here if you have installed Zope already and wish to share the same Zope installation across multiple buildouts. Leave the option blank to have buildout download and build Zope for you.

- The path to an existing directory containing all the Plone products. Again, this lets you share the same code across multiple buildouts and save some time. If you leave it blank, Plone will be downloaded for you.

- The Zope root user and password.

- The port that the Zope HTTP server will run on.

- Whether or not debug mode should be on by default. Note that even if it is off, you can enable debug mode by starting Zope with `./bin/instance fg` instead of `./bin/instance start`.

- Whether "verbose security" should be on by default. Verbose security is very useful for debugging security problems by offering more detailed log messages, but it is best turned off for production servers.

Buildout will create a new environment, containing a generated `buildout.cfg` file and some standard directories. To bootstrap the buildout to get the standard zc.buildout tools, run:

```
$ cd optilux
$ python bootstrap.py
```

This step is only needed once. We are now ready to build the system. Simply run:

```
$ ./bin/buildout
```

This may take a long time, depending on the speed of your computer and internet connection. It will download and build Zope, download and install Plone, and configure the two. When it is finished, you can start Zope by running:

```
$ ./bin/instance start
```

Stop it again with:

```
$ ./bin/instance stop
```

> If Zope fails to start or you cannot find **Plone Site** in the list of addable types in the ZMI, you are most likely missing a dependency such as PIL or elementtree. Start Zope in the foreground using `./bin/instance fg` (with debug mode on) and look out for an error message in the terminal window.

The Buildout Configuration File

That is all that is needed to get started. To understand what is going on, though, let us take a look at the `buildout.cfg` file that was generated for us (slightly abbreviated):

```
[buildout]
parts =
    plone
    zope2
    productdistros
    instance
    zopepy
find-links =
    http://dist.plone.org
    http://download.zope.org/distribution/
    http://effbot.org/downloads
eggs =
    elementtree
develop =
[plone]
```

```
recipe = plone.recipe.plone
[zope2]
recipe = plone.recipe.zope2install
url = ${plone:zope2-url}
[productdistros]
recipe = plone.recipe.distros
urls =
nested-packages =
version-suffix-packages =
[instance]
recipe = plone.recipe.zope2instance
zope2-location = ${zope2:location}
user = admin:admin
http-address = 8080
debug-mode = on
verbose-security = on
eggs =
    ${buildout:eggs}
    ${plone:eggs}
zcml =
products =
    ${buildout:directory}/products
    ${productdistros:location}
    ${plone:products}
[zopepy]
recipe = zc.recipe.egg
eggs = ${instance:eggs}
interpreter = zopepy
extra-paths = ${zope2:location}/lib/python
scripts = zopepy
```

Starting from the top, this file defines various things that will happen when our buildout is run:

- The main [buildout] section sets buildout-wide options. First, it lists several *parts*, which will be executed in order. These refer to sections later on in the file. Then, a number of eggs to install can be listed. By default, this includes elementtree, which is required by Plone. Even if you have elementtree in your system-wide Python installation already, listing it explicitly here will not hurt. The eggs are referenced again in the [instance] section, causing them to be downloaded from the Cheese Shop (or another source, as listed under find-links) and installed when the instance is built and needs to know about them. The empty develop option will let us manage development eggs later.

- The `[plone]` section will download Plone's products and eggs. It also exposes the URL to a "known good" version of Zope, which we will reference in the the `[zope2]` section. To peg Plone to a particular version, you can specify a version for the recipe, e.g. with `recipe = plone.recipe.plone==3.0.1`, which would make sure that we got the version of the release recipe corresponding to Plone 3.0.1, if and when it is released.

- The `[zope2]` section will download and build Zope 2 from the given URL, here supplied by the previously defined `[plone]` section. This will only be present if you did not specify an existing Zope installation above. It may be worth checking the URL to ensure you get the latest appropriate version of Zope.

- The `[productdistros]` section can be used to download and install archives of old-style products; it is referenced again under the `products` option of the `[instance]` section. We will add a few download URLs later in this chapter. The `nested-packages` and `version-suffix-packages` can be used to deal with archives that do not immediately extract to usable product directories. See the comments in the file for more information.

- The `[instance]` section is the most important one. This will create a new Zope instance, and configure it with the appropriate options. The given list of eggs, referring back to the eggs in the main `[buildout]` section (although additional eggs can be added if necessary), will be activated and made available to Zope. Zope is also told where to look for products. The `zcml` section can be used to load ZCML *slugs* — special files that Zope 3-style packages can use to make themselves known to Zope. We will cover slugs in Chapter 9.

- The `[zopepy]` section sets up a custom Python interpreter, which will have available to it all the same eggs as the Zope instance. This is very useful for debugging and quick prototyping.

If for any reason `buildout.cfg` is changed, or if you wish to obtain recent updates to any eggs listed, you should run `./bin/buildout` again. You can often save some time by running buildout in *offline* and *non-updating* mode, where it will not check for updates to eggs and products online, by using:

```
$ ./bin/buildout -No
```

To get a full explanation of the various options available, run:

```
$ ./bin/buildout --help
```

The Buildout Directory

Let us now take a look at the directories zc.buildout creates for us.

- The `bin` directory contains the `instance` control script, `zopepy`, and the `buildout` command itself. `./bin/instance` is equivalent to `$INSTANCE_HOME/bin/zopectl`.

- The `eggs` directory contains eggs that buildout has automatically downloaded. These are enumerated and referenced when needed, for example by the `instance` control script. This is similar to linking packages into `$INSTANCE_HOME/lib/python`, but allows us to use the full power of setuptools and eggs.

- The `develop-eggs` directory contains egg-links to any development eggs specified in `buildout.cfg`. This will be empty for now, but we will make use of development eggs later in the book.

- A `downloads` directory will be created as necessary. Recipes such as `plone.recipe.plone` and `plone.recipe.distros` that fetch archives of products and packages will place their downloads in this directory. If an archive has already been downloaded, it will not be downloaded again.

- The `products` directory can be used for any old-style products that are being developed as part of the project. It is analogous to the aforementioned `$INSTANCE_HOME/Products` directory. Our buildout will also manage various products for us inside the `parts` directory.

- The `src` directory contains the sources of any custom eggs. This is empty now, but we will add packages here in later chapters.

- The `var` directory houses the `Data.fs` file and Zope's logs.

- The `parts` directory is zc.buildout's playground. This is where Zope 2 is downloaded and built, for example — the `$SOFTWARE_HOME` becoming `parts/zope2/lib/python`. The `$INSTANCE_HOME` is in `parts/instance`. You will not typically manage the Zope instance directly when using a buildout. You should not make changes to anything in the `parts` directory, as zc.buildout may stomp on your modifications when you re-run `./bin/buildout`.

Avoiding Duplication between Buildouts

If as a developer you are managing several projects with different buildouts, you may want to share some source code between them. We have already seen the options that allow you to specify shared Zope 2 installations and Plone product directories. This will save considerable disk space, but bear in mind that old-style Zope products are not individually versioned, so any changes or upgrades will affect all instances where they are referenced.

It is also possible to share an `eggs` directory between different buildouts. Unlike products, eggs carry version information, and so it is possible to keep different versions installed simultaneously. For example, if one egg was referenced in `buildout.cfg` as `my.package==0.9` and another buildout used `my.package>=1.0`, two versions could be downloaded and activated as appropriate.

The `eggs` directory to use is controlled by the `eggs-directory` option in the `[buildout]` section of `buildout.cfg`. Rather than having to add this to each project, however, we will put it in the `defaults.cfg` file, which zc.buildout examines to pick up additional options in addition to what is in the `buildout.cfg` file.

In your home directory, create a directory called `.buildout`. Within it, add another directory called `eggs`, and a file called `default.cfg`, containing:

```
[buildout]
eggs-directory = /home/username/.buildout/eggs
```

Similarly, you can specify a shared archive downloads directory, using the `download-directory` option. For example, you can create a directory called `downloads` next to the aforementioned `eggs` directory, and add the following to `default.cfg`:

```
[buildout]
eggs-directory = /home/username/.buildout/eggs
download-directory = /home/username/.buildout/downloads
```

This file can be used for other defaults if necessary. In particular, if you need to use a specific Python interpreter instead of the default system-wide one, use a line like the following:

```
executable = /path/to/python2.4
```

Additional Development Tools

During development, we typically rely on various tools to help us debug our code and inspect Plone and Zope. The oldest of these is the **DocFinderTab**, a Zope product that adds a **Doc** tab to every object in the ZMI. This tab lists the class and base classes for the object being inspected, including methods and their docstrings.

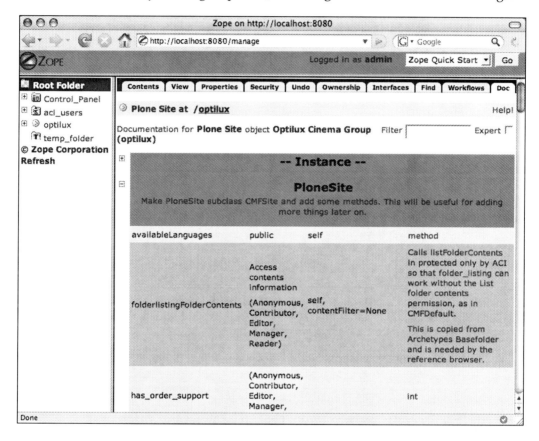

By using a regular expression in the **Filter** box at the top, you can look for specific methods.

If DocFinderTab is old-school, **Clouseau** is hip and happening. It is essentially an in-browser Python shell, using JavaScript and AJAX technologies. It supports two modes:

- A general interpreter prompt, which can be accessed from the **Clouseau** control panel under **Site Setup**.

- An object inspector, which can be invoked on any content object. It is available from the "document actions" shown at the bottom of most content views.

Note that Clouseau makes use of the DocFinderTab to inspect objects, in order to provide auto-complete suggestions for method and attribute names.

Here is an example of Clouseau inspecting the default Plone front page, changing the title and saving the results:

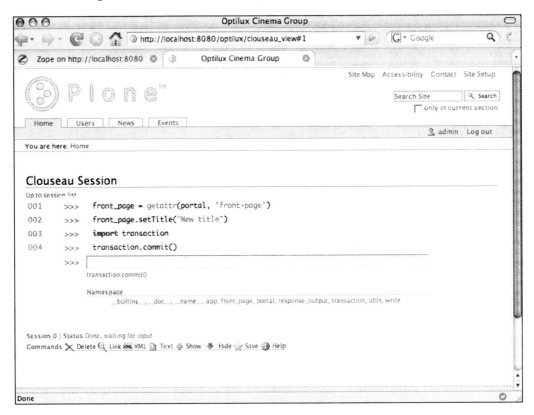

Please refer to the Clouseau help, under the **Clouseau** control panel, for more information.

Clouseau is a full, unprotected interpreter shell with access to all of Zope and the currently installed products and packages. A fine demo of Clouseau is to use it to delete your entire Plone instance. Obviously, it should be kept far, far away from production servers, and by default it is only available when Zope runs in debug mode. Being able to prototype things in the browser, inspect the innards of any object in Zope, and make changes on the fly can be incredibly useful, though. Just keep a backup of your Data.fs file.

Both DocFinderTab and Clouseau are distributed as old-style products in separate archives. To obtain and install them, edit `buildout.cfg` and modify the `[productdistros]` section like this:

```
[productdistros]
recipe = plone.recipe.distros
urls =
  http://www.zope.org/Members/shh/DocFinderTab/1.0.1/
      DocFinderTab-1.0.1.tar.gz
  http://plone.org/products/clouseau/releases/0.7.1/Clouseau.0.7.1.zip
```

These URLs are correct at the time of writing. You may want to check for newer versions, especially of Clouseau, at `http://plone.org/products/clouseau`.

Now, we can re-run buildout and start Zope in debug mode:

```
$ ./bin/buildout -N
$ ./bin/instance fg
```

We should then be able to install Clouseau from the Plone control panel. DocFinderTab requires no explicit installation.

Learning to Help Yourself

During development, there will probably be times when you are stumped. Plone is fairly well-documented, but the documentation is certainly not perfect. The mailing lists and chat room are great resources if you need help, but it is also very important to learn how to help yourself.

Use the Source, Luke!

Python's readability is both a blessing and a curse. A blessing, because it is normally possible to read the source code and find out what is going on. A curse, because this sometimes makes developers a little lax about documentation.

One of the first hurdles new developers should overcome is any undue respect for the Python files that make up Zope and Plone. There is (almost) nothing magical about them. In this chapter, we have seen where the source code lives: core Zope modules in $SOFTWARE_HOME, third-party products in the products folder, and eggs in lib/python or the eggs folder managed by buildout.

Get used to searching for code in these files using `grep` or equivalent graphical tools, opening them, and looking for specific classes and methods. Seeing what a piece of code does can often be faster than looking up documentation or examples. As time goes by, you will find that a few packages come up again and again, and finding code will be easier.

You can of course change these files as well. A backup is advisable, but if you think that temporarily raising an exception or printing a message from somewhere deep inside Zope helps you to solve a problem, go right ahead. It is probably a bad idea to make permanent changes this way, however, because those changes will be overwritten if you upgrade or re-install the particular component. In the next chapter, we will learn more about other ways of customizing code Zope and Plone. However, if you find a bug, please report it, and attach a patch if you can!

 Plone bugs can be reported at `http://dev.plone.org/plone`. Zope bugs are collected at `http://zope.org/Collectors/Zope`, and CMF bugs at `http://zope.org/Collectors/CMF`.

Here are some examples of where you may look for source code if you see an import or a description of a module in this book:

Module	Location
`Products.CMFCore.MembershipTool`	A product bundled with Plone. Found in `$INSTANCE_HOME/Products/CMFCore/MembershipTool.py` for a manual Zope installation, and in `parts/plone/CMFCore/MembershipTool.py` when using a buildout to download and install the tarball containing this package.
`plone.memoize`	A simple package bundled with Plone. Could be anywhere on the `$PYTHONPATH`, but most likely in `$INSTANCE_HOME/lib/python/plone/memoize` when using a manually created instance, or in `eggs/plone.memoize/plone/memoize` if installed as an egg via a buildout.
`AccessControl.ImplPython`	A low-level Zope 2 module, found in `$SOFTWARE_HOME/AccessControl/ImplPython.py`. Recall that when using a buildout, the `$SOFTWARE_HOME` is `parts/zope2/lib/python`.

Module	Location
`Products.Five.browser`	A product bundled with Zope 2 and therefore found within `$SOFTWARE_HOME/Products/Five/browser`. These are less common than products in the `$INSTANCE_HOME`, `Five` being the most common example of something may want to look at.
`zope.component.interfaces`	A package that is part of Zope 3 (as evidenced by the top-level `zope` namespace). This could be anywhere on the `$PYTHONPATH`, but is most likely in `$SOFTWARE_HOME/zope/component/interfaces.py`.

Become Familiar with the Debugger

It is also very important to be familiar with **pdb**, the Python debugger (see `http://docs.python.org/lib/module-pdb.html`). To insert a breakpoint in your code—or in some other code that you are trying to debug—add the following line and (re-)start Zope in the foreground in a terminal:

```
import pdb; pdb.set_trace()
```

When the line is encountered, execution will stop, and the terminal will display:

```
(pdb)
```

This is the interactive pdb prompt. Type *help* and press *Enter* to see available commands: the most important ones are *pp*—to print a variable or the result of an expression, *n*—to step to the next line, *s*—to step into a function call, *l*—to show a listing of the source code around the current execution point, and *c*—to stop debugging and continue execution.

If you want to quickly test syntax or libraries, you can run Python's interactive interpreter. To make sure you have all the same eggs and packages available as Zope will when it starts up, run:

```
$ ./bin/zopepy
>>>
```

Write Tests for Everything

Finally, the biggest favor you can do yourself as a developer is to learn to write unit tests. To learn more about tests, see `http://plone.org/documentation/tutorial/testing`. Without unit tests, there is no telling whether your code is working, and whether you have inadvertently broken it. Since tests are normally small and isolated, they are also a great starting point for diagnosing problems or examining the behavior of other components. Try writing a small test and placing a pdb break point in it, stepping into other code as necessary.

We will make extensive use of tests in this book. The rationale, theory, and tools of unit and functional testing are covered in the next chapter.

Summary

In this chapter, we have seen:

- How to create a Zope instance and install Plone into it manually
- The various elements that make up a Zope installation, including the meaning of the `$SOFTWARE_HOME` and `$INSTANCE_HOME` environment variables
- Some background on Python's setuptools and eggs, and how they differ from Zope products
- How to use `paster` and zc.buildout to automate the creation and building of Zope instances in a repeatable manner
- Some important debugging tools, including pdb, DocFinderTab, and Clouseau
- A few tips on how you can more effectively help yourself by learning to look at source code, using pdb effectively, and prototyping things with `zopepy`

This concludes Part 1 of the book. In Part 2, we will learn more about customizing Plone for our specific needs.

Part 2

Customizing Plone

Customization Basics

Developing a Site Strategy

Security and Workflow

Using Add-on Products

Creating a Custom Theme

4
Customization Basics

To a certain extent, all we ever do when we use *Plone-the-platform* is to customize *Plone-the-product*. Sometimes, that means building a system that barely resembles "out-of-the-box" Plone; and at times, it's just about adding a few bells and removing a few unnecessary whistles.

In this chapter, we will learn about the main types of customization that Plone supports. In the next chapter, we will put these concepts into practice by creating a *policy product* to manage specific customizations relevant to Optilux Cinema case study.

Persistent Settings and the ZODB

The first type of customization most developers encounter is the settings exposed by various tools and Plone control panel forms. Sometimes, they build applications that depend on particular content locations or site structure. In both of these cases, part of the application's configuration is stored in the ZODB, rather than in source code or configuration files.

Relying on persistent database state does not scale or repeat easily. Imagine a team of developers working on the same site. Ideally, each developer would have their own sandbox, much like we saw in the last chapter. This sandbox would need to be separate from the live environment. Replicating or merging settings across such distributed environments is hard and error-prone.

Further, because of the way the ZODB serializes Python objects (using *pickles*, a feature of the Python standard library), persistent objects can only be de-serialized with reference to the code that was used to create them. This means that extra care needs to be taken when renaming or relocating classes in the source code for objects that may be persisted.

These challenges led Tres Seaver, the creator of the Zope Content Management Framework (CMF), to formulate **Seaver's Law**:

> Persistence means always having to say you're sorry.

This is so because any setting that is persisted in a running application requires migration if the underlying code is modified (more on that later in this chapter), and any setting that is made through the Web is ephemeral if it has to be manually translated from a development environment to a production server (or vice-versa).

Configuration Using GenericSetup

GenericSetup (http://plone.org/documentation/tutorial/genericsetup) is the CMF team's answer to Seaver's Law. In particular, it solves the translation-of-settings challenge, and simplifies pre-configuration of persistent objects on the site map.

Each configurable component (such as a tool) provides a pair of *handlers* for importing and exporting its state in an XML format. At any point of time, a particular *profile* is active. The profile specifies a series of import and export steps—the handlers that will be run. Each handler (typically) knows how to read an XML file with a particular name. For example, the skins.xml file will be read by the import handler for the skins tool to set up skin layers (we will cover more on these in the next section).

A **tool** is a singleton persistent object, found in the root of the Plone site. Most tools have names starting with portal_, such as portal_membership or portal_types. They variously expose shared functionality and act as containers for configuration state. Most tools can be configured from the ZMI, and many of the Plone **Site Setup** control panels manage tool settings under the hood.

There are two types of GenericSetup profiles—**base profiles**, and **extension profiles**. Base profiles describe a complete configuration (excluding actual content) for a site—at least in theory.

Because GenericSetup was only introduced in Plone 2.5, there may still be settings for which there are no import/export handlers. We will see in the next chapter how these can be set up using specific Python code.

When a Plone site is created, it is configured from a base profile found in `CMFPlone/profiles/default/`, but you can switch to other profiles later. It is also possible to make changes through the Web and then export a snapshot of those changes as an archive of XML files, which can be re-imported later.

When a base profile has been activated, you can install additional extension profiles. An extension profile is configured in the same way as a base profile and uses the same handlers, but it will normally only contain a subset of the settings that make up the site, either as overrides for those from the base profile, or as new entries. Extension profiles are useful for add-on products that need to be installable independently of the rest of the configuration of the site, as well as where the configuration will not deviate extensively from the base profile.

We will show how to create a profile and set it up programmatically in the next chapter, when we define the policy product for our example application. For now, it is important to know how to take a snapshot of the current state of the portal and manage profiles through the Web. This can be useful for development, since the exported profiles can be adapted for use in an on-disk product. It can also help you *roll back* a site to a previous configuration, and inspect differences between a previous profile and the current state.

GenericSetup configuration is managed through the `portal_setup` tool found in the ZMI at the root of a Plone site. On the **Profiles** tab, you will see the active base profile:

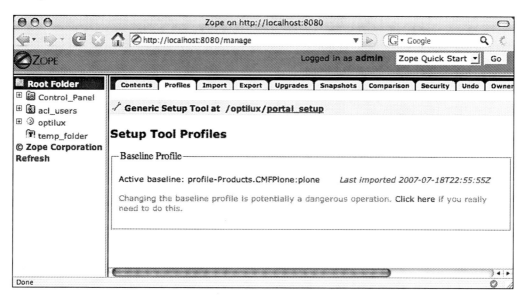

As the text in the screenshot suggests, changing the base profile on a live site can lead to unexpected side effects unless the new base profile closely resembles the current base profile in structure.

The available import steps are listed under the **Import** tab. The default selection allows us to re-run the steps of the current base profile. You can select an appropriate extension profile or snapshot from the drop-down menu, and run some or all of its steps using the buttons at the bottom of the page:

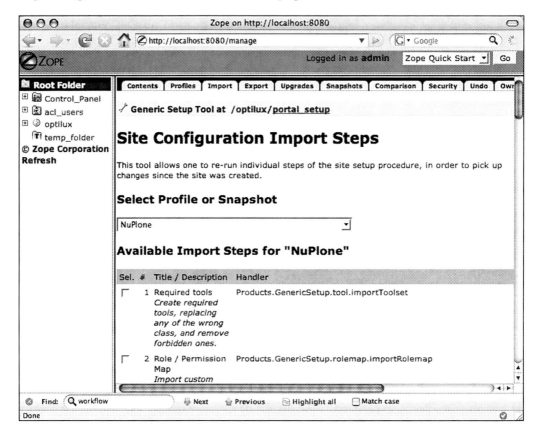

Note that when viewing the available import steps for an extension profile, there may be more handlers listed than the extension profile provides configuration for. Handlers with no corresponding import steps – i.e. with no corresponding XML files in the extension profile – will simply be skipped.

During development, it can be useful to re-run individual steps after making changes to a profile. For example, say we have defined and imported a new workflow using an extension profile (as we will learn to do in Chapter 6). If we subsequently change the profile on disk, this will not be reflected in the site automatically. Rather than re-importing the entire profile and potentially resetting other configuration data, we can re-run the **Workflow Tool** step in isolation.

Lastly, import steps can be run from an uploaded `.tar.gz` archive. Such an archive can be created from the **Export** tab, where we can choose to export some or all of the currently available steps to the local machine.

It is also possible to create a snapshot of the site and store it inside the `portal_setup` tool, rather than downloading it to the local machine. This is done from the **Snapshots** tab. Snapshots at different points in time can be compared using the **Comparison** tab. Here, we have taken a snapshot immediately before and after changing the portal title:

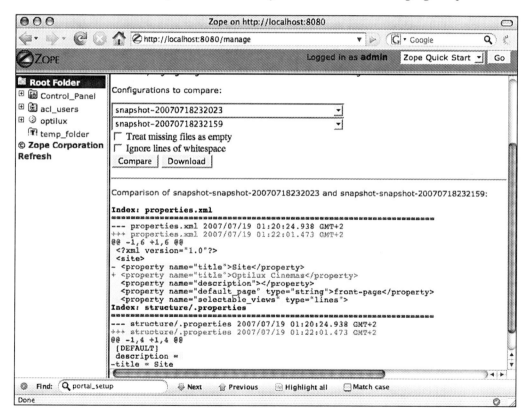

GenericSetup and the Add/Remove Products Control Panel

The user interface of the `portal_setup` tool is not ideal for installing add-on products that use GenericSetup for installation. Luckily, as of Plone 3, `portal_quickinstaller`, the tool that powers Plone's **Add-on Products** control panel, is GenericSetup-aware: if a product registers an extension profile, it will be available for installation in the control panel. The tool also tracks the most common types of changes to the base configuration and is able to undo them upon uninstall.

In previous versions of Plone, installation of third-party products was always done using a script inside the product directory called `Extensions/Install.py`, which the QuickInstaller tool would find and execute. This still works, but most setup tasks are much simpler using GenericSetup. Some operations, such as installing workflows, no longer have feasible non-GenericSetup alternatives.

An `install.py` script may contain one or both of two methods:

```
def install(self, reinstall=False):
    ...
def uninstall(self, reinstall=False):
    ...
```

If present, these will be called upon install and uninstall from the control panel, with the `reinstall` flag set if the user is performing a reinstallation.

Note that as far as the QuickInstaller is concerned, an `Install.py` file takes precedence over an extension profile. In Chapter 7, we will see how to explicitly invoke an extension profile from an `Install.py` file that is responsible for installing various dependencies.

Acquisition and Skin Layers

Acquisition is simultaneously one of best and worst features of Zope 2. Consider that Zope manages a hierarchy of objects, each of which (except the Zope application root) has exactly one parent. In traditional object-oriented programming, a subclass can gain attributes and methods from its super-classes. Zope 2 acquisition wraps Python objects retrieved from the ZODB or being found during URL traversal in such a way that they can also *acquire* attributes from their parents in the hierarchy. For example, some code may read:

```
context.getDefault()
```

Here, `context` may be the current content object, and `getDefault()` could be a method on its containing folder, or another folder higher up. *Closer* attributes always take precedence.

Other types of objects can also be acquired. For example, remember that each CMF tool is a persistent object in the root of the Plone site. Lazily written code thus often looks like this:

```
return context.portal_membership.getAuthenticatedUser()
```

> Note that the safer, more flexible version of this statement looks up the tool by name:
>
> ```
> from Products.CMFCore.utils import getToolByName
> return getToolByName(context,
> 'portal_membership').getAuthenticatedUser()
> ```

Here, we are acquiring the `portal_membership` tool and calling a method on it. Again, `context` could be an object anywhere in the Plone site.

Acquisition also applies to templates and scripts. The following is found at the top of nearly all Plone-specific page templates:

```
<html metal:use-macro="context/main_template/macros/main">
```

This means "find the object `main_template`, be it an attribute on the `context` object, an attribute on one of its parents, or a script or template or other object contained in a parent folder". Normally, of course, the first thing Zope finds in this case is Plone's main page template.

We also see acquisition take place during URL traversal. For example, the URL `/plone-site/front-page/document_view` will cause Zope to look for an attribute, object or template called `document_view` relative to the `front-page` object. As it happens, `document_view` is a page template, written in terms of an abstract context, and thus able to render a document-like object no matter where in the portal it is.

In the early days of Zope 2 development, all objects, including page templates and scripts, would be kept in the ZODB rather than on the file system and edited through the Web. Using acquisition, it is possible to let specific templates and scripts in a subfolder take precedence over more general ones higher up. Using *more local* objects to override general ones higher up in the containment hierarchy is thus a way to customize an application.

Unfortunately, keeping application logic (scripts and templates) in the ZODB quickly becomes a problem: recall Seaver's Law. Therefore, the CMF extends acquisition with a mechanism known as **skin layers**, which lets us manage templates and scripts on the file system.

In the `portal_skins` tool in the ZMI, you will see a number of folders:

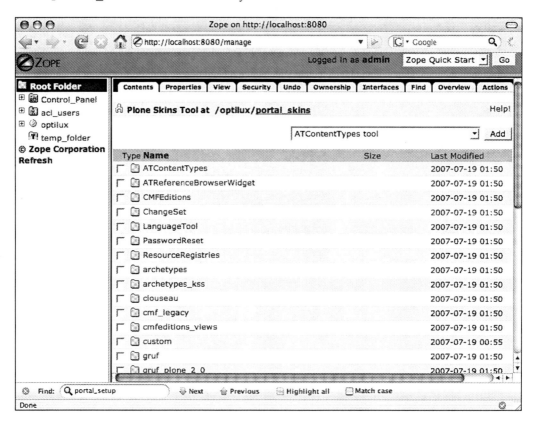

Except for the **custom** folder, which is managed in the ZODB, these are actually just views of directories on the file system, by convention found in a directory called `skins/` inside various products.

On the **Properties** tab of `portal_skins`, you will see a list of **skins**, (also called **themes)** of which one will be currently selected as the default (probably **Plone Default**).

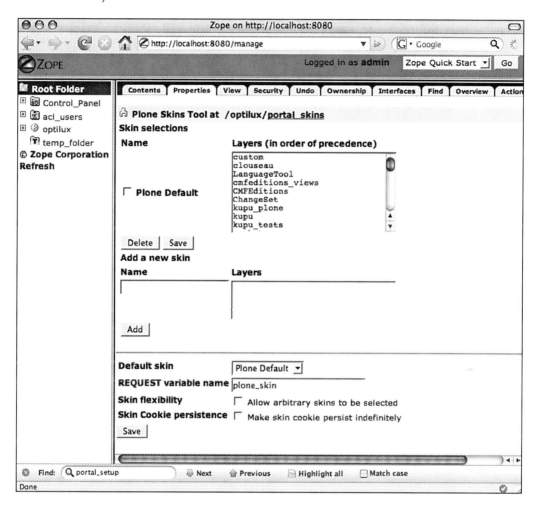

Each theme contains an ordered list of skin layers, referring to the folders in the previous screenshot. As Zope looks for an object to acquire *up* the containment hierarchy, once it comes to the root of the Plone site, CMF will direct it *down* the skin layers, in the order defined for the current skin. Similarly to location-based acquisition, items higher up in the skin layers (i.e. those checked first) will take precedence. This means that a third-party product can install a new skin layer near the top (conventionally, new skin layers are added just beneath **custom**) and override some of Plone's standard templates, for example.

Furthermore, administrators can perform customizations through the Web by placing items in the **custom** folder at the top of the layers. There is even a button to copy a script or template to the **custom** folder when you open an object inside one of the other skin layer folders in portal_skins. For serious development, however, **through-the-web customization** is not recommended, because it robs you of the ability to use source code management tools and has the same problems of deployment and repeatability as persistent settings. In the next chapter, we will show how a policy product can manage customizations more effectively.

Acquisition is very powerful (the same mechanism underpins Zope 2 security, for example), but as you may have guessed, it can sometimes lead to unexpected results. Acquired objects, attributes, and templates essentially form one giant namespace. If an object obj has a method named document_view() it will be called when Zope traverses to obj/document_view. Of course, that may be what was intended (the method could for example explicitly call a different page template to deal with some special case), but it may not be. This also means Plone needs to reserve a number of content IDs to avoid strange errors caused by Zope not finding the right templates or tools.

Perhaps surprisingly, this is not as a big a problem in practice as it may seem. Most of the time, some testing and consideration of naming policies are all that is needed. However, as Plone grows, so does the strain of the single namespace. Luckily, Zope 3 has a solution.

Overriding Zope 3 Components

In the Zope 3 Component Architecture, a **browser view** is a Python class and/or page template (depending on how it is configured) that acts as a page or action. Unlike templates in skin layers, browser views are registered for a particular type of object, described by an interface. They can also be distinguished from content objects and acquirable attributes explicitly. We will learn more about writing and configuring browser views in Chapters 8, 9, and 11, but for now consider the following registration in Zope 3's ZCML (Zope Configuration Meta-Language) syntax:

```
<browser:page
    name="list-contents"
    for=".interfaces.IMyType"
    permission="zope2.View"
    class=".browser.listcontents.ListContentsView"
    template="browser/listcontents.pt"
    />
```

This statement, which could be found in a `configure.zcml` file in some product, configures a new browser view with the name `list-contents`, defined by a particular template and a class to house the view logic related to that template. It is protected by a particular permission, and only available when its context provides the fictitious `IMyType` interface.

The view could be invoked with a URL like `/some-folder/some-content/@@list-contents`. The `@@` part disambiguates `list-contents` as a view. It is optional, but attributes and objects in folders will take precedence if there is a name conflict and the `@@` is omitted. If the `some-context` object did not declare support for the `IMyType` interface, `@@list-contents` would simply not be available and would result in a `NotFound` exception, with a 404 (HTTP Not Found) error being showed to the user.

If we wanted to customize this fictitious view, we could use a special file called `overrides.zcml`. This file, if included in a package, can be used to override registrations from other packages. Note that there can only be one override for each particular declaration (in this case, the specific name and interface combination), so this is not quite as flexible as skin layers. In Chapter 8, we will see how to use Zope 3's concept of **browser layers** (which are different from CMF layers, although they serve a similar purpose) to override views when a particular theme is being used.

More generally, however, component registrations can be overridden for *more specific* interfaces. For example, say `some-context` above was of class `MyType`, which implemented the interface `IMyType` (the one the view is registered for). Let us say we had an object `other-context`, of type `MyOtherType` that was a subclass of `MyType` and happened to also provide an interface `IMyOtherType`. The `@@list-contents` view would be available on `other-context`, because of its super-class, but we could provide a more specific version just for objects providing `IMyOtherType` as follows:

```
<browser:page
    name="list-contents"
    for=".interfaces.IMyOtherType"
    permission="zope2.View"
    class=".browser.listcontents.ListOtherContentsView"
    template="browser/listothercontents.pt"
    />
```

This approach—letting a more specific registration override another, more generic one, as described by the interfaces provided by an object—permeates the Zope 3 Component Architecture. As it happens, views are simply a special case of **adapters**, which are used to encapsulate particular aspects of an object's associated logic (in this case, the display logic). Very specific aspects of an application's behavior can thus be customized and general aspects can be re-used with appropriate component registrations.

All of this will become clearer in Chapter 9. For now, you need only appreciate that Zope 3's concept of customization by interface is an evolution of Zope 2's concept of customization by location and CMF's concept of customization by skin layer.

Customization Best Practices

We will see lots of examples throughout this book of customizations and extensions to Plone's out-of-the-box behavior. Hopefully, these will demonstrate sound working principles and practical patterns. There are a few general concepts that are worth understanding, though.

Using Source Control

In the previous chapter, we learned how to set up a development sandbox containing all the dependencies of our project. Development sandboxes are best treated as dispensable. Tools like zc.buildout make it easy to re-create sandboxes. This, in turn, makes it easier to manage the development process, and start again if things go awry.

It is important to be able to revert to earlier versions of your code base, for example if you discover that you made a mistake at some point, perhaps weeks ago. Any serious project should use a source code management system, and all developers should learn how to use such systems effectively.

The most popular source control system among Plone developers is Subversion (`http://subversion.tigris.org`), which is also used by Plone itself, and works on all modern platforms. This fits the *local sandbox* mode of development, because Subversion, like its predecessor CVS, assumes a distributed network of developers. Each developer checks out a local copy of the code to work on, and commits changes back regularly. If conflicts arise, Subversion will attempt to merge changes. If it fails, it will require the developer to resolve conflicts manually before being allowed to commit the change.

This works well, even for a large project like Plone. However, it requires some discipline, which is good practice even in small or single-developer projects:

- Always update your local sandbox before you begin work. This ensures that you have the latest changes and are less likely to be subject to conflicts later.

- Commit one change at a time. Do not check in code only once a day (or week!). This makes it easier to *revert* (undo) specific changes without affecting other ones.

- Write sensible commit log messages. If you need to find a particular revision again later, you will regret having committed it with a message saying only *"Committed latest changes"*.

- If applicable, reference specific bug/issue numbers or items in the specification when writing commit log messages. This makes requirements and defects traceable.

- Run all the tests for a component (or better yet, the entire project) before checking in any changes. Otherwise, you may have broken something and not realized it. Leaving tests in a broken state for other developers to untangle is an unforgivable sin in large projects like Plone, and should be in your own work as well.

Writing Tests

If source code management tools let you recover from your mistakes, automated unit and integration tests help you make fewer mistakes in the first place. Test-driven development is hugely important, and is a habit that should be second nature to every developer. We will write tests for everything we do in this book, demonstrating several testing techniques.

The basic premise of unit testing is that after writing an interface or stub method for a particular piece of code, you write a test for it—*before* you write the functionality itself. The test should assert the state of the application after the code under test has been called, to prove that the code works as expected.

A **unit** test should be as small as possible, and test the most common cases and edge cases. Tests are run in splendid isolation, and should not depend on one another in any way. The testing framework takes care of resetting the **test fixture** for each test. Tests are combined into a **test suite** and run automatically when the test suite is invoked. The **test runner** reports on which tests fail, and why.

Obviously, if a test is written before the code it tests, it should fail—if it does not, then either the test is invalid, or the code is not actually needed. The challenge is then to write code that makes the test pass, and ensure that it keeps on passing. Thus, if the test coverage is good, developers can be more confident that they do not accidentally break code they thought was working. Unit testing is no substitute for testing by real users (often referred to as *through-the-web testing*), but neither is user testing a substitute for having decent automated test coverage.

Code not covered by tests is by definition incomplete and almost certainly bad for you and your project.

When writing customizations, it is particularly important to have tests that prove that the installation and set-up code is working. As our local sandbox becomes more sophisticated, we may add something to the set-up code to replicate a particular setting initially made manually through the Web while exploring different approaches to solve a particular problem. Tests are the best way to know whether this would work on a new site, such as when the production environment is being set up.

There will be lots of examples of full tests in this book, but here is a short example of what a test may look like. In this case, we are checking that the setTitle() method of a standard *Document* (a.k.a. *Page*) works as expected:

```
from Products.PloneTestCase import PloneTestCase
PloneTestCase.setupPloneSite()

class TestDocuments(PloneTestCase):

    def afterSetUp(self):
        self.folder.invokeFactory('Document', id='d1')

    def testSetTitle(self):
        self.folder.d1.setTitle("New title")
        self.assertEquals("New title", self.folder.d1.Title())

def test_suite():
    suite = unittest.TestSuite()
    suite.addTest(unittest.makeSuite(TestDocuments))
    return suite
```

For more information, the testing tutorial at http://plone.org/documentation/tutorial/testing is essential reading, and will teach you a lot more about how to write tests in different styles and how to run them.

Migration of Persistent State

Recall that the ZODB manages Python **pickles**—serializations of objects that can be stored on disk and resurrected. Pickles may reference specific classes and attributes. This is convenient because it absolves the developer from worrying about how persistent objects are managed. The only requirement is that the persistent class inherits from persistence.Persistent, either directly or indirectly.

However, if we change the code that was the original basis for the pickle, Zope may fail to read back the value that was stored. If a class was moved or removed, Zope may not be able to read the object at all. In this case, the ZMI may list a `BrokenObject`, a special kind of wrapper for broken pickles, instead of the object you were expecting.

A common solution to this problem is to create compatibility aliases to old code and emit deprecation warnings. This means that other code (including the ZODB) that tries to import the old object will still find it. Take a look at the `zope.deferredimport` module, which comes with Zope. Search the Plone source code for calls to `zope.deferredimport.deprecated` to see some examples.

 Hopefully after reading the previous chapter, you will have guessed to look in `$SOFTWARE_HOME/zope/deferredimport`, If you are using zc.buildout, it will be in `parts/zope2/lib/python/zope/deferredimport`, and like most Zope 3 modules comes with a comprehensive `README.txt` file.

Where the persistent parts of classes have changed, you may need to perform ZODB migration. Migration code typically searches for objects that may be in the *old* state and modifies them. This can sometimes be tricky, and requires careful testing.

 If you have this need, a library called `contentmigration` and found in Plone's Subversion repository may be of help. See `http://svn.plone.org/svn/collective/contentmigration/trunk`.

For triggering migrations, Plone itself uses the `portal_migration` tool. For your own packages, you can either write custom migration scripts—perhaps invoking them as part of the re-installation routine for your product—or use the registry of upgrade steps managed by the `portal_setup` tool. We will show how to register such an upgrade step in Chapter 19.

Instead of writing object-modifying migration scripts, you may attempt to write code that degrades gracefully, for example by checking for variables that are no longer used. Here is a reasonably common pattern to avoid the need for explicit migration:

```
def get_value(self):
    # We used to store the value in a variable called '_val'.
    # Now we store it as 'value', and we store the value as a number,
    # not a string
    value = getattr(self, 'value', None)
    if value is None:
        value = getattr(self, '_val', None)
```

```
    try:
        value = int(old_val)
    except ValueError:
        pass
return value
```

In general, if users of your code would need a completely fresh site to ensure it is in a proper state after you have made some change to the source code, you probably need migration when doing new releases. Such persistence can feel a lot like saying sorry indeed.

Summary

In this chapter, we have covered:

- How persistent settings in the ZODB may need to be scripted or described using GenericSetup to make it possible to repeat a configuration across multiple environments.

- The way in which Zope Acquisition and CMF skin layers are used to customize templates and scripts by context and arbitrary priority.

- Briefly, the approach to customization exposed by Zope 3. This will be covered in more detail as we introduce Zope 3 concepts more fully in Chapter 9.

- A few things to bear in mind when writing customizations, including the importance of using source control, writing unit/integration tests and managing migrations.

Next, we will demonstrate how the site infrastructure for our example application is encapsulated in its policy product, making use of these techniques.

5
Developing a Site Strategy

In the previous chapter, we learned about various ways in which a developer can customize Plone without needing to change the source code of Plone itself. In this chapter, we will take a closer look at the requirements from Chapter 2 and create a *policy product*, which will facilitate the customizations necessary to implement these requirements.

Creating a "Policy Product"

Our *policy product* is just a package that can be installed as an add-on component to Plone. We will use a GenericSetup extension profile to *extend* a vanilla Plone installation into one that is configured to our client's needs. We could have used a full-site GenericSetup profile instead, but by using a GenericSetup extension profile we can avoid replicating the majority of the configuration that is done by Plone.

To create the package that houses this product, we will use `paster` with the `plone` template from ZopeSkel, which we installed in Chapter 3. This template creates a simple package inside a namespace of our choosing (in this case the namespace is `optilux.*`), with some boilerplate code to make it a full-blown Zope product.

 To see all installed Paste Script templates,
run `paster create --list-templates`

Go into the `src` directory of the buildout we created in Chapter 3, and run the following command:

```
$ paster create -t plone optilux.policy
```

Enter `optilux` as the namespace package, and `policy` as the package name. Answer `True` when asked to create a Zope 2 product, and `False` when asked whether the package is *zip safe*. Fill in the remainder of the metadata (author name, email address, home page, and so on) as you wish.

 Python can run a *zip safe* package from a compressed archive without unpacking it first. This places some restrictions on the package's use of files, which means that most Zope products are not zip safe.

There should now be a new directory `src/optilux.policy`, containing a `setup.py` file with Python egg information based on the answers given to `paster`, as well as skeletal documentation and other metadata. The real code is in the `optilux/policy` sub-folder.

Before we can use this product, we need to tell the buildout about it. Edit the `buildout.cfg` file, and add the following:

```
[buildout]
...
eggs =
    optilux.policy
develop =
    src/optilux.policy
...
[instance]
zcml =
    optilux.policy
```

This registers a new development egg, makes it available in the instance, and tells buildout to create a ZCML *slug* in `etc/package-includes` in the Zope instance.

 A ZCML *slug* lets Zope find our new package at startup. It contains a line like `<include package="optilux.policy" file="configure.zcml" />`. We will learn more about these in Chapter 9.

Next we must re-run buildout to let the changes take effect. Offline mode will speed it up a little.

```
$ bin/buildout -o
```

We can test that this works using the `zopepy` interpreter:

```
$ bin/zopepy
>>> from optilux import policy
>>>
```

The absence of an `ImportError` tells us that this package will now be known to the Zope instance in the buildout. If you start Zope, go to the ZMI, and look in the **Control_Panel** at the root of the Zope instance, you should see **optilux.policy** listed under **Products**.

Creating an Extension Profile

Let us now register a new extension profile for the policy product. We can do so in our new package's `configure.zcml` file, which is read at Zope start-up thanks to the ZCML slug. Edit `src/optilux.policy/optilux/policy/configure.zcml` to look like this:

```
<configure
    xmlns="http://namespaces.zope.org/zope"
    xmlns:five="http://namespaces.zope.org/five"
    xmlns:genericsetup="http://namespaces.zope.org/genericsetup"
    i18n_domain="optilux.policy">

    <five:registerPackage package="." initialize=".initialize" />

    <genericsetup:registerProfile
      name="default"
      title="Optilux Site Policy"
      directory="profiles/default"
      description="Turn a Plone site into the Optilux site."
      provides="Products.GenericSetup.interfaces.EXTENSION"
      />

</configure>
```

The `<genericsetup:registerProfile />` stanza registers a new profile. The title and description will be shown to the user when installing the policy product. The name is usually `default`, because the full profile name includes the product name where the registration is made. In this case, it will be `optilux.policy:default`. If you have multiple extension profiles registered in the same product, they will need different names, as well as different directories.

The `directory` argument tells GenericSetup where to look for the XML files that the various import handles will read, relative to the package. By convention, this is `profiles/default` for the primary profile. We must create these directories manually:

```
$ mkdir optilux.policy/optilux/policy/profiles
$ mkdir optilux.policy/optilux/policy/profiles/default
```

Writing Tests for Customizations

We will begin by making a simple change: setting the title in the browser window. This is managed as a property called `title` on the root of the Plone site root. You can view it in the ZMI by clicking the **Properties** tab for the site root.

Like good software developers, we will write automated tests before implementing the functionality. Tests conventionally go into the `tests` directory of a package. We also create an insulating base class for all our tests so that we can perform test setup that is shared across multiple test suites.

Create the `tests` module like this:

```
$ cd src/optilux.policy/optilux/policy
$ mkdir tests
$ touch tests/__init__.py
```

The empty `__init__.py` file makes this a Python package. Now create a file called `tests/base.py`, containing:

```python
from Products.Five import zcml
from Products.Five import fiveconfigure

from Testing import ZopeTestCase as ztc

from Products.PloneTestCase import PloneTestCase as ptc
from Products.PloneTestCase.layer import onsetup

@onsetup
def setup_optilux_policy():
    """Set up the additional products required for the Optilux site
    policy.

    The @onsetup decorator causes the execution of this body to be
deferred
    until the setup of the Plone site testing layer.
    """

    # Load the ZCML configuration for the optilux.policy package.

    fiveconfigure.debug_mode = True
    import optilux.policy
    zcml.load_config('configure.zcml', optilux.policy)
    fiveconfigure.debug_mode = False

    # We need to tell the testing framework that these products
    # should be available. This can't happen until after we have loaded
```

```
    # the ZCML.

    ztc.installPackage('optilux.policy')

# The order here is important: We first call the (deferred) function
# which installs the products we need for the Optilux package. Then,
# we let PloneTestCase set up this product on installation.
setup_optilux_policy()
ptc.setupPloneSite(products=['optilux.policy'])
class OptiluxPolicyTestCase(ptc.PloneTestCase):
    """We use this base class for all the tests in this package. If
necessary,
    we can put common utility or setup code in here.
    """
```

This notifies Zope and the Zope 3 Component Architecture of our package by loading its `configure.zcml`. This is done so that we do not depend on the test runner having read the ZCML slug that buildout installed for us. The test layer extends the default `PloneSite` layer, which means that we will get the test setup for all of Plone as well. The `_setup()` method, which is called before each test, ensures that the product is installed, using the `portal_quickinstaller` tool.

The tests themselves are straightforward. Add the following to `tests/test_setup.py`:

```
import unittest
from optilux.policy.tests.base import OptiluxPolicyTestCase

class TestSetup(OptiluxPolicyTestCase):

    def test_portal_title(self):
        self.assertEquals("Optilux Cinemas", self.portal.
getProperty('title'))

    def test_portal_description(self):
        self.assertEquals("Welcome to Optilux Cinemas",
                          self.portal.getProperty('description'))
def test_suite():
    suite = unittest.TestSuite()
    suite.addTest(unittest.makeSuite(TestSetup))
    return suite
```

We should now be able to run the tests. Both of these tests should fail, since we have not yet written the functionality to make them pass.

```
$ ./bin/instance test -s optilux.policy

Running tests at level 1

...

AssertionError: 'Welcome to Optilux Cinemas' != ''

...

AssertionError: 'Optilux Cinemas' != 'Plone site'

  Ran 2 tests with 2 failures and 0 errors in 0.311 seconds.
```

The actual output is a little more verbose, but these lines tell us that both our tests failed, as expected.

 Refer to Chapter 4, and to http://plone.org/documentation/ tutorial/testing if you are unfamiliar with testing concepts and APIs.

Making a Change with the Extension Profile

Now, create a file inside src/optilux.policy/optilux/policy/profiles/ default called properties.xml, containing the following:

```
<?xml version="1.0"?>
<site>
 <property name="title">Optilux Cinemas</property>
 <property name="description">Welcome to Optilux Cinemas</property>
</site>
```

This is taken from the corresponding file in CMFPlone/profiles/default, reduced to include only the properties we want to change. One of the import steps in Plone's base profile, *Site Properties*, knows how to read this file and set properties on the portal root accordingly.

Hopefully, the tests should pass now:

```
$ ./bin/instance test -s optilux.policy

Running tests at level 1

...

  Ran 2 tests with 0 failures and 0 errors in 0.648 seconds.
```

Installation through the Web

Finally, we should verify that we can install the product through the Plone interface. Start Zope and go to the Plone interface. Under **Site Setup**, in **Add/Remove Products**, the new package should have appeared:

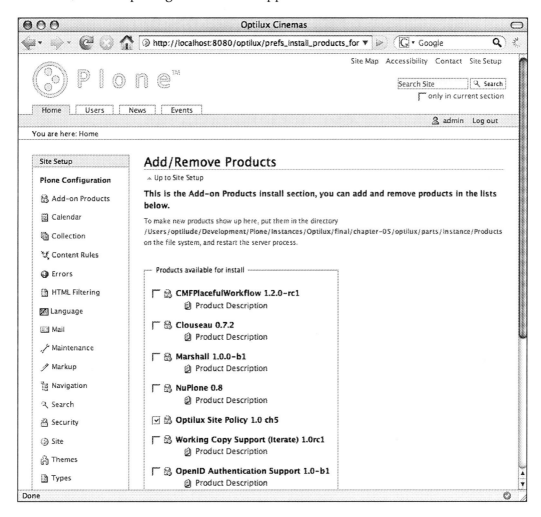

Install it, and verify that installing it causes the title in the browser to change.

Information Architecture

Let us now re-visit the requirements from Chapter 2. Several of them have implications for the site's information architecture. Here are the relevant parts of the list again, highlighting in bold those items that suggest that the site may need to provide a particular section or page:

	Requirement	Importance
2	The site should show information about all of Optilux's **cinemas**.	High
4	The site should allow staff to highlight **promotions** and special events. These may apply to **one or more cinemas**.	High
5	Cinema staff should be able to publish information about new **films**. It should be possible to update this information after publication.	High
6	Customers should be able to find out in which cinemas a particular film is showing (a **screening**), and which films are showing at a particular cinema. Note that the scheduling of films at cinemas is managed in an existing relational database.	High
9	Customers should be able to reserve **tickets** online. Tickets will be picked up and payment taken at the cinema. Reservations must use Optilux's existing relational database-based ticketing system.	Medium
10	Cinema managers should be able to view **reports** on reservations and site usage.	Medium
12	Logged-in customers should have easy access to their **preferred cinema or cinemas**, e.g. those in their area.	Medium
14	Customers should be able to **discuss** and **rate** movies.	Low
15	The site should support cinema staff in developing future programming and promotions through a private **collaborative workspace**.	Low

The site design mock-up gives some clues as to how these elements may be related.

The links across the top and in the left-hand side navigation will most likely expose the main functionality of the site. Different options may appear for logged-in customers, cinema staff, or managers, as appropriate. Note that the labels in the mock-up are suggestions from the graphic designer. The actual information architecture may be different, depending on how the site administrator wishes to set it all up.

The following outline shows the initial information architecture for the site, based on the requirements specification.

Section	Purpose	Content types	Visibility
Home	Front page, contains general information	*Folder, Page*	All
About Optilux	General information about Optilux Cinemas	*Folder, Page*	All
About membership	Information about membership benefits	*Folder, Page*	All
Films	Container for films, including film listing	*Film Folder*	All
First film	Information about a film currently showing	*Film*	All
Unpublished film	A film not yet visible to the public	*Film*	Staff
Cinemas	Container for cinemas, including listings	*Cinema Folder*	All
Region one	Container for cinemas in one region	*Cinema Folder*	All
Promotion	A promotion specific to *Region one*	*Promotion*	All
Cinema one	A cinema in *Region one*	*Cinema*	All
Screening times	Listing of screening times for films	*(Screening)*	All
Reserve	Form to reserve tickets for a screening	*(Reservation)*	Member
Cinema two	Another cinema in *Region one*	*Cinema*	All
Promotion	A promotion specific to *Cinema two*	*Promotion*	All
Future promotion	A promotion not yet visible	*Promotion*	Staff
Region two	Container for cinemas in another region	*Cinema Folder*	All
Corporate information	General corporate information	*Folder, Page*	All
Workspaces	A staff-only are where projects are hosted	*Folder*	Staff
Project one	A project, visible to all staff	*Workspace*	Staff
Project two	Another project, private to one group	*Workspace*	Some staff

This outline should translate more or less to a site map of the content hierarchy. There are a number of custom content types envisaged here. We therefore cannot create this structure yet, but we could create the ones that only rely on standard folders and pages. Typically, a folder may represent a section, and have a *front page* set as its default view, using the **Display** menu in Plone.

This is also the pattern that will be used for custom content types. For example, we will create a *Cinema Folder* type to contain cinemas. The default view of the cinema folder will allow users to browse for cinemas. These will be built in Chapter 10. In Chapter 13, we will show how to add private collaborative workspaces to one area of the site.

We will not encode the site structure in our policy product. Plone is flexible enough to leave this decision up to site administrators, who may create the root content and arrange it as appropriate. If each top-level section is a folder or a folder-like object in the root of the portal site, the tabs across the top will be automatically generated. The left-hand side navigation may reflect the content items as it does in the standard Plone navigation tree. We will address this as part of the site theme, in Chapter 8.

Summary

In this chapter, we have shown:

- How to create a "policy product" to encapsulate a specific policy for a site
- How to use a GenericSetup extension profile to customize various aspects of Plone
- An example of how to translate the requirements and high-level modeling into the information architecture for the site

As we build new functionality throughout the book, we will continue to add to the policy product. In the next chapter, we will extend it with custom workflow and security settings.

6
Security and Workflow

Security should never be an afterthought, particularly when building web applications. Luckily, Zope and Plone provide a robust and flexible security model that lets you concentrate on building your application instead of worrying too much about how to lock it down. That is, so long as you understand a few basics.

In this chapter, we will explain the building blocks of Zope security — users, roles, and permissions — as well as workflows, the usual way to manage permissions in Plone. As a demonstration, we will build a custom workflow for the Optilux website and add it to the policy product we created in the previous chapter.

Security Primitives

Zope's security is *declarative*. Views, actions, and attributes on content objects are protected by **permissions** and Zope takes care of verifying that the current user has the appropriate access rights. If not, an `AccessControl.Unauthorized` exception will be raised.

Permissions are not given directly to users. Instead, permissions are assigned to **roles**. Users can be given any number of roles, either globally in the portal, or in the context of a particular folder. Global and local roles can also be assigned to **groups**, in which case all users in that group will have the particular role. This makes security settings much more manageable than if they were assigned to individual users.

Users and Groups

Users and groups are kept in a **user folder**, called `acl_users`. There is one at the root of the Zope instance, typically containing only the default Zope-wide administrator. There is also an `acl_users` folder inside Plone, which manages Plone's users and groups.

Since version 2.5, Plone has used the **Pluggable Authentication Service** (**PAS**), a particularly flexible kind of user folder. In PAS, users, groups, their roles, and their properties are constructed using various interchangeable plug-ins. For example, an LDAP plug-in could allow users to be found in an LDAP repository. We will revisit PAS in Chapter 13, when we look at more advanced member management, and again in Chapter 18, when we configure LDAP authentication.

You can manage users and groups from `acl_users` in the ZMI, but the user interface here can be a little confusing. A much better place to create users and groups is Plone's **Users and Groups** control panel, under **Site Setup**.

Permissions

Plone relies on a large number of permissions to control various aspects of its functionality. To see for yourself, go into the ZMI and click the **Security** tab at the root of the Plone site. This tab lets you assign permissions to roles at a particular object. Note that for most permissions, the **Acquire permission settings** checkbox is checked, meaning that permissions cascade down from the parent. Role assignments are additive when permissions are set to acquire.

Sometimes, it is appropriate to change permission settings at the root of the site, but managing permissions from the **Security** tab anywhere else is almost never a good idea. Keeping track of which security settings are made where in a complex site can be a nightmare.

Permissions are the most granular piece of the security puzzle, and can be seen as a consequence of a user's roles in the particular context.

 Security-aware code should almost always check for permissions, rather than roles. Checking for specific user or group names is rarely a good idea, because roles can change depending on the current context and security policy of the site.

Permissions come in three main flavors:

- Permissions that relate to basic content operations, such as *View* and *Modify portal content*. These are used by almost all content types, and defined as constants in `Products.CMFCore.permissions`. Core permissions are normally managed by workflow.

- Permissions that control the creation of particular types of content objects, such as *ATContentTypes: Add Image*. These may be set at the portal root to apply to the whole portal, or they may be managed by folder-level workflow.

- Permissions for site-wide policy. For example, the *Portlets: Manage portlets* permission is given to the *Manager* role, because this is a manager-only operation. These permissions are usually set at the portal root and acquired everywhere else. Occasionally, it may be appropriate to change them at the site root. For example, the *Add portal member* permission controls whether anonymous users can add themselves (i.e. *join* the site). In Plone 3, however, there is a control panel setting for this, under **Security** in **Site Setup**.

Developers can create new permissions when necessary, although they are encouraged to re-use the ones in `Products.CMFCore.permissions` if at all possible. We will see examples of declaring new permissions (controlling the ability to add content of various types) when we create custom content types in Chapter 10, and again in Chapter 12.

The most commonly used permissions are:

Permission	Constant	Zope 3-style name	Controls
Access contents information	`AccessContents-Information`	`zope2.AccessContents-Information`	Low-level Zope permission controlling access to objects.
View	`View`	`zope2.View`	Access to the main view of a content object.
List folder contents	`ListFolderContents`	`cmf.ListFolderContents`	Ability to view folder listings.
Modify portal content	`ModifyPortalContent`	`cmf.ModifyPortalContent`	Edit operations on content.
Manage portal	`ManagePortal`	`cmf.ManagePortal`	Operations typically restricted to the *Manager* role.
Add portal content	`AddPortalContent`	`cmf.AddPortalContent`	Ability to add new content in a folder. Note that many content types have their own "add" permissions. In this case, both this permission and the type-specific permission are required.

The **Constant** column refers to constants defined in `Products.CMFCore.permissions`. The **Zope 3-style name** column lists the equivalent names found in `Products.Five`'s `permissions.zcml`, which contains directives such as:

```
<permission
  id="zope2.View"
  title="View"
  />
```

This is how new permissions are defined in pure Zope 3. Sometimes, we will use ZCML directives, which expect a `permission` attribute, such as:

```
<browser:page
    name="some-view"
    class=".someview.SomeView"
    for="*"
    permission="zope2.View"
    />
```

The `permission` here must be a Zope 3 permission `id`. In Zope 2 with Five, the `title` of the `<permission />` directive is used to map Zope 2 permissions (which are really just strings) to Zope 3 permissions. In fact, permissions in Zope 3 are named utilities providing `IPermission`, but you don't need to worry about that.

Roles

Roles can be assigned to users and/or groups from the **Users and Groups** control panel. It is usually easier to create logical groups that can be assigned a set of roles once, rather than to manage those roles for each and every user. The *Administrators* and *Reviewers* groups that are created by default have the *Manager* and *Reviewer* roles, respectively.

Local role assignment is usually managed via the **Sharing** tab that appears on most content items. You can search for a user or group to assign local roles. Note that the set of roles on the sharing tab is limited to those explicitly white-listed.

 See the `plone.app.workflow` module, in particular the `localroles.py` file and the related entries in `configure.zcml`. You can use similar declarations in your own product to make more roles available through the sharing tab.

Other local roles can be granted from the **Security** tab in the ZMI. However, you should only do this if absolutely necessary. Again, workflow is normally a more appropriate way of managing local security assignments.

There are six key roles in a default Plone installation.

- *Member* is the default role for a portal user. Quite a few permissions that normally apply to logged in uses are given to this role, so it makes sense to re-use it where possible.

- *Manager* is the super-user role. Members of the *Administrators* group will have this role.

- *Reviewer*, granted to the *Reviewers* group, allow users to view and approve content that has been submitted for review.

- *Reader* is intended to be used as a local role only. It can be assigned from the **Sharing** tab. When granted the *Reader* role, a user will (almost) always be allowed to view the content object, even when normal *Members* cannot.

- *Editor*, the counterpart to *Reader*, is used to assign modification rights locally. This allows content owners to delegate edit permissions selectively to other users.

- *Contributor* is used to delegate permission to add content items in folders. It appears on the **Sharing** tab under the title **Can add**.

 If you create a new content type with a custom *add* permission, you should normally grant this to the *Contributor* role. Similarly, if you have any custom permissions necessary to view an object, they should normally be granted to the *Reader* role, while any permissions necessary to modify an object should be granted to the *Editor* role.

In addition, Zope defines three automatically assigned roles:

- *Owner* is given to the owner of the current content item. Normally, this is the user who created it.

- *Authenticated* is given to all logged-in users. This is more low-level than the *Member* role and cannot be revoked or granted explicitly. Therefore, it is usually better to rely on the *Member* role when designing a permission scheme for logged-in users.

- *Anonymous* refers to non-logged in users. There is a special user object, also called *Anonymous*, which is always granted this role.

In addition, there is a pseudo-group called *Logged-in users*, which automatically includes all authenticated users. This appears on the **Sharing** tab to allow the site administrators to assign local roles to all logged-in members. For example, you could give the *Contributor* role to this pseudo-group in the default **News** folder to allow any user to create new news items in that folder and submit them for review.

It is possible to create new roles, either through a `rolemap.xml` import handler in a GenericSetup profile, or through the **Security** tab in the ZMI. Think carefully before doing so, however. A large number of custom roles is normally a sign that the security policy is not well thought-through. When adding roles, it is usually necessary to amend the site's workflows to incorporate them.

Manipulating Permissions and Roles Programmatically

Most low-level security operations are provided by the `AccessControl.Role.`
`RoleManager` mix-in class, which is included in all content objects, including the
Plone Site object itself. Take a look at it on the **Doc** tab (assuming you have the
DocFinderTab installed):

RoleManager			
An object that has configurable permissions			
ac_inherited_permissions	Change permissions (Manager)	self, all=0	method
aclAChecked	(Anonymous, Contributor, Editor, Manager, Reader)		str
aclEChecked	(Anonymous, Contributor, Editor, Manager, Reader)		str
aclPChecked	(Anonymous, Contributor, Editor, Manager, Reader)		str
acquiredRolesAreUsedBy	Change permissions (Manager)	self, permission	Used by management screen.

To validate a permission in a particular context—such as the current content object—
for the current user, you can do:

```
from AccessControl import getSecurityManager
from Products.CMFCore.permissions import ModifyPortalContent
sm = getSecurityManager()
if sm.checkPermission(ModifyPortalContent, context):
    # do something
```

Permissions are identified by strings, so you could write `"Modify portal content"`
instead of importing and using `ModifyPortalContent`, but using the constant makes it
less likely that you will make a mistake.

To grant a particular permission to a list of roles, you can use:

```
context.manage_permission("Portlets: Manage portlets",
                          roles=['Manager', 'Owner'], acquire=1)
```

Of course, it would be better to use a constant (provided there is one defined), but as the example shows, strings work too. Set `acquire=0` to turn off acquisition of role assignments.

To find out if the current user is logged-in or not (i.e. whether the user is *anonymous*), you can use the `portal_membership` tool:

```
from Products.CMFCore.utils import getToolByName
mtool = getToolByName(context, 'portal_membership')
if mtool.isAnonymousUser():
    # do something
```

Similarly, you can obtain the current member from this tool:

```
member = mtool.getAuthenticatedMember()
user_id = member.getId()
```

You can also find members by ID using:

```
admin_user = mtool.getMemberById('admin')
```

Take a look at the **Doc** tab of the `portal_membership` tool in the ZMI, or see `Products.CMFCore.MembershipTool` for more information about its API.

Keeping Control with Workflow

As we have alluded to before, managing permissions directly anywhere other than the portal root is normally a bad idea. Every content object in a Plone site is subject to security, and will in most cases inherit permission settings from its parent. If you start making special settings in particular folders, you will quickly lose control.

However, if settings are always acquired, how can we restrict access to particular folders or prevent authors from editing published content while still giving them rights to work on items in a draft state? The answer to both of these problems is workflow.

Workflows are managed via the `portal_workflow` tool. If you view it in the ZMI, you will see a mapping of workflows to content types, including the default workflow used by a number of standard content types.

The workflow definitions themselves are found inside the `portal_workflow` tool, under the **Contents** tab. Each workflow consists of **states**, such as *private* or *published*, and **transitions** between them. Transitions can be protected by permissions or restricted to particular roles. Some transitions are automatic, which means that they will be invoked as soon as an object enters a state that has this transition as a possible exit (provided the guard conditions are met), but normally transitions are invoked following some user action, via the **state** drop-down menu in Plone's user interface.

> Although it is fairly common to protect workflow transitions by role, this is actually not a very good use of the security system. It would be much more sensible to use an appropriate permission. The exception is when custom roles are used solely for the purpose of defining roles in a workflow.

States are sometimes just metadata. For example, it may be useful to be able to mark a content object as *published* and be able to search for all published content. However, when an object enters a particular state (either the initial state when it is first created, or as a result of a workflow transition), the workflow tool will set a number of permissions on that object. The exact permissions that are managed are listed under the **Permissions** tab on the workflow definition:

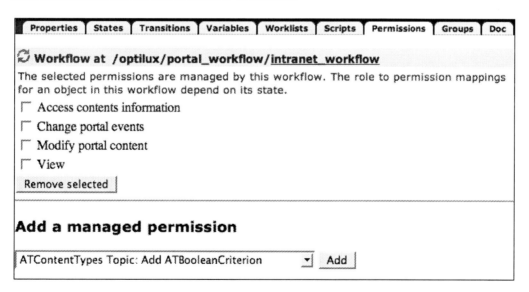

Navigate to the **intranet_workflow** under **portal_workflow** (via the **Contents** tab) click on the **States** tab, and find the **pending** state. Click the **Permissions** tab for the state, and you should see the permission map:

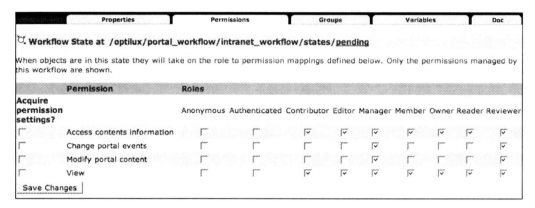

Compare that to the permissions in another state, say **private**:

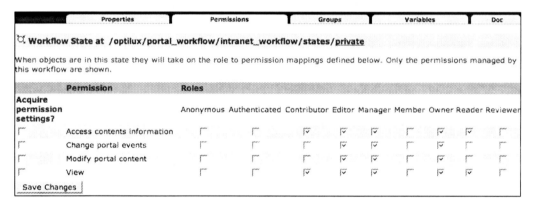

Note that if you change security settings for workflow states, they will not take effect immediately. You need to click the **Update security settings** button, at the bottom of the **Workflows** tab of the **portal_workflow** tool. On large sites, this can take a long time, because it needs to find all content items using the old settings and update their permissions. Therefore, it is preferable to get the workflow right before the site grows very large.

The workflow system is very powerful, and can be used to solve many kinds of problems where objects of the same type need to be in different states. Learning to use it effectively can pay off greatly in the long run.

Using Workflow from Python

Interacting with workflow from your own code is usually straightforward. To get the workflow state of a particular object, you can do:

```
from Products.CMFCore.utils import getToolByName
wftool = getToolByName(context, 'portal_workflow')
review_state = wftool.getInfoFor(context, 'review_state')
```

Note that if you are doing a search using the `portal_catalog` tool, the results it returns already have the review state as metadata:

```
from Products.CMFCore.utils import getToolByName
catalog = getToolByName(context, 'portal_catalog')
for result in catalog(portal_type = ('Document', 'News Item',),
                review_state=('published', 'public', 'visible',)):
    review_state = result.review_state
    # do something with the review_state
```

The catalog tool will be covered in more detail in Chapter 9.

To change the workflow state of an object, you can use:

```
wftool.doActionFor(context, action='publish')
```

The `action` here is the name of a transition, which must be available to the current user, from `context`'s current state. There is no (easy) way to directly specify the target state. This is by design: recall that transitions form the paths between states, and may involve additional security restrictions or the triggering of scripts.

Again, the **Doc** tab for the **portal_workflow** tool and its sub-objects (the workflow definitions and their states and transitions) should be your first point of call if you need more detail. The workflow code can be found in `Products.CMFCore.WorkflowTool` and `Products.DCWorkflow`.

Custom Workflow Installation

It is fairly common to create custom workflows when building a Plone system. Plone 3 ships with several useful workflows, such as an *intranet* workflow and a *community site* workflow, but security and approvals processes tend to differ from site to site, so you will often find yourself modifying these stock workflows to fit your particular use case.

It can be convenient to experiment with workflows in the ZMI, but as we learned in Chapter 4, you should create the final version on the file system using GenericSetup. This can be done from scratch, by copying an existing GenericSetup profile, or by exporting the **Workflow Tool** step from `portal_setup` in the ZMI.

Designing a New Workflow

In the previous chapter, we considered the information architecture for the Optilux Cinemas site, consisting of several custom content types as well as some stock ones. The custom content types will be considered in Chapter 10. For now, we will show how to set up a customized default workflow for the core content types.

It is important to get the design of a workflow policy right, considering the different roles that need to interact with the objects, and the permissions they should have in the various states. The information architecture implies that only cinema staff should be creating content. Draft content should be visible to cinema staff, but not customers, and should go through review before being published.

The following diagram illustrates this workflow:

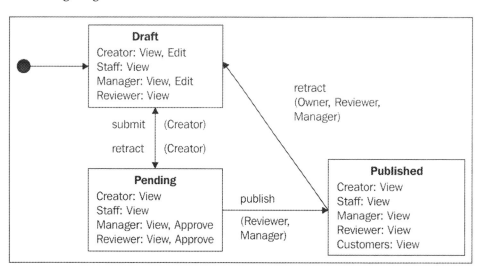

Because we need to distinguish between logged-in customers and staff members, we will introduce a new role called *StaffMember*. We will let the *Manager* role represent site administrators, and the *Reviewer* role represent content reviewers, as they do in a default Plone installation. We will create a new group, *Staff*, which is given the *StaffMember* role.

Amending the Policy Product

In the `optilux.policy` package that we created in Chapter 5, add a file called `rolemap.xml` under `profiles/default`. This file will be read by the **Role/ Permission Map** import step, and can be used to create new roles and map roles to permissions at the root of the site:

```xml
<?xml version="1.0"?>
<rolemap>
  <roles>
    <role name="StaffMember" />
  </roles>
  <permissions>
      <permission name="View"
                 acquire="True">
        <role name="Reader" />
        <role name="Editor" />
        <role name="Contributor" />
        <role name="StaffMember" />
    </permission>
  </permissions>
</rolemap>
```

This will create our new role, and ensure that by default, staff members can view any content (i.e. where the *View* permission is acquired). Note that when we assign roles to a permission with the `<permission />` directive, it overwrites existing role assignments for this permission at the portal root. Therefore, we specify `acquire="True"` for the *View* permission and grant it to the *Reader*, *Editor*, and *Contributor* roles, as is the case in a default Plone installation.

Next, we will add a file called `workflows.xml` in the same directory. This is read by the **Workflow Tool** import step, and can be used to define new workflows as well as to change the mapping of workflows to content types:

```xml
<?xml version="1.0"?>
<object name="portal_workflow" meta_type="Plone Workflow Tool">
 <object name="optilux_sitecontent_workflow" meta_type="Workflow"/>
 <bindings>
  <default>
   <bound-workflow workflow_id="optilux_sitecontent_workflow"/>
  </default>
  <type type_id="File" remove="remove" />
  <type type_id="Image" remove="remove" />
  <type type_id="Plone Site" />
 </bindings>
</object>
```

This will create a new workflow called `optilux_sitecontent_workflow`, and set it as the default. Hence, any content type listed in `portal_workflow` as having a **Default** workflow will now use our new workflow.

As Plone 3 comes configured, the *File* and *Image* types do not have an associated workflow at all. Therefore, we make them use the default workflow explicitly, by removing the special *no workflow* setting. For completeness, we also show how to ensure that the *Plone Site* type remains workflow-less. If you need to set a particular workflow for a particular content type, you can do so with a binding such as this:

```
<type type_id="SomeType">
  <bound-workflow workflow_id="some_workflow"/>
</type>
```

Finally, we need to define the states and transitions for our new workflow. Create the directories `profiles/default/workflows/optilux_sitecontent_workflow` (the name must match the ID of the workflow in `workflows.xml`). Inside this directory, add a file called `definition.xml`. This is shown below, abbreviated to save space. You can find the full version in the book's accompanying source code.

```xml
<?xml version="1.0"?>
<dc-workflow workflow_id="optilux_sitecontent_workflow"
             title="Optilux Site Content"
             state_variable="review_state"
             initial_state="draft">

  <!-- These are the permissions being managed -->
  <permission>Access contents information</permission>
  <permission>Change portal events</permission>
  <permission>List folder contents</permission>
  <permission>Modify portal content</permission>
  <permission>View</permission>

  <!-- The various workflow states, with their permission maps -->
  <state state_id="draft" title="Draft">
   <exit-transition transition_id="publish"/>
   <exit-transition transition_id="submit"/>
   <permission-map name="Access contents information" acquired="False">
    <permission-role>Editor</permission-role>
    <permission-role>Manager</permission-role>
    <permission-role>StaffMember</permission-role>
    <permission-role>Owner</permission-role>
    <permission-role>Reader</permission-role>
    <permission-role>Contributor</permission-role>
   </permission-map>
   <permission-map name="Change portal events" acquired="False">
```

```
 <permission-role>Editor</permission-role>
 <permission-role>Manager</permission-role>
 <permission-role>Owner</permission-role>
</permission-map>
<permission-map name="List folder contents" acquired="False">
 <permission-role>Editor</permission-role>
 <permission-role>Manager</permission-role>
 <permission-role>StaffMember</permission-role>
 <permission-role>Owner</permission-role>
 <permission-role>Reader</permission-role>
<permission-role>Contributor</permission-role>
</permission-map>
<permission-map name="Modify portal content" acquired="False">
 <permission-role>Editor</permission-role>
 <permission-role>Manager</permission-role>
 <permission-role>Owner</permission-role>
</permission-map>
<permission-map name="View" acquired="False">
 <permission-role>Editor</permission-role>
 <permission-role>Manager</permission-role>
 <permission-role>StaffMember</permission-role>
 <permission-role>Owner</permission-role>
 <permission-role>Reader</permission-role>
 <permission-role>Contributor</permission-role>
 </permission-map>
</state>
<state state_id="pending" title="Pending review">
 <exit-transition transition_id="publish"/>
 <exit-transition transition_id="reject"/>
 <exit-transition transition_id="retract"/>
 ...
</state>
<state state_id="published" title="Published">
 <exit-transition transition_id="retract"/>
 ...
</state>
<!-- Transitions between states, including guard conditions -->
<transition transition_id="submit"
            title="Author submits for review"
            new_state="pending" trigger="USER"
            before_script="" after_script="">
 <action url="%(content_url)s/content_status_
                  modify?workflow_action=submit"
        category="workflow">Submit for review</action>
```

```
        <guard>
          <guard-permission>Request review</guard-permission>
        </guard>
      </transition>
      ...
    </dc-workflow>
```

First, we define some general properties about the workflow — its ID, title, the name of the initial state, and the name of the variable holding the review state. The latter should always be `"review_state"`. Next, we enumerate the permissions being managed. Notice the `Change portal events` permission. This is something of a relic from CMF, which protects write operations on the *Event* type.

We then define various states and transitions. For each state, we set the possible *exit transitions* — the ones that will be available in the **State** menu — as well as a mapping of permissions to roles in that particular state. We need to make sure that we include the *Reader, Editor,* and *Contributor* roles as appropriate here. In general, the *Reader* role can view an object when the *Owner* role can; the *Editor* role can view and edit where the *Owner* role can; and the *Contributor* role can always view and add unless a folder is locked down and unable to accept new content.

Transitions are given an ID, a title, and a trigger type — either `"USER"` or `"AUTOMATIC"`. The `<action />` tag contains the name that will be displayed in the **State** menu, and the URL that will be invoked if the user selects this transition. Normally, this uses the `content_status_modify` script as shown. Finally, we set a `guard` permission. If this is not granted to the current user, the transition will not be available.

The omitted code defines the full permission maps, the remaining transitions, as well as a work list (used by the review list portlet) and some standard workflow variables (used in the workflow history). These tend to be the same across all workflows.

Using GenericSetup and defining new workflows is not difficult, but sometimes it can be cumbersome to get all the permissions right. It often helps to draw a table of who can do what in which states and use this to double-check that the security settings are as intended. Some developers also prefer to make changes in the ZMI and then use the GenericSetup export facility to generate a first draft of the `workflows.xml` file, possibly tweaking it on the file system later.

Finally, we must add the staff member group. Here, we have a problem, because there is currently no standard import handler for creating groups. In other words, we cannot just create an XML file. Therefore, we will create a special import step that will invoke some custom setup code for us. This will not cover export of the group configuration, but it will suffice in our case.

Create a new file in `profiles/default` called `import_steps.xml`. This is the file that GenericSetup consults to find out which steps to execute on import. Since we are creating an extension profile, we have been piggy-backing on Plone's import steps up until now. We do not need to re-define the steps that Plone defines, so the file contains only:

```
<?xml version="1.0"?>
<import-steps>
 <import-step id="optilux-various" version="20070308-01"
              handler="optilux.policy.setuphandlers.importVarious"
              title="Additional Optilux site policy setup">
  <dependency step="rolemap"/>
 </import-step>
</import-steps>
```

The import step ID needs to be unique. The version should be unique and incremental over time, and using the date-based format shown is the accepted convention. We also specify that the `rolemap` step must come before this one — otherwise, we would not have enough context to add the group. The `handler` attribute specifies a function that will be called when the import step is run.

A setup handler normally reads an XML file and configures the site accordingly. There are several examples in Plone and the CMF, for example in `Products.CMFCore.exportimport`. In this case, however, we are not writing a generic handler, so we can perform the specific steps in Python. The `optilux.policy.setuphandlers` module contains:

```python
from Products.CMFCore.utils import getToolByName

def setupGroups(portal):
    acl_users = getToolByName(portal, 'acl_users')
    if not acl_users.searchGroups(name='Staff'):
        gtool = getToolByName(portal, 'portal_groups')
        gtool.addGroup('Staff', roles=['StaffMember'])

def importVarious(context):
    """Miscellanous steps import handle
    """
    if context.readDataFile('optilux.policy_various.txt') is None:
        return

    portal = context.getSite()
    setupGroups(portal)
```

Note the explicit check for the file `optilux.policy_various.txt` in the import context.

The `import context` is just the directory that holds the profile files, e.g. the `profiles/default` folder.

A blank file with this name can be found in `profiles/default`. We need this *flag file* because of the way GenericSetup executes import steps. If an import step handler has been registered and run once, it will be called for any subsequent profiles (even from different products) that are imported. Normally, this is harmless because the handler will do nothing if the appropriate XML file cannot be found in the current import context. Here, we do not have an XML file, but we still need to look for a file in the current import context to decide whether the step should be run or not.

If you write an *import various*-type import handler that executes Python code, do not forget to check a *flag file* in the current import context to determine if the import steps should actually be run.

Writing the Tests

Of course, we must not forget the tests for this functionality. Since we are still concerned with site setup, we amend `test_setup.py`, as follows:

```
...
from Products.CMFCore.utils import getToolByName
class TestSetup(OptiluxPolicyTestCase):
    def afterSetUp(self):
        self.workflow = getToolByName(self.portal, 'portal_workflow')
        self.acl_users = getToolByName(self.portal, 'acl_users')
        self.types = getToolByName(self.portal, 'portal_types')

    ...

    def test_role_added(self):
        self.failUnless("StaffMember", self.portal.validRoles())
    def test_workflow_installed(self):
        self.failUnless(
            'optilux_sitecontent_workflow' in self.workflow.objectIds())
    def test_workflows_mapped(self):
        self.assertEquals(('optilux_sitecontent_workflow',),
                          self.workflow.getDefaultChain())
        for portal_type, chain in self.workflow.listChainOverrides():
            if portal_type in ('File', 'Image',):
                self.assertEquals(('optilux_sitecontent_workflow',), chain)
```

```
def test_view_permisison_for_staffmember(self):
    # The API of the permissionsOfRole() function sucks -
    # it is bound too closely up in the permission management
    # screen's user interface
    self.failUnless('View' in [r['name'] for r in
    self.portal.permissionsOfRole('Reader') if r['selected']])
    self.failUnless('View' in [r['name'] for r in
    self.portal.permissionsOfRole('StaffMember') if r['selected']])

def test_staffmember_group_added(self):
    self.assertEquals(1, len(self.acl_users.searchGroups(
                                            name='Staff')))

...
```

These tests make use of the `RoleManager` and `WorkflowTool` APIs to inspect the security settings in the portal after creation. We should also test adding content through the Web, to make sure the security settings behave as expected. It is often easier to visualize the impact of different configuration options by interacting with the site rather than with abstract code and configuration files.

Protected and Trusted Code

The techniques that we have covered — managing roles and permissions at the portal root — managing detailed permissions with workflows — are the staple of security configuration for integrators and customizers. As we progress to develop new functionality, we will of course ensure that it is properly protected by appropriate permissions, normally relying on the *core* permissions such as *View* and *Modify portal content*, for which we have defined a policy in this chapter.

It is important, however, to understand when and how permissions are enforced. In particular, permissions are *not* generally enforced in file system Python code. The exceptions are a few methods — notably `restrictedTraverse()`, which can be used to explicitly traverse to an object, and `invokeFactory()`, which is available on *folderish* content types and used to create new sub-objects — that explicitly check the permissions of the current authenticated user, using the patterns shown earlier in this chapter.

Security is principally applied to things that are either created or accessed through the Web. It is invoked on URL traversal when the browser requests a particular resource, or on *path traversal* in untrusted code. A *resource* here can mean a view of a content object, a particular method on a content object that returns something to the browser, a style sheet, or indeed anything else that is published by Zope. We will look at the process of URL traversal and object publishing in more detail in Chapter 9.

Security assertions are made in one of three places:

- Zope 3-style browser components, such as browser views and resources, are declared in ZCML with an associated permission. We saw an example of declaring a view with `<browser:page />` earlier. These resources will not be available unless the current user has the given permission. We will see more examples of this in Chapters 9, 10, and 11.

- Page templates and other resources in skin layers may explicitly restrict access to particular roles. For example, the page template `prefs_install_products_form.pt` from the `plone_prefs` skin layer has an associated `prefs_install_products_form.pt.metadata` file containing the following lines:

  ```
  [security]
  View = 0:Manager
  ```

- Attributes and methods on content items, tools, and other persistent objects can be protected by permissions. This is either done in ZCML, using the `<class />` and `<require />` directives, or in Python code using an `AccessControl.ClassSecurityInfo` object. We will see examples of both in Chapter 10.

In addition the variable `__allow_access_to_unprotected_subjects__` is set to `True` by one of the common base classes used for all Plone content types. This informs the security machinery that any attribute (whether originally part of the class or acquired from a parent) that does not have an explicit security assertion will be accessible. This is necessary to enable the kind of generic user interface that Plone exposes, but it does mean that it is important to protect attributes of custom content types and other components.

Restricted Python

Zope allows sufficiently privileged users to create Page Templates, DTML methods and, *Python Scripts* through the Web. This was traditionally the way to build Zope applications, with scripts and templates co-existing with data objects in the ZODB. In Chapter 4, we saw that the `portal_skins` tool allows us to manage acquirable resources such as page templates and scripts on the file system, and that this is generally preferable. To the underlying Zope architecture, however, resources in skin layers are no different to resources created in the ZMI. In both cases, expressions are subject to the controls imposed by **Restricted Python**.

The Python classes and Page Templates used in Zope 3 browser views are *file system* code, and thus not subject to Restricted Python. Other file system code, such as methods of content types, tools, adapters, or utilities are also oblivious to Restricted Python.

Restricted Python ensures that users cannot create scripts or templates that access resources or perform operations they would not normally be allowed to invoke. Permissions are automatically checked when a script or template traverses the object graph or calls a method.

It is possible to define a **proxy role** for individual templates or scripts, either in the ZMI or via a `.metadata` file. For example, the `send_feedback.cpy` script needs to be able to access the site's email configuration, even if it is invoked by users not normally allowed to do so. The associated `send_feedback.cpy.metadata` contains:

```
[default]
proxy=Manager,Anonymous
[security]
View=0:Authenticated
```

Restricted Python also ensures that scripts created through the Web cannot access the server's file system, nor can they import unauthorized modules, which may be used to compromise the server's security. Only those modules explicitly allowed, using the `allow_module()` and `allow_class()` methods from `AccessControl`, may be imported. In addition, methods and variables with names beginning with an underscore are considered private, and cannot be accessed. Lastly, any published class or method must have a docstring.

Restricted Python is becoming less important as developers begin to prefer Zope 3-style browser views and resources. Here, the primary means of enforcing security is through the permission that applies to the entire view or resource, set with ZCML. Persistent objects such as content items also need to set appropriate permissions for their methods. We will see how in Chapter 10.

Summary

In this chapter we have taken a look at Plone's approach to security, including:

- Key concepts such as users, groups, roles, and permissions
- Some examples of how to manipulate security settings in code
- The role played by workflows in managing security
- How to create a custom workflow and install it, using GenericSetup
- How security is invoked during URL traversal and in Restricted Python

In the next chapter, we will learn how to find and install third-party add-on components.

7
Using Add-on Products

Throughout this book, we aim to develop re-useable components. Of course, it is not very likely that someone else would want to re-use the Optilux site theme or policy, but developing for re-usability encourages good practice. Besides, the client could come back next year wanting another site with the same basic look and feel.

Plone developers have created add-on products that do everything from making small improvements to core content types to providing new functionality like forums, blogs, and database integration tools. Sometimes developers will factor components developed for customers into a re-usable base product and another with customer-specific integration code. In the spirit of the Plone community, the vast majority of these products are made available free under open-source licenses.

In this chapter, we will discuss how to find, evaluate and test add-on products, demonstrating the inclusion of the RichDocument product in the Optilux application. We will also issue a few warnings: not all add-on products are created equal, and due diligence is usually required.

Finding and Evaluating Products

The main place to look for Plone add-on components is the products area on the Plone website: `http://plone.org/products`. The Plone community encourages developers to list their products here, and make use of the tools provided, such as issue trackers, roadmaps, and release management.

Many products listed on the Plone website — and quite a few more — use the **Collective**, a community Subversion repository, to host their code. The Collective is located at `http://svn.plone.org/svn/collective`, and can be browsed through `http://dev.plone.org/collective/browser`. If you have code you want to contribute to the Collective, you should ask on the mailing lists or chat room and then file a ticket with a request in the `plone.org` issue tracker (see `http://plone.org/support` and `http://dev.plone.org/plone.org`). The criteria for getting commit privileges to the Collective are not very onerous. Getting commit access to the repository that hosts the core Plone source code involves a little more scrutiny, but not very much.

This also applies if you want to make fixes or improvements to other developers' code. If you are making changes to code you do not own, make sure you contact the maintainer of the product. For non-trivial changes, you should work on a branch. Members of the community in the chat room or on the mailing lists will be able to advise you if you are unsure about the etiquette of working with code in the Collective.

There is no centralized review of add-on products. The Plone community thrives on contributions, and encourages developers to share their code. The downside to this is that sometimes products overlap in scope or vary in quality.

 In general, you cannot assume that an add-on product has gone through the same quality control procedures as the Plone core. Though there are plenty of add-on products that are rock solid, there are also those that simply do not work or, worse, could damage your site when installed, for example by making unwise configuration changes.

Therefore, it pays to conduct some due diligence before choosing add-on products to rely on. Often, the best way to evaluate the quality of a particular add-on product is to ask around for other community members' experiences with particular products or ask for recommendations on how to achieve a particular goal.

You may also wish to consider how well the product presents itself: is there a page in the products section of `plone.org`? Is there a release? Is it a final release, a release candidate, or a less mature pre-release? Has the product author taken the time to explain the functionality of the product clearly, and is there a mention of outstanding issues or missing features? You could also take a look at the issue tracker and roadmap pages, if available, to get a flavor for how many outstanding issues there are and, perhaps more importantly, how quickly they are being resolved.

As you become a more experienced developer, however, the first thing you are likely to do is to browse through the source code. Over time, you will learn to spot when a product is using good practices or not. A good initial benchmark is whether the product has any automated tests.

Playing it Safe

When you have found one or more candidate products to solve a particular problem, you will need to try them out. In doing so, there is one very important thing to remember:

Never, *ever* install someone else's add-on product directly onto a live server without first testing it in your development environment. Even then, always, *always* take a backup of your Data.fs file before installing new software on a production server.

A product could be perfectly stable on its own, but could still cause problems if it conflicts with other components that you have installed or developed.

The usual procedure is to copy the Data.fs file from the live server to a test or staging environment that has exactly the same software configuration as the live server (e.g. using the same buildout) and install the product here. Then, run the automated tests for your own code, as well as those for the product itself if applicable. These may tell you of conflicts that may not be obvious. You should of course also test it in the browser to ensure the new component behaves as expected.

Installing a Product

At the time of writing, most add-on products are still old-style Zope 2 products. However, the Plone community has recently begun to use Python eggs to distribute software. Therefore, eggs are likely to become more important as a distribution mechanism for Plone products in the near future.

We have already seen how to install an egg: list it in the buildout.cfg file under the eggs option, as we did with the optilux.policy egg in Chapter 5. This works so long as an egg is available in the Python Cheese Shop. If it is packaged for download somewhere else, you can enter the URL of a web page linking to it under the find-links option. Alternatively, if you want to track a development egg, check it out to the src/ directory and reference it in the develop option in addition to the eggs option. This is equivalent to the way in which the optilux.policy egg is set up at the moment. Remember to re-run ./bin/buildout after any changes to buildout.cfg.

If you are installing an old-style product, you need to add it to Zope's Products directory. In the buildout, the safest way of doing so is to reference it in the [productdistros] section, so that it will be downloaded and installed automatically. Alternatively, if there is no release or you need to track a development version, you can check it out into the products/ directory in the root of the buildout.

Adding RichDocument

In the Optilux site, we now choose to make use of the **RichDocument** (http://plone.org/products/richdocument) product for the elements of the information architecture that suggest static pages of text and images. RichDocument is an extension of the standard *Page* type in Plone, which adds the ability to attach images and files.

First, we need to add the RichDocument download to buildout.cfg. We do this by listing an additional URL in the [productdistros] section. At the time of writing, the latest release is 3.0:

```
[productdistros]
...
urls =
   ...
  http://plone.org/products/richdocument/releases/3.0/
                                  RichDocument-3.0.tar.gz
```

After making this change, we must of course re-run buildout:

```
$ ./bin/buildout
```

We will then amend the optilux.policy product to install RichDocument, and disable Plone's default *Page* type. We will also give the Rich Document type a title of *Web page* to better reflect its purpose.

Let us first add some tests to optilux.policy.tests.test_setup:

```
class TestSetup(OptiluxPolicyTestCase):

    ...

    def test_richdocument_installed(self):
        self.failUnless('RichDocument' in self.types.objectIds())

    def test_plain_document_disabled(self):
        # the internal name for "Page" is "Document"
        document_fti = getattr(self.types, 'Document')
        self.failIf(document_fti.global_allow)

    def test_richdocument_renamed_to_page(self):
        rich_document_fti = getattr(self.types, 'RichDocument')
        self.assertEquals("Web page", rich_document_fti.title)

    ...
```

We also need to amend the bootstrapping code in `tests/base.py` to inform the test runner about the newly added `RichDocument` product, and its bundled dependency `SimpleAttachment`:

```
from Products.Five import zcml
from Products.Five import fiveconfigure

from Testing import ZopeTestCase as ztc

from Products.PloneTestCase import PloneTestCase as ptc
from Products.PloneTestCase.layer import onsetup

# These are traditional products (in the Products namespace). They'd normally
# be loaded automatically, but in tests we have to load them explicitly. This
# should happen at module level to make sure they are available early enough.
ztc.installProduct('SimpleAttachment')
ztc.installProduct('RichDocument')

@onsetup
def setup_optilux_policy():
    """Set up the additional products required for the Optilux site policy.

    The @onsetup decorator causes the execution of this body to be deferred
    until the setup of the Plone site testing layer.
    """

    # Load the ZCML configuration for the optilux.policy package.
    fiveconfigure.debug_mode = True
    import optilux.policy
    zcml.load_config('configure.zcml', optilux.policy)
    fiveconfigure.debug_mode = False

    # We need to tell the testing framework that these products
    # should be available. This can't happen until after we have
    # loaded the ZCML.
    ztc.installPackage('optilux.policy')

# The order here is important: We first call the (deferred) function
# which installs the products we need for the Optilux package. Then,
# we let PloneTestCase set up this product on installation.
setup_optilux_policy()
ptc.setupPloneSite(products=['optilux.policy'])
```

```
class OptiluxPolicyTestCase(ptc.PloneTestCase):
    """We use this base class for all the tests in this package.
    If necessary, we can put common utility or setup code in here.
    """
```

This illustrates a few important differences between old-style products in the `Products` namespace and products in regular Python packages:

- We must inform the test runner about old-style products at module level, using the `installProduct()` method from `ZopeTestCase`. This executes as soon as the module is imported; the deferred `setup_optilux_policy()` method executes too late.

- Any `configure.zcml` files in old-style products are automatically loaded when the test runner starts up. Hence the need to have loaded the products already at module level.

- For regular Python packages, we need to use a deferred test setup method that explicitly loads the package's `configure.zcml` (and any `overrides.zcml` or `meta.zcml` files, if applicable) and then installs the product using the `installPackage()` method, instead of `installProduct()`. We cannot do this at module level, because we need to wait for the test runner to load Five and other core Zope components.

However, if you use the preceding boilerplate setup code and adjust it for your own packages, you should be safe.

Predictably, all of these tests fail when first run, so let us write the code to make them pass. We will use the QuickInstaller to install `RichDocument` during installation of `optilux.policy`.

Unfortunately, we cannot use a GenericSetup import step in one product to install a different product. Therefore, we must change the way in which `optilux.policy` is installed: in addition to registering an extension profile responsible for performing site customizations, we will add an installation script in `Extensions/Install.py`. As we learned in Chapter 4, if this script is present, the QuickInstaller will use it instead of automatically applying the extension profile.

`Install.py` should contain a method called `install()` and optionally a companion method called `uninstall()`. These are called during installation and un-installation, respectively.

```
import transaction
from Products.CMFCore.utils import getToolByName

PRODUCT_DEPENDENCIES = ('RichDocument',)
EXTENSION_PROFILES = ('optilux.policy:default',)
```

```
def install(self, reinstall=False):
    portal_quickinstaller = getToolByName(self,
'portal_quickinstaller')
    portal_setup = getToolByName(self, 'portal_setup')
    for product in PRODUCT_DEPENDENCIES:
        if reinstall and portal_quickinstaller.isProductInstalled(
            product):
            portal_quickinstaller.reinstallProducts([product])
            transaction.savepoint()
        elif not portal_quickinstaller.isProductInstalled(product):
            portal_quickinstaller.installProduct(product)
            transaction.savepoint()
    for extension_id in EXTENSION_PROFILES:
        portal_setup.runAllImportStepsFromProfile(
                'profile-%s' % extension_id, purge_old=False)
        product_name = extension_id.split(':')[0]
        portal_quickinstaller.notifyInstalled(product_name)
        transaction.savepoint()
```

Using this boilerplate code, we can install additional dependencies simply by changing the PRODUCT_DEPENDENCIES variable. After all the dependencies have been installed, we explicitly invoke our own extension profile.

We must also amend the importVarious step of the optilux.policy extension profile, so that it renames *Rich Document* to *Web page* and disables the built-in *Page* type. In setuphandlers.py, we now have:

```
from Products.CMFCore.utils import getToolByName

...


def renameRichDocument(portal):
    portal_types = getToolByName(portal, 'portal_types')
    rich_document_fti = getattr(portal_types, 'RichDocument')
    rich_document_fti.title = "Web page"


def disableDocument(portal):
    portal_types = getToolByName(portal, 'portal_types')
    document_fti = getattr(portal_types, 'Document')
    document_fti.global_allow = False


def importVarious(context):
    """Miscellanous steps import handle
    """
```

```
portal = context.getSite()
setupGroups(portal)
renameRichDocument(portal)
disableDocument(portal)
```

In renaming the *Rich Document* content type, we have effectively customized a third-party product, which in itself could be seen as a customization of the default *Page* content type. To Zope or the CMF, the product `RichDocument` is no different than the product `CMFPlone`. RichDocument will install its own skin layer in `portal_skins`, which can be customized just like Plone's bundled skins. This type of re-use is very powerful, and makes it easier to separate generic functionality from customer-specific integration logic or styling.

Summary

In this chapter, we have looked at:

- What add-on products are, and how they relate to the Plone core
- Where to find add-on products
- Some tips for evaluating the viability of add-on products
- Some caveats around the use of add-on products, and how to stay safe when evaluating a new product for the first time
- Installing products automatically, using our buildout and site policy product
- How extending add-on products is no different than extending Plone itself

In the next chapter, we will begin to build the visual look-and-feel of the Optilux site.

8

Creating a Custom Theme

Plone's default look and feel is best described as *functional*. It has evolved over several years to facilitate a wide range of features and user interface metaphors. If Plone is being deployed as an internal content management solution, it is probably a good choice. However, custom branding is normally required for public-facing systems such as the Optilux website.

In this chapter, we will demonstrate how to create a new **theme** for Plone. We will add a new style sheet to change the visual appearance of various parts of the Plone site, change the default page layout, and customize a few templates to provide alternative markup where necessary.

Background

We mentioned themes (sometimes also called *skins*) briefly in Chapter 4. Recall from that chapter that the `portal_skins` tool manages a list of skin layers, which contain templates, style sheets, images, and other resources. Skin layers are collected and ordered in themes (skins). The order is important, since items in skin layers nearer to the top of the list can override more general items from skin layers further down.

The process of building a custom look and feel for a site typically begins by defining a new theme with one or more skin layers near the top of the list providing theme-specific graphics and style sheets, as well as overrides for standard Plone templates. As we will see later in this chapter, it is also possible to tie specific versions of Zope 3-style views and **viewlets** to a theme. Viewlets are fragments that provide different elements of the page, such as the logo or the row of tabs across the top of the site. Viewlets can be hidden or re-ordered on a theme-by-theme basis as well.

By keeping all our registrations and overrides collated into a single theme, we can easily switch back to the default look and feel. The theme's package is also the natural home for all customized templates, making it easier to keep track of which parts of Plone have been overridden for a particular application.

The Theme Package

As with the `optilux.policy` product from Chapter 5, we will use `paster` to create the package containing the theme. This time, we will use the `plone3_theme` template. Go to the `src/` directory of our buildout, and run:

```
$ paster create -t plone3_theme optilux.theme
```

Enter `optilux` as the namespace of the package, and `theme` as the package name. The skin name should be `Optilux Theme`, the skin base should be left as `Plone Default`, and the *zip safe* flag should be set to `False`. The answers to the other questions are less important unless you plan to release the theme to the Python Cheese Shop, in which case you should enter a contact name and email address, as well as the package's license.

There should now be a new egg in `src/optilux.theme`. We need to add this to our buildout, so edit `buildout.cfg`, and add the following:

```
[buildout]
...
develop =
    src/optilux.policy
    src/optilux.theme
...
eggs =
    optilux.policy
    optilux.theme
...
[instance]
zcml = optilux.policy
```

Then re-run buildout with:

```
$ ./bin/buildout -o
```

This should make the package available in the build environment. For the package to work, we also need to tell Zope to read its `configure.zcml` file at startup. We could install a ZCML *slug* as we did for `optilux.policy`, but it is easier to let the policy product orchestrate all the other custom products we use. Therefore, we will include the `optilux.theme` package as a dependency of `optilux.policy`. In `src/optilux.policy/optilux/policy/configure.zcml`, we have the following:

```
<configure
    xmlns="http://namespaces.zope.org/zope"
    xmlns:five="http://namespaces.zope.org/five"
    xmlns:genericsetup="http://namespaces.zope.org/genericsetup"
```

```
        i18n_domain="optilux.policy">
        <!-- Include direct package dependencies -->
        <include package="optilux.theme" />
        ...
</configure>
```

If we now start Zope, the `optilux.theme` package should show up in the **Product Management** screen, under the **Control_Panel** in the ZMI root.

We must also ensure that the theme product is installed automatically when the policy product is installed. We will add the following near the top of `src/optilux.policy/optilux/policy/Extensions/Install.py`:

```
PRODUCT_DEPENDENCIES = ('RichDocument',
                        'optilux.theme',)
```

The boilerplate we added to this file in Chapter 7 takes care of the rest.

Adding a Test to the Policy Product

There should be a test in `optilux.policy` to ensure that the theme is installed properly when the policy product is installed. In `optilux.policy`, we must first add the following line to `tests/base.py`:

```
from Products.Five import zcml
from Products.Five import fiveconfigure

from Testing import ZopeTestCase as ztc

from Products.PloneTestCase import PloneTestCase as ptc
from Products.PloneTestCase.layer import onsetup

ztc.installProduct('SimpleAttachment')
ztc.installProduct('RichDocument')

@onsetup
def setup_optilux_policy():
    fiveconfigure.debug_mode = True
    import optilux.policy
    zcml.load_config('configure.zcml', optilux.policy)
    fiveconfigure.debug_mode = False

    ztc.installProduct('optilux.policy', package=True)
    ztc.installProduct('optilux.theme', package=True)

setup_optilux_policy()
ptc.setupPloneSite(products=['optilux.policy'])

    ...
```

This ensures that after the `optilux.policy` ZCML file—which includes `optilux.theme`—has been loaded, we install `optilux.theme` as a product. Without this, the installation of `optilux.theme` from the `optilux.policy Install.py` file would fail.

The test itself, found in `optilux.policy.tests.test_setup.py`, is simple:

```
def test_theme_installed(self):
    skins = getToolByName(self.portal, 'portal_skins')
    layer = skins.getSkinPath('Optilux Theme')
    self.failUnless('optilux_theme_custom_templates' in layer)
    self.assertEquals('Optilux Theme', skins.getDefaultSkin())
```

Theme Product Contents

Let us take a look at the contents of our new theme product. As with all egg-based packages, there is a `setup.py` file in the root directory, used to pull in dependencies and provide release metadata. The real code lives in `src/optilux.theme/optilux/theme`, and includes the following files and directories.

- The `configure.zcml` file includes another file called `profile.zcml`—which registers the GenericSetup profile used to install the product—and the `browser` sub-package, where Zope 3-style browser views, viewlets, and portlets will be registered.

- The GenericSetup extension profile is found in `profiles/default` as usual. It installs the new theme and registers its style sheet. There are also example files for registering new Java Script resources and re-ordering or hiding viewlets. We will cover the latter in more detail below.

- The file `setuphandlers.py` contains a blank `setupVarious()` method, which can be used to perform additional setup operations using Python code when the theme product is installed. We will not need this.

- In `browser/interfaces.py`, there is an interface called `IThemeSpecific`, which is associated with the `Optilux Theme` theme in `browser/configure.zcml`. We can reference this interface from the `layer` attribute of various ZCML directives to register visual components as specific to this theme. More on that later in this chapter.

- The `browser/` directory also includes two sub-directories that are registered as *resource directories* in `browser/configure.zcml`: `stylesheets` and `images`. We will see how to use these shortly.

- The `skins` directory houses various custom skin layers, which are installed in the `portal_skins` tool and associated with the `Optilux Theme` theme.

By default, there are three theme-specific skin layers: one for style sheets (`optilux_theme_styles`), one for images (`optilux_theme_custom_images`), and one for templates (`optilux_theme_custom_templates`). The separation into several skin layers is arbitrary, but encourages good practice.

It is a good idea to keep customized (overridden) resources separate from bespoke ones. This makes it easier to keep track of what you have changed from an out-of-the-box Plone installation, which is especially useful if you upgrade Plone in future. When building a new theme, you should generally prefer to create images, style sheets, and templates as Zope 3-style browser resources in the `browser` sub-package, using the theme-specific skin layers to override existing skin layer-based resources only.

If you install the Optilux theme using the **Add-on products** control panel in Plone, you should see the three new layers installed in `portal_skins` in the ZMI. Take a look at `profiles/default/skins.xml` to better understand how they are configured.

Tools and Techniques

When working on a theme product, make sure that Zope is running in debug mode. This is set in `zope.conf`. In Chapter 3, we added the appropriate configuration to `buildout.cfg` to ensure debug mode is enabled in our development environment. When Zope is in debug mode, you can modify resources in skin layers without having to re-start Zope. The same goes for Zope 3-style templates (but not view classes: as a rule of thumb, anything in a skin layer can be modified at run time while in debug mode, as can any page template file (.pt) on the file system).

When working with CSS, you should also go into the `portal_css` tool in the ZMI and enable **Debug/development mode**. When this is off—as it should be in a production scenario—CSS files may be merged and cached to improve performance. During development, this can mean that changes do not get properly propagated to the browser.

The `portal_css` tool has two siblings: `portal_javascripts`, and `portal_kss`. Both of these support the same debug mode feature.

Finally, you should get Mozilla Firefox and the Firebug extension (`http://getfirebug.com`). Firebug is an incredible productivity tool for web developers, allowing you to inspect any element in the page, determine which CSS styles are being applied to it, experiment with changes to styles and structure *live*, watch HTTP traffic, profile your pages for performance problems, and much more.

Building the Theme

Most themes begin life as a design mockup. Developers then break visual elements of the design up into small image files used as backgrounds and fillers, or represent them using stylized HTML. This process gets easier with experience, as you learn to visualize how a page can most easily be represented with HTML and CSS. It often helps to draw guidelines on the mockup to identify how it can be represented as floating boxes, tables, and lists.

Let us take a look at the mockup from chapter 2. We have annotated this to pick out some standard design features:

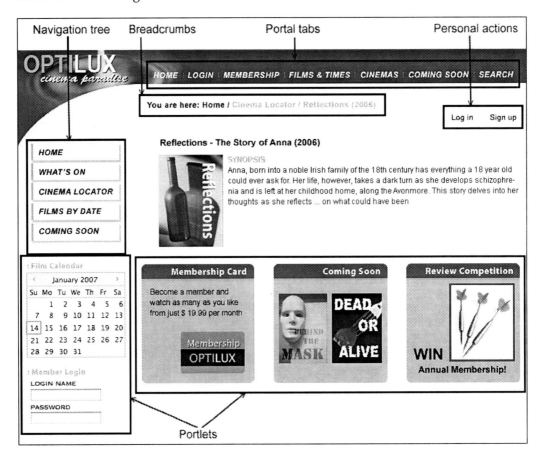

Here is a picture of Plone's default look and feel, with the same features highlighted:

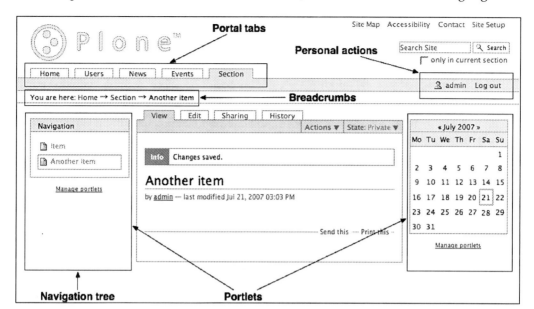

As far as possible, we will aim to re-use these elements, styling them as necessary.

Plone's standard markup is almost entirely structural. Colors, borders, spacing, and positioning are all controlled by CSS. Furthermore, each of the main page elements is managed by a viewlet. As we will see, it is possible to re-order, hide, and re-assign viewlets.

Thus, building a theme is usually an iterative process:

- If your theme will deviate radically from Plone's look and feel, consider disabling one or more of Plone's public-facing style sheets. It is usually a good idea to keep the authoring style sheets intact, since reproducing the CSS for forms and other editing UI is a lot of work.

- Add your own style sheet, images, and other resources, and apply them to the HTML markup that comes out of Plone to get as close to the desired look and feel as possible without changing any HTML.

- Re-order, hide, or re-assign any viewlets for page elements that are not where you need them to be.

- Consider creating new viewlets in the existing viewlet managers if you want to plug in some generic user interface elements.

- If the viewlets infrastructure does not give you enough control over the page layout, consider customizing Plone's `main_template`. This page template is used by most views to invoke the page layout. Making radical changes to `main_template` can sometimes make it harder to upgrade in the future, so be careful, and document your changes if you go down this route.

- If specific templates, views, or viewlets cannot be made to look the way you want with CSS, you can customize (override) them individually.

The remainder of this chapter will follow the process above to achieve a final theme for the Optilux website. It can be seen in the image below, showing an almost fresh Plone instance with the policy product installed:

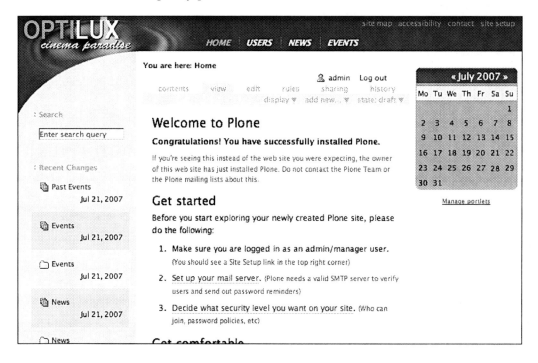

The author will not pretend to be a great web designer. We could do a lot more with the theme's CSS to make it look more professional, but we have opted to keep things reasonably simple for the purposes of this book.

Custom CSS Style Sheets

Plone's style sheets are managed by a tool in the ZMI called **portal_css**. It looks like this:

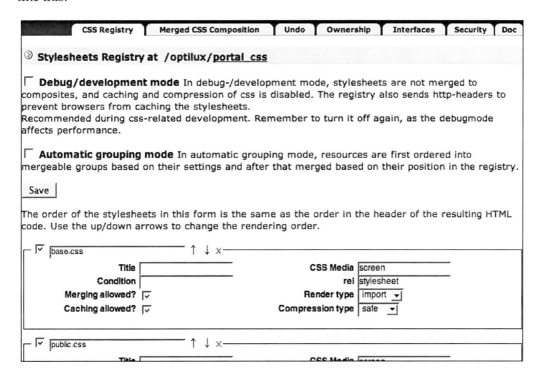

As mentioned, you should enable **Debug/development** mode during development. The **Automatic grouping mode** option can improve performance if you use a lot of custom style sheets, but introduces a small risk of style sheets being included in a different order to what the designer intended. Turn this on if it does not cause any problems for your theme.

The various style sheets listed will be collated (and possibly concatenated, if development mode is off) and rendered in the page sent to the web browser. The installer for the optilux.theme package will have added a new item called ++resource++optilux.theme.styles/main.css near the bottom of this list.

The name ++resource++optilux.theme.styles/main.css refers to the file main.css in the directory browser/stylesheets. This is registered as a **resource directory** with the name optilux.theme.styles, in browser/configure.zcml. You can add other style sheets here and refer to them in the same way if you need to.

Style sheets are rendered in order. This means that styles in later style sheets may override those in earlier style sheets, according to the usual CSS rules.

It may be educational to turn off one or more of the style sheets here and observe the effects on Plone in your browser. The first two style sheets in particular — `base. css` and `public.css` — contain styles for basic tags and public-facing page elements. Most theme authors prefer to re-use Plone's `authoring.css` and most of the other style sheets. Plone is a complex system, and styling it all from scratch can take a lot of time.

By default, a package generated using the `plone3_theme` template will have blank overrides for `base.css` and `public.css` in its *styles* skin layer, which is only installed for the new theme. As we saw in Chapter 4, this means that these overrides apply only when the theme is selected.

This is useful if your theme deviates a lot from Plone's standard look and feel, since you will not need to counteract any of Plone's public-facing styles. For the purposes of the Optilux example, it was easier to let Plone's public styles apply, and override only when necessary. Therefore, we have removed these files from `skins/optilux_theme_styles`, making the skin fall back on Plone's defaults.

If Zope is running in debug mode (e.g. it was started with the command `./bin/instance fg`), you should be able to make changes to `browser/ stylesheets/main.css`, and see the changes immediately. You may need to perform a hard refresh each time, if your browser caches aggressively. Here is a short extract from the file:

```
h1, h2 {
    border: none;
    border-bottom: solid transparent 1px;
}
```

Consult a CSS reference to learn more about the rules of CSS. There are plenty of good references available online for free.

If you are inexperienced with CSS-based design, you will undoubtedly hit problems where things look great in one browser, but wrong in another. Unfortunately, web browsers have subtle bugs and inconsistencies that can cause a lot of pain for web developers. Worse still, the most popular browser — Internet Explorer — not only causes the most headaches, but also has the fewest free tools to help you debug problems.

Cross-browser web design is outside the scope of this book, but a few tips are in order:

- The author prefers to work with Mozilla Firefox (and the Firebug extension) in the first instance, cross-checking with Safari and Internet Explorer regularly.

- A lot of time has gone into making Plone's CSS as cross-browser friendly as possible. It usually makes sense to reuse styles from Plone where possible.

- Plone has a special style sheet called `IEFixes.css`, which is conditionally included in `main_template.pt`. You may want to re-use or customize this for your own themes, if you need to make Internet Explorer-specific overrides.

- If you ever find that floating elements disappear temporarily or permanently in Internet Explorer for no good reason, you may have been stung by the infamous **peekaboo** bug. Try to use the `visualIEFloatFix` class from Plone's CSS on the disappearing element, or its parent.

For more general tips and examples of how to deal with browser inconsistencies in your own templates, consult a good, modern web design guide. Again, there is a multitude of resources on the Internet, as well as a few documents at `http://plone.org/documentation`.

Using "base_properties" and DTML Variables in Style Sheets

You may have seen style sheet files in skin layers that have an extension of `.dtml` instead of `.css`. This extension is not carried forward to the resource name in Zope, but it signifies that the file should be processed as a **DTML** document. DTML is a legacy template language for Zope, largely superseded by Zope Page Templates (ZPT). It is still quite useful for non-XML files such as style sheets, however.

The only feature of DTML commonly used in style sheets is variable interpolation. For example, `CMFPlone/skins/plone_styles/base.css` contains:

```
/* <dtml-with base_properties> (do not remove this :) */
/* <dtml-call "REQUEST.set('portal_url', portal_url())"> */

body {
    font: &dtml-fontBaseSize; <dtml-var fontFamily>;
    background-color: &dtml-backgroundColor;;
    color: &dtml-fontColor;;
    margin: 0;
    padding: 0;
```

```
}

...

/* </dtml-with> */
```

The dtml-with and dtml-call tags are ignored by CSS parsers, but will pull
in various variables from a property sheet called base_properties.props.
This contains definitions of standard colors, border styles, and fonts. There is a
theme-specific customization of this file in the optilux_theme_styles layer, which
looks like this:

```
title:string=Optilux Theme's color, font, logo and border defaults

plone_skin:string=Optilux Theme

logoName:string=logo.jpg

fontFamily:string="Lucida Grande", Verdana, Lucida, Helvetica, Arial,
sans-serif
fontBaseSize:string=69%
fontColor:string=Black
fontSmallSize:string=85%

...

globalBorderColor:string=#8cacbb
globalBackgroundColor:string=#f0f0f0
globalFontColor:string=#436976

...

contentViewBorderColor:string=transparent
contentViewBackgroundColor:string=#f0f0f0
contentViewFontColor:string=#fe9900

...

portalMinWidth:string=70em
columnOneWidth:string=181px
columnTwoWidth:string=16em
```

We can bring the Plone color scheme in line with our site branding simply by
editing this file.

 Note that the main.css style sheet that we use for theme-specific
styling is not a DTML document and thus does not support such
variable interpolation.

Image Resources

The `browser/images` directory is analogous to the `brower/stylesheets` directory, intended to store theme-specific images. Both are registered as resource directories in `browser/configure.zcml` like this:

```
<!-- Resource directory for stylesheets -->
<browser:resourceDirectory
    name="optilux.theme.stylesheets"
    directory="stylesheets"
    layer=".interfaces.IThemeSpecific"
    />

<!-- Resource directory for images -->
<browser:resourceDirectory
    name="optilux.theme.images"
    directory="images"
    layer=".interfaces.IThemeSpecific"
    />
```

To render an image `myimage.jpg` placed in the `images` directory using a standard HTML image tag, we could use a construct such as:

```
<img tal:attributes="src portal/++resource++optilux.theme.images/
myimage.jpg" />
```

Here, `portal` is a globally available variable, which refers to the portal root object. If for some reason this is not available, we could have used the `context` variable instead. However, it is generally preferable to render image resources using a fixed path relative to the portal root, as this makes it easier for browsers and proxies to cache the image.

In `main.css`, we use an image in the resource directory as the background of the left-hand side column:

```
#portal-column-one {
    background-image: url(++resource++optilux.theme.images/
                          column-one-bg.jpg);
    background-position: top-left;
    background-repeat: no-repeat;
    background-color: #f0f0f0;
    padding-top: 60px;
}
```

Since the style sheet is always rendered with the same path via the `portal_css` tool, we do not need to explicitly reference the portal root here.

Managing Viewlets

Plone 3 uses viewlets to manage various standard page elements, such the logo, the navigation breadcrumbs, and the personal bar. Viewlets are registered to a **viewlet manager**, which controls which viewlets are displayed, and in which order they are rendered.

 If you want to learn more about how viewlets are implemented, see the interfaces, and documentation in the `zope.viewlet` package. We will cover viewlets in more detail in Chapters 9 and 11.

To see which viewlet managers and viewlets are used to compose a page, append `/@@manage-viewlets` to a URL.

 Note that this only works with viewlet managers based on the `plone.app.viewletmanager` package. All of Plone's viewlet managers use this, but third-party products may come with simpler managers that sort viewlets alphabetically or according to some other means.

Here is how it looks:

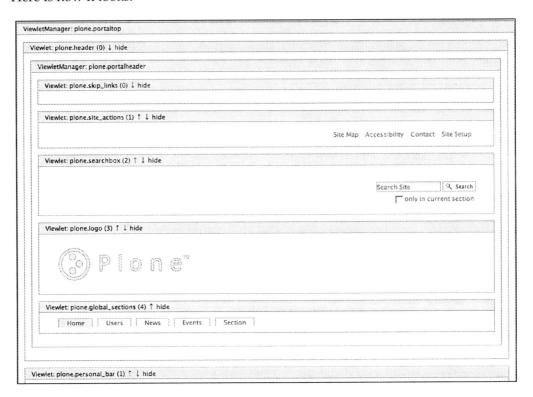

You can see the name of each viewlet manager and its viewlets. Use the arrows and the **hide** link to re-order and hide viewlets. Any changes will be persisted in the ZODB immediately.

Of course, as we learned in Chapter 4, we should make changes in a repeatable, controllable way, and not rely on settings stored only in the ZODB. Therefore, we use a GenericSetup import step, found in `profiles/default/viewlets.xml`:

```
<object>

  ...

  <!-- Header - contained within plone.portaltop -->
  <order manager="plone.portalheader" skinname="Optilux Theme"
    based-on="Plone Default">
    <viewlet name="plone.skip_links" />
    <viewlet name="plone.site_actions" />
    <viewlet name="plone.logo" />
    <viewlet name="plone.global_sections" />
  </order>

  <hidden manager="plone.portalheader" skinname="Optilux Theme">
    <viewlet name="plone.searchbox" />
  </hidden>

  ...

</object>
```

The `<order />` directive can be used to define the order of viewlets in a manager for a particular theme (specified with `skinname`). You can get the name of the viewlet manager, set in the `manager` attribute, from the `@@manage-viewlets` screen. The `based-on` attribute can be used to copy the default settings from another skin—usually `"Plone Default"`.

It is often easiest to list all the eligible viewlets in order, as we have done above. However, if you want to specify the order of a viewlet relative to an existing one, you can use a line such as:

```
<viewlet name="my.viewlet" insert-before="another.viewlet" />
```

You can write `insert-before="*"` to place a viewlet first in the list, or use `insert-after` to place a viewlet after another one.

The `<hidden />` directive is used to hide (disable) viewlets in a particular viewlet manager. Again, this is tied to a specific `skinname`, and you can use a `based-on` attribute to copy settings from an existing theme.

Defining Viewlet Managers

Viewlet managers are declared in ZCML. All of Plone's standard viewlet managers are in the `plone.app.layout.viewlets` package, where you will see lines such as this in `configure.zcml`:

```
<browser:viewletManager
    name="plone.portaltop"
    provides=".interfaces.IPortalTop"
    permission="zope2.View"
    class="plone.app.viewletmanager.manager.OrderedViewletManager"
    />
```

The interface is defined in `plone.app.layout.viewlets`' `interfaces.py` file:

```
from zope.viewlet.interfaces import IViewletManager

class IPortalTop(IViewletManager):
    """A viewlet manager that sits at the very top of the
    rendered page
    """
```

We will see in a moment how this is used to tie viewlet registrations to specific managers.

Plone's `main_template`, found in `CMFPlone/skins/plone_templates`, asks the viewlet manager to render itself, with a line such as:

```
<div tal:replace="structure provider:plone.portaltop" />
```

You can use similar constructs in your own themes to define new viewlet managers. Of course, a viewlet manager does not need to be rendered in `main_template` — it could be invoked from any page template, such as the view of a particular content object.

Reassigning Viewlets

For the Optilux theme, we need to move the breadcrumbs and personal bar from `plone.portaltop` manager down to the `plone.contentviews` manager, which is inside the main content area.

We cannot reassign viewlets between portlet managers using `viewlets.xml`, but we can re-register a viewlet for a new manager. In `browser/configure.zcml` in the `optilux.theme` package, we have:

```
<browser:viewlet
    name="optilux.personal_bar"
```

```
manager="plone.app.layout.viewlets.interfaces.IContentViews"
layer=".interfaces.IThemeSpecific"
class="plone.app.layout.viewlets.common.PersonalBarViewlet"
permission="zope2.View"
/>
```

This is taken from the corresponding statement in the `plone.app.layout.viewlets` `configure.zcml` file. We have given it a new name, and registered it for a different viewlet manager interface, but we still reference the same implementation, using the `class` attribute with an absolute package name.

To ensure that this registration only affects the Optilux theme, we use the `layer` attribute to reference the `IThemeSpecific` interface. This interface is registered earlier in `browser/configure.zcml`, with a block of code generated by the `plone3_theme` template:

```
<interface
    interface=".interfaces.IThemeSpecific"
    type="zope.publisher.interfaces.browser.IBrowserSkinType"
    name="Optilux Theme"
    />
```

The name here should match our theme name (see Chapter 9, and the `plone.theme` package for more information on how this works).

Finally, we hide the viewlet in its original viewlet manager—otherwise, we would get the personal bar twice. This is done in `viewlets.xml`:

```
<hidden manager="plone.portaltop" skinname="Optilux Theme">
  <viewlet name="plone.app.i18n.locales.languageselector" />
  <viewlet name="plone.path_bar" />
  <viewlet name="plone.personal_bar" />
</hidden>
```

Creating New Viewlets

Let us now add a brand-new viewlet. We will do so using a page template only. In Chapter 11, we will learn how to write a class to encapsulate any complex logic that may lie behind the viewlet.

The new viewlet must be registered in `browser/configure.zcml`:

```
<browser:viewlet
    name="optilux.footer"
    manager="plone.app.layout.viewlets.interfaces.IPortalFooter"
    layer=".interfaces.IThemeSpecific"
```

```
template="templates/footer.pt"
permission="zope2.View"
/>
```

We have to specify a unique name, the interface for the viewlet manager we want it to be displayed in, and a required permission. As before, the `layer` attribute ensures that this viewlet only shows up for this particular theme. We then reference a page template file called `footer.pt` in a newly created `templates` directory, which contains:

```
<div class="discreet">
    All content copyright Optilux Corporation.
</div>
```

To learn more about TAL and Zope Page Templates, see `http://plone.org/documentation/tutorial/zpt`.

 If we needed to, we could have added an `<order />` directive to `viewlets.xml` to control the appearance of the new viewlet more precisely.

Overriding Visual Elements

The relative ease with which Plone's visual elements can be customized without having to modify Plone's own source code is one of the greatest advantages in using Plone as a development platform. Broadly speaking, visual elements can come from one of these four different sources:

- A page template, style sheet, script, or other file in a skin layer. This is the most common type of resource (although Zope 3-style browser views and viewlets are becoming more and more prevalent). These can be found in `portal_skins` in the ZMI. Plone's standard skins are mostly in `CMFPlone/skins`, though other packages provide their own skin layers too.

- A Zope 3 browser view. These are registered in a `configure.zcml` file, using a `<browser:page />` directive. When invoked, they are normally prefixed with `@@` (e.g. the `manage-viewlets` view is normally seen at the end of a URL as `/@manage-viewlets`). Views consist of a Python class and/or a page template, and live on the file system only. They are typically defined in the same package as the functionality they relate to. The `portal_view_customizations` tool provides a listing of most registered browser views (and allows them to be customized through the Web).

- A Zope 3 viewlet is similar to a browser view in that it may consist of a class and/or a template. Viewlets are registered for a particular viewlet manager. Most of Plone's standard viewlets are defined in the `plone.app.layout` package, in the `viewlets` module.

- Portlets have *renderers*, which are similar to viewlets in that they render a part of the page. However, portlet renderers are aware of additional components such as their associated **portlet data provider** holding configuration data (settings made from the **Manage portlets** screen). Portlets are rendered inside **portlet managers**, which are similar to viewlet managers. All of Plone's standard portlets are defined in the `plone.app.portlets` package, under the `portlets` module.

Apart from resources in skin layers, overrides for visual components involve a registration in ZCML, and either a template or a class containing the actual customizations. We will focus on template customizations in this chapter.

As mentioned in Chapter 4, blanket overrides can be made using an `overrides. zcml` file. However, it is usually preferable to provide overrides for a particular theme (using the `layer` attribute as we have seen already), or perhaps for a particular type of context content object (using the `for` attribute).

Note that for Zope to process an `overrides.zcml` in the root of your package, you will need a ZCML slug. In `buildout.cfg`, this would mean a line like `zcml = my.package-overrides` under the `[instance]` section.

Templates and Other Resources in Skin Layers

We have already seen how to override skin layer resources by using skin layers *higher up*. Again, it is a good idea to keep track of any customized elements separately from new page templates, style sheets, and images.

The login, logout, and signup templates all look a little strange under the Optilux theme, because they clear the left-hand side column. Therefore, we will copy the relevant templates from `CMFPlone/skins/plone_login` into the `optilux_theme_custom_templates` skin layer folder.

Each of these templates has an associated `.metadata` file, which we must also copy. For example, `join_form.cpt.metadata` is associated with `join_form.cpt`. As we will learn in Chapter 11, these files contain page flow information, though they can also contain page titles as well as cache and security settings.

Page templates, images, and style sheets in skin layers may have associated *metadata* files. These have the same name as the file, with a suffix of `.metadata`. Zope will only be able to find these if they are in the same directory as the file they refer to.

The actual template customizations we require are quite simple. For example, in `login_form.cpt`, we have commented out this line:

```
<!-- <metal:block fill-slot="column_one_slot" /> -->
```

Before it was commented out, this statement would fill the `column_one_slot` in `main_template` with an empty tag, essentially removing the table cell that houses the left-hand side column. Of course, if it were necessary, we could have customized the template much more extensively.

Zope 3-Style Browser Views

Zope 3 browser views are typically rendered with page templates as well. However, such templates live in a folder on the file system—conventionally in a sub-package called `browser` in the package the view belongs to—not in a skin layer in `portal_skins`. We will use a ZCML declaration that ties the skin to our particular theme (using the `layer` attribute as seen earlier) to customize these.

We would like staff members to be able to use Plone's **Dashboard** to manage personal portlets. However, like the login-related templates alrealdy mentioned, these clear the left and right columns to utilize the full width of the screen. We will customize them to clear the right column only.

The two views we want to customize are `@@dashboard` (the main dashboard view), and `@@manage-dashboard` (the edit tab for the **dashboard**). One way to discover which packages these templates are defined in is to look in the **portal_view_ customizations** tool in the ZMI. Hover your mouse cursor over the name of a view, and you should see the package and file name.

Alternatively, you can search Plone's source code for files with extension `.zcml` containing the view names.

In this case, the views are defined in two different packages: `plone.app.layout.dashboard` and `plone.app.portlets.browser`. First, `plone.app.layout.dashboard`'s `configure.zcml` file contains this:

```
<browser:page
    for="Products.CMFCore.interfaces.ISiteRoot"
    name="dashboard"
    permission="plone.app.portlets.ManageOwnPortlets"
    class=".dashboard.DashboardView"
    template="dashboard.pt"
    />
```

Second, `plone.app.portlet.browser`'s `configure.zcml` file has:

```
<browser:page
   for="Products.CMFCore.interfaces.ISiteRoot"
   class=".manage.ManageDashboardPortlets"
   name="manage-dashboard"
   template="templates/manage-dashboard.pt"
   permission="plone.app.portlets.ManageOwnPortlets"
   />
```

These reference both a `template` and a `class`. Some views do not need a companion class to manage their display logic, and so only use a template. Others either do not use page templates for rendering, or explicitly invoke a template from their view class. We will learn more about these in Chapters 9 and 11.

To customize the two views, we will add the following to `optilux.theme.browser`'s `configure.zcml` file:

```
<browser:page
    for="Products.CMFCore.interfaces.ISiteRoot"
    name="dashboard"
    permission="plone.app.portlets.ManageOwnPortlets"
    class="plone.app.layout.dashboard.dashboard.DashboardView"
    template="templates/dashboard.pt"
    layer=".interfaces.IThemeSpecific"
    />

<browser:page
    for="Products.CMFCore.interfaces.ISiteRoot"
    name="manage-dashboard"
    permission="plone.app.portlets.ManageOwnPortlets"
    class="plone.app.portlets.browser.manage.ManageDashboardPortlets"
    template="templates/manage-dashboard.pt"
    layer=".interfaces.IThemeSpecific"
    />
```

In both cases, we use `layer=".interfaces.IThemeSpecific"` to provide an override for this particular theme only, and keep the `name`, `for`, and `permission` attributes the same.

In the `class` attribute, we use an absolute dotted name to reference the original class containing the display logic used by the template. We could of course have used a custom class (perhaps a subclass of the original one) or no class at all. In this case, we want to use a template that is very similar to the original, so it makes sense to tie this to the default view class.

The two templates—`dashboard.pt` and `manage-dashboard.pt`—have been copied into the `browser/templates` directory in the `optilux.theme` package, and modified in a way analogous to the customizations for the login templates, by commenting out this line:

```
<!-- <metal:left fill-slot="column_one_slot" /> -->
```

Again, we could have modified the templates much more extensively if it were necessary.

Viewlets

The mechanism for overriding viewlets is similar to that for overriding views. To change the rendering of the breadcrumbs, we have the following registration in `browser/configure.zcml`:

```
<browser:viewlet
    name="optilux.path_bar"
    manager="plone.app.layout.viewlets.interfaces.IContentViews"
    layer=".interfaces.IThemeSpecific"
    class=".viewlets.PathBarViewlet"
    permission="zope2.View"
    />
```

Since we hide the default `plone.path_bar` viewlet in `viewlets.xml`, we can register this one with a unique name to make it clear that it is different. To ensure that the viewlet only shows up for the Optilux theme, we use the same `layer` specification as seen before. We then reference a class that is responsible for updating and rendering the viewlet, found in `browser/viewlets.py`:

```
from zope.component import getMultiAdapter
from Products.Five.browser.pagetemplatefile import
ViewPageTemplateFile
from plone.app.layout.viewlets import common

class PathBarViewlet(common.PathBarViewlet):
    """A custom version of the path bar (breadcrumbs) viewlet, which
    uses slightly different markup.
    """

    render = ViewPageTemplateFile('templates/path_bar.pt')

    # The update() method, inherited from the base class, takes care
    # of initializing various variables used in the template
```

This is simply an extension of the equivalent class from `plone.app.layout.viewlets`, referencing a different template as its `render()` method. In Chapter 11, we will learn how to add custom logic to the viewlet class.

The template `path_bar.pt` lives in the `templates` directory, and is referenced with a relative path. It was originally copied from `plone.app.layout.viewlets`.

```
<div id="portal-breadcrumbs"
     i18n:domain="plone">

    <span id="breadcrumbs-you-are-here"
            i18n:translate="you_are_here">You are here:</span>
    <a id="breadcrumbs-home" i18n:translate="tabs_home"
```

```
            tal:attributes="href view/navigation_root_url">Home</a>
    <span tal:condition="view/breadcrumbs" class="breadcrumbSeparator">
        /
    </span>
    <span class="breadcrumbItem"
          tal:repeat="crumb view/breadcrumbs"
          tal:attributes="dir python:view.is_rtl and 'rtl' or 'ltr'">
        <tal:last tal:define="is_last repeat/crumb/end">
            <a href="#"
                tal:omit-tag="not: crumb/absolute_url"
                tal:condition="python:not is_last"
                tal:attributes="href crumb/absolute_url"
                tal:content="crumb/Title">
                 crumb
            </a>
            <span class="breadcrumbSeparator"
                    tal:condition="not: is_last">
                /
            </span>
            <span tal:condition="is_last"
                    tal:content="crumb/Title">crumb</span>
        </tal:last>
    </span>
</div>
```

Here, we have added a few CSS IDs and classes, which are used in the `main.css` style sheet. We have also changed the separator from an arrow to a forward slash.

Portlets

Finally, we will customize the view of the search portlet, which we will use in the left-hand side column to display a search box. In `configure.zcml`, we have:

```
<configure
    xmlns="http://namespaces.zope.org/zope"
    xmlns:browser="http://namespaces.zope.org/browser"
    xmlns:plone="http://namespaces.plone.org/plone"
    i18n_domain="optilux.theme">

    <include package="plone.app.portlets" />

    ...

    <plone:portletRenderer
        portlet="plone.app.portlets.portlets.search.ISearchPortlet"
```

```
        layer=".interfaces.IThemeSpecific"
        template="templates/search_portlet.pt"
        />

</configure>
```

We have to make sure that we include the `plone` XML namespace as well as the more common `zope` and `browser` ones. We also include the `plone.app.portlets` package, to make sure that its ZCML directives are processed before the new renderer is defined. This is because the `<plone:portletRenderer />` directive makes use of the initial portlet registration to provide some defaults for the new renderer. This saves a lot of typing, and reduces the chance of subtle errors.

 For regular browser views and viewlets—which are architecturally simpler—it is not necessary to ensure that the original registration is processed before the customization.

The `<plone:portletRenderer />` directive references a portlet by its interface. All of Plone's standard portlets are found `plone.app.portlets.portlets`. As before, we specify a `layer`, and then reference a `template`.

Unlike the `<browser:page />` and `<browser:viewlet />` directives, we will actually get the original portlet renderer class if we do not specify a `class` directly. This is available to the template using the implicit variable `view`. The template, `search_portlet.pt`, is based on `search.pt` in `plone.app.portlets.portlets`, and looks like this:

```
<dl class="portlet portletSearch"
    i18n:domain="plone">

  <dt class="portletHeader">
      <span class="portletTopLeft"></span>
      <a class="tile"
         tal:attributes="href view/search_form"
         i18n:translate="box_search">Search</a>
      <span class="portletTopRight"></span>
  </dt>

  <dd class="portletItem odd">
    <form name="searchform" action="search"
          tal:define="livesearch view/enable_livesearch;"
          tal:attributes="action view/search_action">
      <div class="LSBox">
        <input class="portlet-search-gadget"
           name="SearchableText"
           type="text"
```

```
                    size="15"
                    title="Enter search query"
                    i18n:attributes="title title_search_title;"
                    tal:attributes="value request/SearchableTest|nothing;
                                class python:livesearch and 'inputLabel
  portlet-search-gadget' or 'inputLabel portlet-search-gadget-nols'"
                    class="inputLabel" />
              <div class="LSResult" style="" tal:condition="livesearch">
                <div class="LSShadow"></div>
              </div>
            </div>
          </form>

          <dd class="portletFooter">
        </dd>
      </dl>
```

This is mostly a simplification of the original template.

Summary

In this chapter, we have learned:

- How to create a new package for a custom theme and integrate it into our build environment
- How to put Zope and the `portal_css` tool into development mode
- That Firebug is the greatest thing since sliced bread
- How to apply new CSS in a theme
- How to re-order, hide, and register new viewlets
- How to override templates from CMF skin layers
- How to override Zope 3-style views
- How to override the rendering of a viewlet
- How to customize the rendering of a portlet

These constitute the main techniques for adding a custom look and feel to Plone. If you have not done so already, it is probably instructive to look at the code in the `optilux.theme` package in detail to understand how the various pieces fit together.

We have not spent a lot of time discussing fundamental web technologies such as HTML and CSS. Demonstrating how to create usable, accessible, maintainable, standards-compliant, and cross-browser compatible designs with HTML and CSS deserves a book in its own right. There are plenty of good resources online as well.

If you are the type of web developer who uses a `<font />` tag every now and then, manages all layout with `<table />`s and is not quite sure how to float a box to the right of a block of text, you owe it to yourself to spend some time with a quality CSS reference.

We have also not spent much time on the syntax of **Zope Page Templates** (**ZPTs**), their **Template Attribute Language** (**TAL**), and their Macro Extensions (**METAL**). If you are not familiar with these, please see the ZPT tutorial at `http://plone.org/documentation/tutorial/zpt`. The documentation section on `plone.org` also features tutorials, and useful "how-to" documents describing approaches to theming, and visual customizations.

Bear in mind that some of the documentation on `plone.org` may have been written for earlier versions of Plone.

This concludes Part 2 of the book. In Part 3, we will sink our teeth into Python, as we learn how to develop new content types, views, and other components.

Part 3

Developing
New Functionality

9

Nine Core Concepts of Zope Programming

Now that we have learned how to set up and customize Plone, we are nearly ready to start developing brand-new functionality. This often means writing new content types, with custom views and forms to manage them. Sometimes, we will also create forms and pages that are not connected to any particular content type.

Before we continue with the Optilux Cinemas example, however, we will take a look at the core principles that underpin Zope programming. Writing software for Zope is a little different than writing software for other web programming platforms such as PHP or ASP.NET. Having a solid understanding of Zope's core concepts will help you understand the examples that follow, and help you apply what you learn to your own applications.

The examples in this chapter are intentionally frivolous, and demonstrate concepts in isolation. They use Python doctest syntax, and most can be found again in the `optilux.codeexamples` package that accompanies this book. You can run these tests as shown in Chapter 5, using:

```
$ ./bin/instance test -s optilux.codeexamples
```

If you are brand new to Zope and Plone programming, you may find this chapter a little intense on first reading. If so, do not get discouraged! It may be easier to skim this chapter first, and come back to it as you encounter different concepts again in subsequent chapters. Alternatively, you may want to explore and play with the `optilux.codeexamples` package to gain some experience with the various techniques demonstrated.

1. Object Publishing and Traversal

Consider a URL: `http://guitarsrus.com/guitars/fender/strat.html`. If this server was running Apache serving up HTML pages, then `guitars` and `fender` would probably be directories, and `strat.html` would be a static HTML page. If the server was using PHP, then perhaps `strat.html` would be called `strat.php` and consist of HTML with PHP code for branching, looping, and other logic. Languages such as ASP.NET and Cold Fusion are similar. Other frameworks, such as Ruby on Rails or Django rely on URL pattern matching to dispatch a request to a particular controller.

In Zope, the different parts of the URL are (in most cases) related to **object publishing**. For example, `guitars` and `fender` may be **folderish** objects, and `strat.html` could be the name of an object inside the `fender` folder. Similarly, `strat.html` could be the name of an attribute or method on `fender`, a view (more on those in a little while), or a **method alias**. As we saw in Chapter 4, the last part of the path could be acquired from a skin layer or parent folder.

 In the words of Jon Stahl, one of this book's reviewers: "Data in Zope is like a flowchart. Data in other web application frameworks is like a spreadsheet."

The process of determining which object to publish is called **URL traversal**. Zope will start at the **application root** — the root node in the ZODB, normally the place where a Plone site lives — and look for an item matching the first part of the URL, in this case an object called `guitars`. Zope will then look at the next part of the URL — `fender` — and try to find it, using the following logic:

- If `fender` is an attribute on the `guitars` object, traversal will continue from this attribute.

- If `fender` is a callable (i.e. method) on `guitars`, it will be called, and the return value used.

- If `guitars` is dictionary-like, and `fender` is a valid key in it, the value at that key will be used.

- If none of the above applies, but `fender` can be looked up as a view that is registered for `guitars`, this will be used.

- If `fender` cannot be found, a `NotFound` exception is raised, which in Plone will result in an error page.

When an object is found, Zope will attempt to call it and render it as a stream of data that will be sent to the browser. Page templates and other items implement a `__call__()` method accordingly, in order to render themselves.

Plone has some additional logic that determines the default view for a content object when the URL does not explicitly include the name of a page template, script, or method alias to use. It works as follows:

- If an object provides the Plone-specific `IBrowserDefault` interface (normally using `Products.CMFDynamicViewFTI.browserdefault.BrowserDefaultMixin` as a base class), then the currently selected *layout* (as managed via the **display** menu in Plone) or, if applicable, the current *default page* (an object set as the default view of a folder, also from the **display** menu) will be used.

- If there is a `(Default)` method alias for the content type of the object that is being displayed, this will be queried to find a page template (normally) to display. Method aliases are defined in the Factory Type Information (FTI) of an object, as found in `portal_types` in the ZMI.

- If there is no `(Default)` alias, but there is a `view` action in the FTI (this is the action that gets rendered as the **view** tab on the object when viewed in Plone), this will be resolved to find out which page template to display.

Because this logic is already in place for the base classes used by virtually all content objects in Plone, you will rarely need to worry about the details, but it is important to understand how attributes and containment can be used to influence what will be displayed.

Containment

URL traversal thus normally walks the **containment hierarchy**, also known as the **object graph**, in the ZODB. Each object has exactly one parent, and everything is ultimately a child of the application root. Two methods, available on all regular content objects, are used to reference the containment hierarchy:

- `absolute_url()` returns an absolute URL to an object, which can be safely rendered as a link to the user. It will take into account the actual URL that the server has assumed.

  Note that it includes the server name, so it is normally not a good idea to persist the string it returns. If it is saved in the ZODB, and that ZODB instance is moved to another server, all such links will be broken. Plone normally stores relative links and converts them to absolute links during rendering.

- `getPhysicalPath()` returns a tuple that includes each element of the path, all the way to the application root.

Note that in most hosting scenarios, the application is hosted in such a way that the Plone site appears to be the root of the server, even though to Zope, it lives one level down, inside the Zope application root. Therefore, it is not safe to construct URLs manually from paths. However, such paths are useful as unique identifiers of objects (at least until those objects are moved by the user), and are frequently used when constructing catalog searches. A common construct for converting the physical path tuple to a /-separated string is `'/'.join(context.getPhysicalPath())`. In particular, this is what we pass to the catalog when searching its `path` index (see later).

Hence, if an object called `taylor` is found inside a Plone site called `guitarsrus`, in a folder called `acoustic`, its absolute URL could be `http://localhost:8080/guitarsrus/acoustic/taylor`. As we will learn in Chapter 17, it could also be exposed using *virtual hosting*, for example assuming the URL `http://guitarsrus/acoustic/taylor`. In both cases, the physical path would be `/guitarsrus/acoustic/taylor`, so `taylor.getPhysicalPath()` would return a tuple `('', 'guitarsrus', 'acoustic', 'taylor')`.

In the ZODB object graph, nodes (or rather, objects capable of acting as containers) are known as **folderish** objects, and leaves are called **non-folderish** objects. A folderish object has a special attribute `isPrinicipiaFolderish` set to `True`; non-folderish objects have this set to `False`.

Plone also introduces the concept of a **non-structural folder**, which is just a folderish object that does not appear to be a folder in Plone's user interface. The *Rich Document* type we installed in Chapter 7 is a non-structural folder, containing its attachments and images, but appearing to the user as a standard object. Non-structural folders are distinguished by providing the interface `Products.CMFPlone.interfaces.INonStructuralFolder`. You will sometimes see the term **structural folder** used to refer to *real* folders, i.e. those folderish items that are not non-structural.

Recall that traversal checks for attributes before anything else. In Zope 2, folderish objects, specifically those that derive from `OFS.ObjectManager.ObjectManager`, implement `__getattr__()` in such a way that any attempt to get an attribute that is not directly found on the folderish object itself will result in an attempt to retrieve a contained object. As you may have guessed, this sometimes leads to naming conflicts between contained objects and methods, and attributes on folders. In Plone, names that would lead to conflicts are treated as *reserved*, and any object that is added will be renamed to create an unambiguous name. In pure Zope 3, containment is managed by mapping semantics, i.e. `__getitem__()`, instead of attribute semantics. Each containable object has an ID that is unique in its folder. This can be obtained by calling `getId()` on the contained object.

Here is an example of using getattr() and getId() to retrieve an object from its container. We first create a document with ID *guitars* inside the folder that is set up by the unit testing framework, and then we obtain it as an attribute on that folder. The invokeFactory() method, available on any standard folder, comes from Products.CMFCore.PortalFolder, and takes as arguments a portal type name (as found in the portal_types tool) and an ID, as well as any initial properties, passed as keyword parameters. Please note below that the variable _ here is used to ignore the return value from invokeFactory() in the doctest; otherwise, we would have to account for this to make the test pass. The name of the variable is arbitrary.

```
>>> _ = self.folder.invokeFactory('Document', 'favorites',
...                               title=u"Favorite Guitars")
>>> obj = getattr(self.folder, 'favorites', None)
>>> obj.getId()
'favorites'
```

To discover the parent of an object, you can use the aq_parent() function or, slightly less efficiently, the aq_parent attribute:

```
>>> from Acquisition import aq_parent
>>> aq_parent(obj) is self.folder
True
>>> obj.aq_parent is self.folder
True
```

Acquisition Chains

As you may have guessed from the previous examples, containment hierarchies are linked to Zope 2 acquisition. Recall from Chapter 4 how acquisition allows attributes on objects to come from parents—normally through the containment hierarchy—in what is known as an **acquisition chain**. In fact, it is possible for an object to have more than one acquisition chain, for example if it is being explicitly *wrapped* into a new chain as we will see in a moment. This is why it is normally safer to ask for the innermost chain when you want to walk the containment hierarchy:

```
>>> from Acquisition import aq_inner
>>> containment_parent = aq_parent(aq_inner(obj))
>>> also_containment_parent = obj.aq_inner.aq_parent
>>> containment_parent is also_containment_parent
True
```

There are two base classes that signal an object's participation in acquisition. Most content objects inherit `Acquisition.Implicit`, which means that `__getattr__()` is implemented in such a way that if an attribute is not found on the object, the parents in the (outermost) acquisition chain will be queried. This is the type of acquisition we saw in Chapter 4. Bear in mind that this applies both to containment, and to attributes defined in code. Using implicit acquisition (e.g. during URL traversal), an object contained in a parent folder may be returned if it matches the name of the requested attribute.

If you need to temporarily *turn off* implicit acquisition, you can use the `aq_explicit` attribute, which is provided by `Acquisition.Implict`. We use the `aq_base` function to discard the acquisition wrapper and get the raw object when testing object reference equivalence. Without `aq_base`, we would be comparing the object references of the acquisition wrappers themselves, not the objects they wrap.

```
>>> from Acquisition import aq_base
>>> favorites = getattr(self.portal, 'favorites')
>>> acquiring = getattr(self.folder, 'favorites', None)
>>> aq_base(acquiring) is aq_base(favorites)
True
>>> non_acquiring = getattr(self.folder.aq_explicit, 'favorites',
None)
>>> non_acquiring is None
True
```

The other type of acquisition is explicit acquisition, provided by the `Acquisition.Explicit` base class. Here, attributes are not acquired from parents in the chain implicitly as they are with `Acquisition.Implicit`. Explicit acquisition still maintains an acquisition chain, which is crucial for Zope 2 security and containment. Methods such as `absolute_url()` and `getPhysicalPath()`, which rely on acquisition to construct a path, continue to work.

An object's acquisition chain is constructed dynamically, during traversal or inspection from code. If an attribute on an acquisition-aware object returns another acquisition-aware object, then the former object is the immediate acquisition chain parent of the returned object. The acquisition chain can be inspected using the `aq_chain` function:

```
>>> from Acquisition import aq_chain, aq_inner
>>> aq_chain(self.portal.favorites)
[<ATDocument at /plone/favorites >, <PloneSite at /plone>,
<Application at >, <ZPublisher.BaseRequest.RequestContainer object at
...>]
>>> aq_chain(self.folder.favorites)
```

```
[<ATDocument at /plone/favorites used for /plone/Members/test_user_
1_>, <ATFolder at /plone/Members/test_user_1_>, <ATBTreeFolder at /
plone/Members>, <PloneSite at /plone>, <Application at >, <ZPublisher.
BaseRequest.RequestContainer object at ...>]
```

Notice how the acquisition chain for `favorites` is different depending on whether it was acquired from `self.portal` (which also happens to be its containment parent) or `self.folder` (via implicit acquisition). We can explicitly request the innermost chain, which is normally the containment chain:

```
>>> aq_chain(aq_inner(self.folder.favorites))
[<ATDocument at /plone/favorites>, <PloneSite at /plone>, <Application
at >, <ZPublisher.BaseRequest.RequestContainer object at ...>]
```

Also, notice how the final parent in the acquisition chain that results from URL traversal is a special request container object. This is why you will sometimes see this:

```
request = context.REQUEST
```

Here, the `REQUEST` variable is implicitly acquired from the context.

The example above shows a nice and tidy acquisition chain, based on the containment hierarchy. Now consider another common piece of code:

```
from Products.Five.browser import BrowserView

class MyView(BrowserView):

    def __init__(self, context, request):
        self.context = context
        self.request = request

    def use_context(self):
        context = self.context
        # Use 'context' or 'self.context' for something
        ...
```

We will learn about Zope 3 style browser views later in this chapter, but the important points here are that `context` is a content object, part of the containment hierarchy, and `Products.Five.browser.BrowserView` inherits from `Acquisition.Explicit`. Therefore, when we access `self.context`, it will have two acquisition chains: the innermost chain, which is the containment chain, and the outermost chain that contains the `MyView` object.

If the `use_context()` method uses the `context` variable in a way that relies on containment hierarchy acquisition, for example because it conducts an explicit security check or because it needs to acquire a skin layer template or script, it may encounter spurious `AttributeErrors`. Therefore, you will often see code like this:

```
def use_context(self):
    context = aq_inner(self.context)
    # Now use 'context' in place of 'self.context'
    ...
```

Sometimes you need to control the acquisition chain explicitly. This generally occurs when you are trying to make an object appear as if it came from somewhere other than where it was originally stored, either as part of a security scheme, or to fool implicit acquisition. To do so, you can use the `__of__()` method, which is part of any acquisition-aware object.

In the following example, we instantiate a content object in memory, without connecting it to the containment hierarchy, and then wrap it in the acquisition context of the portal:

```
>>> from Products.ATContentTypes.content.document import ATDocument
>>> temp_document = ATDocument('temp_document')
>>> aq_chain(temp_document)
[<ATDocument at temp_document>]
>>> aq_chain(temp_document.__of__(self.portal))
[<ATDocument at /plone/temp_document>, <PloneSite at /plone>,
<Application at >, <ZPublisher.BaseRequest.RequestContainer object at
...>]
```

Path Traversal

In page templates or actions, you will sometimes see expressions such as `context/guitars/fender`. This is using traversal relative to a particular object, employing a similar heuristic to the one described for URL traversal. In fact, path expressions in page templates can also *traverse* to elements inside dictionaries and lists. This does not apply to the `restrictedTraverse()`/`unrestrictedTraverse()` methods. Acquisition is taken into account here too.

Path traversal can be invoked from Python code relative to a content object, using this syntax:

```
>>> self.setRoles(('Manager',))
>>> _ = self.portal.invokeFactory('Folder', 'guitars')
>>> _ = self.portal.guitars.invokeFactory('Document', 'fender')
>>> self.portal.unrestrictedTraverse('guitars/fender')
```

```
<ATDocument at /plone/guitars/fender>
>>> fender_path = '/'.join(self.portal.guitars.fender.
getPhysicalPath())
>>> fender_path
'/plone/guitars/fender'
>>> self.portal.unrestrictedTraverse(fender_path)
<ATDocument at /plone/guitars/fender>
```

There is also a `restrictedTraverse()`, method, which has the same semantics, but performs security checks for each traversal step, in the same way as skin layer page templates and scripts are subject to *untrusted code* security checks as explained in Chapter 6.

2. ZODB Persistence

When working with Zope, developers are largely free from having to worry about persistence. Zope begins a new transaction for each request. If an error occurs (i.e. an uncaught exception is raised), the transaction is rolled back and no changes are written. If no error occurs, the transaction is committed, and any changes to objects connected to the ZODB object graph are saved.

Transactions

Transactions are managed by the `transaction` module. It is possible to manually begin and end transactions, but in practice the only operation you are likely to perform is to set a **savepoint**. A savepoint is like a sub-transaction. It is required before certain operations, but it also helps free memory by writing the partial transaction to a disk cache.

 Note that a very small number of functions require a savepoint to run in combination. Most commonly, if you need to use the `manage_cutObjects()` and `manage_pasteObjects()` methods from `OFS.CopySupport` in the same transaction, you may need to place a savepoint between them.

To set a savepoint, use:

```
import transaction
savepoint = transaction.savepoint()
```

It is now possible to call `savepoint.rollback()` to roll back this sub-transaction. If you are only interested in freeing up memory, use an *optimistic* savepoint:

```
transaction.savepoint(True)
```

This still returns a value, but rolling back an optimistic savepoint will result in an error.

If you need to abort a transaction, you should raise an unhandled exception. Note that the ZODB error handling machinery uses a special exception called a `ConflictError` to deal with write conflicts when multiple threads attempt to modify the same object. A conflicted transaction can almost always be resolved automatically, but you must let this exception go uncaught, allowing Zope to re-attempt the failed transaction.

Do not use a bare `try...except` clause around code that could cause a ZODB write, and thus could raise a `ConflictError`. Always let a `ConflictError` go unhandled. Of course, you should try to avoid bare excepts in general.

To ensure `ConflictErrors` are not swallowed, you will often see code like this:

```
from ZODB.POSException import ConflictError
try:
    # some unpredictable operation that may cause a write
except ConflictError:
    raise
except:
    # Swallow other errors or handle in some other way
```

Object Persistence

For an object to be persisted, it must either be a primitive (e.g. an integer or string) or of a class deriving from `persistence.Persistent`.

Take a look at the `persistence` module, in particular `interfaces.py`, if you want to know the gritty details of object persistence.

All Plone content types ultimately derive from this base class. The base classes we will use in Chapter 10 to build new content types properly derive from `Persistent` as well.

To be saved, an object must be connected to the ZODB object graph by being set as an attribute of another persistent object. This is what happens when a content object is added to a folderish parent in Plone, for example. When an attribute is accessed later, the ZODB will transparently load the associated object from disk if necessary.

The ZODB will automatically detect when a persisted object has been changed. Those changes will be saved when the transaction is committed. The exception is that if an object has a standard list or dict as an attribute, and a value in that list or dict is changed, Zope will not be able to detect it. If no other changes took place for that object, the changes may be lost.

To explicitly tell the ZODB to persist an object, you can set the _p_changed property to True:

```
>>> someobj.somedict['key1'] = "new value"
>>> someobj._p_changed = True
```

Alternatively, you can use either of the two classes: persistent.dict. PersistentDict or persistent.list.PersistentList. These act exactly like standard dicts and lists, but derive from Persistent, and will set _p_changed as necessary:

```
>>> from persistent.dict import PersistentDict
>>> someobj.somedict = PersistentDict()
>>> someobj.somedict['key1'] = "new value"
```

The PersistentDict, and PersistentList types are not recommended for large data sets (hundreds of items or more). This is because each time the ZODB saves an object, it will essentially write out a new copy of it (at least with the default File Storage). Every time an item in one of these data structures is changed, the entire dict or list is versioned.

Writing a new copy of the object while saving it allows the **Undo** tab in the ZMI to work. It also makes the ZODB very fast. On frequently changing sites, the ZODB should be *packed* regularly. You can do so from the **Maintenance** control panel in Plone, or the **Control_Panel** in the ZMI. In Chapter 16, we will look at how to automate this process.

For large data sets, the BTrees module provides several optimized data structures, which do not suffer from this problem. They come in sets (IOSet, OOSet, OISet, IISet), sorted sets (IOTreeSet, OOTreeSet, OITreeSet, IITreeSet), and mappings (IOBTree, OOBTree, OIBTree, IIBTree), designed for integer or object keys or values. For example, BTrees.IOBTree.IOSet is an unordered set with integer keys, while BTrees.OIBTree.OIBTree is a mapping with object keys, and integer values. See Interfaces.py in that module for more information.

Finally, it is possible to use **volatile attributes**, which are explicitly not saved. They will only remain as long as the object is in memory. Since there is no guarantee of how long an object will remain in memory until it is ghosted by the ZODB, you can never rely on volatile attributes being there, but they are sometimes useful as a simple cache.

Volatile attributes have names beginning with _v_. They must be used defensively:

```
>>> someobj._v_saved = expensive_operation()
>>> # do something else for a while
>>> saved = getattr(someobj, '_v_saved', None)
>>> if saved is None: # in case we lost it ...
>>>     saved = expensive_operation()
```

3. Searching Objects Using the Catalog

So far, we have discussed the object graph of the ZODB. We can walk this graph, using `getattr()` to retrieve acquisition-wrapped objects, and we can scan folderish objects using methods such as `objectIds()`, which returns a list of all the IDs in that container, and `objectValues()`, which returns a list of contained objects.

Walking the entire ZODB every time we want to find an object is not ideal. In particular, functions such as `objectValues()` should be avoided if possible, because they can *wake up* a large number of objects from the ZODB—unpickling them, and swapping them into the ZODB cache. *Waking up* objects is a relatively slow process, and waking up lots of objects will make your code very slow.

Zope mitigates this problem with **ZCatalog**s—relational database-like tables of objects. In Plone, there is a ZCatalog called **portal_catalog** in the root of the site, which indexes all content objects. You can get a hold of it using:

```
>>> from Products.CMFCore.utils import getToolByName
>>> catalog = getToolByName(context, 'portal_catalog')
```

Here, `context` must be an object inside the Plone site, or the Plone site root itself.

The catalog is configured with **indexes**—which can be used to search various attributes of indexed objects—and **metadata**—copies of certain attributes that can be examined without fetching the underlying content object. Sometimes, the same attribute is used both in an index, and as metadata. You can think of an index as something you use to find an object, and a metadata item as something you use to inspect the search results.

Where an object does not provide a particular attribute, the value of any corresponding metadata item may be `None` (or it could be acquired from a parent). Note that if too many attributes are listed in the metadata table, the catalog will grow in size, and become slower, counteracting the efficiency benefits of using metadata instead of fetching full objects.

To see the complete list of metadata columns, look at `portal_catalog` in the ZMI, under the **Metadata** tab. Indexes are listed on the **Indexes** tab. We will see an example of adding additional indexes and metadata columns via the `catalog.xml` import step in the next chapter.

Plone's catalog has an implicit search parameter that ensures that only those content objects that are viewable by the current user are returned, and since non-content objects (e.g. CMF tools found in the portal root) are not indexed, they will not be found when searching the catalog. However, if you want to find objects that are not viewable by the current user regardless, you can use the `unrestrictedSearchResults()` function of `portal_catalog`.

When we search the catalog, it returns a lazy list of items known as **brains**. Catalog brains have attributes consisting of values of the various columns in the metadata table. Brains also contain a few useful methods for inspecting the object that was cataloged. Most importantly, retrieving a catalog brain does not wake up the indexed content object itself. To get the full object, you can use the `getObject()` method on the brain.

For further information about ZCatalogs, see the **Searching and Categorizing Content** chapter of the Zope Book, which can be found at `http://www.zope.org/Documentation/Books/ZopeBook`. You will find examples of using the catalog in the subsequent chapters, and all throughout Plone's source code. Below are a few examples of common catalog usage.

To retrieve all published news items in the site, use:

```
>>> for brain in catalog(portal_type='News Item', review_
state='published'):
...     print brain.getPath()
/plone/Members/test_user_1_/guitars/strat
/plone/Members/test_user_1_/guitars/lp
```

Here, we call the catalog object directly to execute a query. For the purposes of testing, we simply print the path, as returned by the brain-specific `getPath()` function. This is equivalent to using `'/'.join(obj.getPhysicalPath())` on a regular object.

To prove this, we will use `getObject()` to retrieve such an object. Note that normally, we would try *not* to do this to avoid a performance hit:

```
>>> for brain in catalog.searchResults({'portal_type' : 'News Item',
...                                      'review_state' : 'published'}):
...     print '/'.join(brain.getObject().getPhysicalPath())
/plone/Members/test_user_1_/guitars/strat
/plone/Members/test_user_1_/guitars/lp
```

Here we also use the `searchResults()` method, which is equivalent to calling the catalog object, and pass a dict of search terms instead of keyword parameters. The keys refer to the names of indexes, while the values are the things to search for.

The `getURL()` method of a brain is complementary to `getPath()`. It returns the referenced object's URL. As with the `absolute_url()` method on a regular object, this takes into account the current server URL (which may be different from the server URL at the time that the object was indexed):

```
>>> for brain in catalog(portal_type='News Item', review_
state='published'):
...         print brain.getURL() == brain.getObject().absolute_url()
True
True
```

Different types of indexes accept different types of search parameters. The most common kinds are the `FieldIndex`, which indexes a single field, and the `KeywordIndex`, used when a field contains a list of values, and you would like to be able to search for a subset of them. For example, the `Subject` index refers to the Dublin Core subject (aka keywords) field. To find any documents (pages) or news items that refer to Guitars or Fender, we could write:

```
>>> results = catalog(portal_type=('Document', 'News Item',),
...                   Subject=('Guitars', 'Fender'))
>>> sorted([r.getId for r in results])
['fender', 'lp', 'tele']
```

Here, we assume that there are three objects, *fender*, *lp*, and *tele*, which match the given criteria. We also make use of the `getId` metadata attributes (which stores the return value of the method with the same name), and reduce the lazy list of results to a sorted list of string IDs for the purposes of validating the output reliably.

The `path` index can be used to search for objects by location. By default, it will match the specified path and all sub-paths. By passing a dictionary with keys `query` and `depth` to the index, we can search either for just a specific path (depth 0) or just sub-paths of specified path (depth 1):

```
>>> guitars_path = '/'.join(self.folder.guitars.getPhysicalPath())
>>> results = catalog(path=guitars_path)
>>> sorted([r.getId for r in results])
['basses', 'fender', 'guitars', 'jagstang', 'lp', 'pbass', 'strat',
'tele']
>>> results = catalog(path=dict(query=guitars_path, depth=0))
>>> sorted([r.getId for r in results])
['guitars']
>>> results = catalog(path=dict(query=guitars_path, depth=1))
>>> sorted([r.getId for r in results])
['basses', 'fender', 'jagstang', 'lp', 'strat', 'tele']
```

In these examples, *pbass* is a child of *basses*, which is why it shows up when searching for all items under *guitars*, but not when searching for only those objects directly inside *guitars*. Also notice that with no depth restriction, the *guitars* folder is included in the search results, but it is excluded when searching for items at depth 1 (i.e. those objects directly inside the folder).

We can control the order of the returned items using the special `sort_on` and `sort_order` parameters, and the maximum number of returned objects using `sort_limit`. When using `sort_limit`, we could potentially get a few more items back—it is only a hint to the search algorithms, and the lazy nature of the returned list makes it possible that complex searches will cause them to overshoot a little. Therefore, we normally also explicitly limit the number of items we iterate over:

```
>>> results = catalog(portal_type='Document', sort_on='sortable_
title')
>>> [r.Title for r in results]
['Favorite guitars', 'Fender', 'Precision bass']
>>> results = catalog(portal_type='Document',
...                    sort_on='sortable_title', sort_
order='descending')
>>> [r.Title for r in results]
['Precision bass', 'Fender', 'Favorite guitars']
>>> limit = 5
>>> results = catalog(portal_type='Document',
...                    sort_on='sortable_title', sort_limit=limit)[:limit]
>>> [r.Title for r in results]
['Favorite guitars', 'Fender', 'Precision bass']
```

This returns the last five published objects, sorted on title. The `sort_order` parameter can be `"ascending"` or `"descending"`, with `"reverse"` being an alias for `"descending"`. The `sortable_title` index is a special version of the `Title` index that uses some clever string manipulation to make sure that titles will sort the way people normally expect them to.

When objects change, they need to be reindexed for the catalog to be updated. This is done automatically when content is manipulated via the Plone user interface. When making changes in code, however, we sometimes need to reindex manually.

```
>>> self.folder.favorites.setDescription("Contains a list of
favorites")
>>> len(catalog(Description="list of favorites"))
0
>>> self.folder.favorites.reindexObject(idxs=['Description'])
>>> len(catalog(Description="list of favorites"))
1
>>> self.folder.favorites.setDescription("My favorites!")
```

```
>>> self.folder.favorites.setTitle("My favorite guitars")
>>> self.folder.favorites.reindexObject()
>>> len(catalog(Title="My favorite guitars"))
1
```

The `reindexObject()` function comes from the `CMFCatalogAware` mix-in class, used in nearly all content objects. It tells the catalog to reindex the given object. Without parameters, it reindexes all indexes, but we can save a bit of processing by passing a list of indexes to re-index if we are certain nothing else has changed. There is also `reindexObjectSecurity()`, which will automatically refresh the permission-related indexes for the current object, and any children it may have.

4. Describing Functionality with Interfaces

Thus far, we have described the core concepts of Zope 2 programming. The remainder of this chapter will focus on concepts that are new with Zope 3: interfaces, utilities, adapters, views, and events.

Interfaces are a key part of most Zope 3 techniques. They are best thought of as verifiable documentation—descriptions of components and their behavior that can be inspected at run time. The simplest form of an interface—known as a **marker interface**—is one that describes the type of a component without promising any methods or attributes.

Because Python does not have a language construct for interfaces, we define them using classes inheriting from `zope.interface.Interface`:

```
>>> from zope.interface import Interface
>>> class IBelievable(Interface):
...     """An item which can be believed
...     """
```

Often, reading a package's interfaces is the best way of understanding how the components of that package are meant to fit together. By convention, interfaces are found in a module called `interfaces`, and have names starting with the letter *I*. Interfaces should always include a meaningful docstring.

Program design can be modeled using interfaces, using constructs such as specialization (inheritance) and association (composition). For example, here is a specialization of the `IBelievable` interface:

```
>>> class IUndeniable(IBelievable):
...     """Something that is so believable it cannot be denied
...     """
```

Interfaces can also describe methods and attributes. Note that methods in interfaces do not have the `self` parameter, nor do they have method bodies, although they *do* have docstrings; again, they serve as documentation. Of course, when the interface is implemented by a class, that class will use the `self` parameter, and have a method body, as we will see below.

Attributes can be described using `zope.interface.Attribute`. We can also make more precise statements about the valid contents of attributes with the `zope.schema` package, which we will cover in Chapter 11 when we look at how Zope can auto-generate forms from this information. In Zope 3-style code, there is usually a preference for using attributes and Python properties over separate *get* and *set* methods when modeling attributes of an object.

Note that if you are using Python `property` syntax, you will not have an acquisition context. Since property getters and setters tend to be simple, this is not usually a problem, but if you find yourself needing one, look at Zope 2's `ComputedAttribute` class.

```
>>> from zope.interface import Attribute
>>> class IMessage(Interface):
...     """A message being communicated
...     """
...
...     def shout(noise_level=5):
...         """Shout the message
...         """
...
...     content = Attribute("The actual text of the message")
```

Interfaces are typically **implemented** by classes. Objects of these classes are then said to **provide** those interfaces. This implies that the object exposes all the methods and attributes promised by the interface.

```
>>> from zope.interface import implements
>>> class StandardMessage(object):
...     implements(IMessage)
...
...     def __init__(self, content):
...         self.content = content
...
...     def shout(self, noise_level=5):
...         print self.content * noise_level
>>> class StrongMessage(StandardMessage):
...     implements(IBelievable)
```

Interfaces are inherited from base classes, and a class can implement multiple interfaces by passing several parameters to implements().

The zope.interface package contains methods for manipulating interfaces on classes and objects. Interfaces themselves contain methods that can be used to verify their relevance to classes and objects.

```
>>> IMessage.implementedBy(StandardMessage)
True
>>> IMessage.implementedBy(StrongMessage)
True
>>> IBelievable.implementedBy(StandardMessage)
False
>>> IBelievable.implementedBy(StrongMessage)
True
```

Here, the implementedBy() method is used to determine if objects of a particular class will comply with the given interface. More commonly, we inspect objects directly, using the providedBy() method:

```
>>> fender = StandardMessage("All Fender guitars rock")
>>> strats = StrongMessage("Stratocasters are great!")
>>> telecaster = StrongMessage("Telecasters are awesome!")
>>> IMessage.providedBy(fender)
True
>>> IMessage.providedBy(strats)
True
>>> IBelievable.providedBy(fender)
False
>>> IBelievable.providedBy(strats)
True
```

We can also apply interfaces directly to objects. Here, the IUndeniable interface is being applied selectively to messages:

```
>>> from zope.interface import alsoProvides
>>> alsoProvides(telecaster, IUndeniable)
>>> IUndeniable.providedBy(fender)
False
>>> IUndeniable.providedBy(telecaster)
True
```

It is also possible to let a class object *provide* (as opposed to *implement*) an interface, in which case we are making a statement about the type of the class, rather than the type of objects of that class. We can even apply interfaces to other interfaces to group them logically, or apply interfaces to modules, to describe their public functions and variables. In normal programming, these constructs are rarely needed, but you may come across them in framework code.

Here, we describe mechanisms for creating messages as *communication factories*. Because we are applying the interface to the *class object*, there is no notion of inheritance between the StrongMessage and the StandardMessage declarations — we have to declare the interface on both classes explicitly.

```
>>> class ICommunicationFactory(Interface):
...     """A Python callable (e.g. classes) which is able to produce
...     communication devices (e.g. messages).
...     """
>>> alsoProvides(StandardMessage, ICommunicationFactory)
>>> alsoProvides(StrongMessage, ICommunicationFactory)
>>> ICommunicationFactory.implementedBy(StandardMessage)
False
>>> ICommunicationFactory.providedBy(StandardMessage)
True
>>> ICommunicationFactory.providedBy(StrongMessage)
True
```

The documentation in zope.interface.interfaces describes in detail the various ways in which interfaces can be applied, inspected, and manipulated.

Using Interfaces in Catalog Searches

In the previous section, we demonstrated how to use the catalog to search for objects by their portal_type, a string. This pattern is quite common, but has a few drawbacks:

- There can only ever be one content type installed with the same portal_type name. We can search for multiple portal types, but the code that searches needs to be aware of all such types in advance.

- Although it is uncommon, portal_type names can be changed.

Interfaces are a better way to describe the semantic type of a content object. In Plone 3, the object_provides catalog index can be used to search for objects providing a particular interface. This takes into account interfaces inherited from parent objects, as well as generalizations of specific interfaces provided.

Note that this index only stores the names of the interfaces an object held when it was being cataloged. Changes in code or ZCML may mean that an object's interfaces change after it has been indexed, in which case the catalog would not be aware of this until the object is reindexed.

```
>>> from Products.ATContentTypes.interface import ITextContent
>>> results = catalog(object_provides=ITextContent.__identifier__)
>>> sorted([r.getId for r in results])
['favorites', 'fender', 'lp', 'pbass', 'strat', 'tele']
```

In this example, we search for all standard *text content*. Interfaces for Plone's standard content types can be found in `Products.ATContentTypes.interface`.

 Normally, the interfaces would be found in an `interfaces` module, but by historical accident, this name was already taken in the `ATContentTypes` package, so here had to use the name `interface` instead for its Zope 3 interfaces.

5. Component Configuration with ZCML

ZCML (Zope Component Meta-Language) is an XML format used by Zope 3 to configure components such as utilities, adapters, and views. We have already seen ZCML files in the `optilux.policy` package, and they are found throughout Plone and Zope.

ZCML files are usually rooted in a `<configure />` node, which includes directives from one of several XML namespaces, including `zope` for core component configuration, `browser` for configuration of views and browser resources, and `five` for Zope 2 integration directives.

```
<configure
    xmlns="http://namespaces.zope.org/zope"
    xmlns:five="http://namespaces.zope.org/five"
    xmlns:browser="http://namespaces.zope.org/browser">

    ...

</configure>
```

We will normally describe specific ZCML directives alongside the concepts that they relate to. One important generic directive, however, is `<include />`. This can be used to trigger the processing of other ZCML files, and allows us to manage interdependencies between packages' configuration or split long ZCML files into more manageable chunks. Common examples include:

```
<include package="zope.annotation" />
<include package=".browser" />
<include file="permissions.zcml" />
```

The first example will cause the ZCML parser to proceed to the `configure.zcml` file in the `zope.annotation` package if it has not been processed already. The second includes the `browser` sub-package inside the current package, again looking for a `configure.zcml` file there. The third example includes a file called `permissions.zcml` in the same directory as the current file. Relative paths are also allowed.

At Zope startup, the `etc/site.zcml` file in the *instance home* is read. This triggers the loading of Five, which in turn will scan all old-style products for `meta.zcml` and `configure.zcml` files, and execute these, before executing any `overrides.zcml` files. A `meta.zcml` file is used to define new ZCML directives, mostly by core Zope 3 packages. `overrides.zcml` is used to override settings made by `configure.zcml` files in other packages. Generic packages should only use `overrides.zcml` when absolutely necessary, to avoid confusion and configuration conflicts.

The `site.zcml` file then includes all files in `$INSTANCE_HOME/etc/package-includes` with names that end in `-meta.zcml`, `-configure.zcml`, and finally `-overrides.zcml`. These files are known as ZCML **slugs**, and typically contain one-line `<include />` statements referencing particular packages. Note that only `configure.zcml` is loaded implicitly, so a slug meant to load `overrides.zcml` from a particular package would need to use:

```
<include package="my.package" file="overrides.zcml" />
```

Conventionally, this file would be called `my.package-overrides.zcml`. The regular slug for `my.package` would be called `my.package-configure.zcml`, and contain only:

```
<include package="my.package" />
```

In Chapter 5, we saw how to use zc.buildout to install a slug for the `optilux.policy` egg automatically, ensuring that its configuration gets loaded at startup.

6. Component Registries Using Utilities

The Zope 3 Component Architecture can be seen as a collection of registries. Code in one component can look up other components by interface and possibly a name, and use them to perform some function. Interfaces are thus the main contract between components, and the Component Architecture is responsible for locating an appropriate implementation of a particular interface for a particular purpose.

Broadly, there are two main types of components:

- *Utilities*, which are context-less. Utilities can either act as singletons, looked up by interface, or as registries of similar components, looked up by interface and name.

- *Adapters*, which are contextual. Adapters allow code expecting components providing a particular interface to *adapt* objects of some other type to this interface. Seen differently, adapters are used to provide a particular *aspect* of an object without modifying the original object itself.

Global Utilities

The simplest type of component is a global unnamed **utility**. Such utilities act as singletons—components that are instantiated exactly once and re-used wherever they are needed.

Consider a message broadcaster, which we want to use in various parts in some program:

```
>>> from zope.interface import Interface
>>> class IBroadcaster(Interface):
...     """A component capable of broadcasting a message to the world
...     """
...
...     def __call__(message):
...         """Broadcast the given message
...         """
>>> from zope.interface import implements
>>> class RadioBroadcaster(object):
...     implements(IBroadcaster)
...
...     def __call__(self, message):
...         print "And now for a special announcement:", message
```

We could, of course, instantiate a RadioBroadcaster each time we wanted to broadcast something, but this would mean a hard dependency on this specific implementation. Really, all we are interested in is something that complies with the IBroadcaster interface, and we can leave it up to application configuration to decide which specific implementation is appropriate. Such configuration is done in ZCML like this:

```
<utility factory=".broadcaster.RadioBroadcaster" />
```

Alternatively, we could explicitly specify the provided interface. This is necessary if the class does not have an `implements()` declaration, or if the class implements more than one interface.

```
<utility
    provides=".interfaces.IBroadcaster"
    factory=".broadcaster.RadioBroadcaster"
    />
```

The ZCML examples in this chapter are hypothetical only. Here, we assume that `IBroadcaster` is in a module called `interfaces` in the current package, and the implementation is in a module called `broadcaster`. In the doctests, we use a Python API to register the utilities instead of ZCML, and we define all the interfaces and classes as part of the test.

Specifically, zope.component.provideAdapter, zope.component. provideUtility, and zope.component.provideHandler are meant for tests only. See zope.component.interfaces for further descriptions.

With this in our `configure.zcml`, we can write:

```
>>> from zope.component import getUtility
>>> broadcaster = getUtility(IBroadcaster)
>>> broadcaster("Jimi Hendrix played a Stratocaster")
And now for a special announcement: Jimi Hendrix played a Stratocaster
```

We could also have used `zope.component.queryUtility`, which acts the same as `getUtility()` but will return `None` if no suitable utility can be found. `getUtility()` will raise a `zope.component.interfaces.ComponentLookupError`.

Common uses for unnamed utilities include:

- Providing services through singletons. This is analogous to the *Service Locator pattern*, if you have ever come across that.

- Providing access to commonly used utility functionality in a more formalized, implementation-exchangeable way.

- Storing policy decisions or global configuration settings in such a way that they can be overridden, for example using `overrides.zcml` or local utilities (see later).

Named Utilities

An unnamed utility is actually a special case of a **named utility**, having the name
u"" (an empty Unicode string). Named utilities allow us to use the utility registry as
a general registry for any kind of homogenous components. Here, *homogenous* just
means "that provide the same interface".

For example, suppose we needed an abstraction for a channel used to transmit
a message:

```
>>> class IChannel(Interface):
...     """A channel through which a message could be transmitted
...     """
...
...     def transmit(source, destination, message):
...         """Transmit a message between two destinations
...         """
```

There could be a number of different types of channels, such as FTP or HTTP, each
with different configurations. Let us assume that we do not want the application to
make a single decision in this case, but rather allow the choice to be made at run time.
To achieve this, we could register the various types of channels as named utilities.

```
>>> class Channel(object):
...     implements(IChannel)
...
...     def __init__(self, port):
...         self.port = port
...
...     def transmit(self, source, destination, message):
...         print "Sending", message, "from", source, \
...             "to", destination, "on", self.port
>>> http = Channel(80)
>>> ftp = Channel(21)
```

In this example, we are actually instantiating objects to act as utilities, rather than
providing a factory to let the Component Architecture instantiate them for itself.
It would be perfectly feasible to write different factories (e.g. different classes) and
register a utility for each one, but we can save some code by using a parameterized
class instead.

To register these objects in ZCML, we could use something like:

```
<utility
    provides=".interfaces.IChannel"
    component=".channel.http"
```

```
    name="http"
    />
<utility
    provides=".interfaces.IChannel"
    component=".channel.ftp"
    name="ftp"
    />
```

To look up these utilities, we still use `getUtility()` or `queryUtility()`, providing an additional `name` parameter.

```
>>> from zope.component import queryUtility
>>> chosen_channel = u"ftp" # perhaps selected by the user
>>> channel = queryUtility(IChannel, name=chosen_channel)
```

Named utilities can be used when:

- We need a registry of similar components (providing a particular interface) identifiable by name. This saves us from writing a custom registry, ties the component lookup explicitly to a formalized interface, and allows us to use a standard API to enumerate or access the registry.

- We want other packages and applications to be able to *plug in* new components. For example, the list of addable portlets in Plone is constructed by querying the utility registry for named utilities providing `IPortletType`. This allows third-party packages to tell Plone about a new portlet simply by registering a utility carrying the necessary information. Here, the name of each utility needs only be unique—the framework code is more interested in the interface. To get back a list of name-utility pairs for all utilities providing a particular interface, use `zope.component.getUtilitiesFor`.

- We require the user to choose among a number of possible components, say to influence the policy used by a particular process. The user's choice is then translated to a utility name, and an appropriate utility is found.

Local Utilities

A **site manager** keeps track of component registrations. The default site manager, which is what we have been using up until now, is known as the **global site manager**. Components in the global site manager are usually configured with ZCML.

A particular location in the containment hierarchy may have a **local site manager**, where local components are persisted. When a local site manager is active, it will take precedence over the global site manager or a local site manager further up in the containment hierarchy, but will fall back on a parent or the global site manager if it does not have an appropriate registration for some requested component. This is similar to how Zope 2 acquisition allows local overrides, except that it only pertains to component registrations.

The Plone site root is a **site** in the Zope 3 sense, meaning that it has a local site manager. During URL traversal, this is activated so that whenever a component is looked up by code invoked inside the Plone site, local components are allowed to override global ones. This is purely a configuration issue — the code performing the component lookup will use the same APIs, such as `getUtility()` and `queryUtility()`.

 In fact, any `OFS.ObjectManager` is a **possible site** in Zope 3 jargon. See `sitemanager.txt` in `Products.Five` or `site.txt` in `zope.app.component` for information on how to turn a container into a site.

Unlike global utilities, however, **local utilities** are stored in the ZODB and thus can be used to persist the state. Therefore, they are often used not as overrides for default global utilities, but as storage for configuration data. For example, the `plone.app.redirector` package registers a local utility that keeps track of where content objects used to live when they are moved.

The easiest way of registering a local utility is to use the `componentregistry.xml` import step with GenericSetup. Plone's version of this file is a good point of reference. Below is a short extract:

```
<componentregistry>
 ...
 <utilities>
  <utility
     interface="five.customerize.interfaces.IViewTemplateContainer"
     object="/portal_view_customizations"/>
  <utility
     interface="plone.app.redirector.interfaces.IRedirectionStorage"
     factory="plone.app.redirector.storage.RedirectionStorage"/>
 </utilities>
 ...
</componentregistry>
```

In the first example, we register an object that is already in the ZODB (in the portal root) as a local utility. This is done because the `portal_view_customizations` tool should be navigable from the ZMI. In the second example, we register the aforementioned redirection storage, allowing the site manager to instantiate it for itself using the supplied factory.

Note that unlike ZCML directives, which are processed every time Zope is started, the GenericSetup profile is run only when the Plone site is created. Thus, while global components are created and kept in volatile memory, local components are instantiated once and persisted.

To access the redirection storage, we would use exactly the same syntax as if we were accessing a global utility:

```
>>> from plone.app.redirector.interfaces import IRedirectionStorage
>>> redirector = getUtility(IRedirectionStorage)
```

This would work so long as we were in a view or other object being executed as a result of Zope traversing to some object inside the Plone site, thus activating the local component registry.

When programming for Plone, this is almost always the case. The exception is in a general event handler for an IObjectMovedEvent or a sub-type, which may be invoked when the portal object itself is renamed or deleted. In this case, we are operating from outside the Plone site, in the ZMI root, and the local registry is not invoked. In these cases, it may be safer to use queryUtility() and check for a None return value. You may also encounter this problem from code that is executed outside the Plone site, for example during a ./bin/zopectl debug session.

Tools

CMF **tools** were the precursors to local utilities. They are persistent objects, typically deriving from OFS.SimpleItem.SimpleItem, a common base class for non-folderish plain Zope objects. Tools are by convention stored in the root of the Plone site, and have names beginning with portal_, such as portal_membership or portal_types. They are used to store configuration information or expose common utility methods. Use the **Doc** tab in the ZMI or see the relevant interfaces to find out more about what each tool does.

Because they are persisted in the root of the site, tools may be acquired as attributes of any object inside the portal or obtained using URL or path traversal. The safest way to obtain tools, however, is to use the getToolByName() function. This is especially true as some tools are being refactored into more appropriate components such as local utilities and views. As this happens, getToolByName() may be used to provide backwards compatibility.

```
>>> from Products.CMFCore.utils import getToolByName
>>> membership_tool = getToolByName(context, 'portal_membership')
```

Here, `context` must be an object inside the Plone site (or the site itself). Sometimes, you do not have an appropriate context to acquire the tools from. In that case, you can use this trick:

```
>>> from zope.app.component.hooks import getSite
>>> site = getSite()
>>> from Products.CMFCore.utils import getToolByName
>>> types_tool = getToolByName(site, 'portal_types')
```

This works because the `getSite()` method returns the current component registry site, which should be the Plone site root or an object inside it.

> In common with local components, it will only work if the request involves traversing *over* the Plone site root. The only likely scenario in which this would not be the case would be an event handler triggered when the Plone site itself was deleted. In this case, the request originates from the ZMI root and does not involve traversing over the Plone site.

The standard tools are crucial to Plone, but they are largely being superseded by local utilities, which do not need to live in *content space*, and which can be looked up more easily using `getUtility()` rather than being acquired from a context. Moreover, some tools were written mainly to provide view logic, to be called from a page template that needed to be executed as trusted file system code. Such tools are now better implemented using template-less Zope 3 browser views with appropriate security declarations.

7. Aspect-oriented Programming with Adapters

When modeling design with interfaces, we should always endeavor to adhere to the principle of *separation of concerns*. A component, as described by an interface, should do one thing and one thing only, providing the minimum necessary operations (methods) and attributes (properties) to support that function.

In complex systems such as Plone, we often need to provide general functionality that can act on different types of objects. Continuing with our earlier examples, consider an instrument that is playable.

```
>>> class IPlayable(Interface):
...     """An instrument that can be played
...     """
...
...     def __call__(tune):
...         """Play that tune!
...         """
```

We may write some general code that expects an `IPlayable`. An object-oriented programming approach could be to use a mix-in or base class and relying on polymorphism:

```
>>> class PlayableMixin(object):
....     implements(IPlayable)
...     def __call__(self, tune):
...         print "Strumming along to", tune
>>> class BassGuitar(PlayableMixin):
...     pass
>>> class ClassicalGuitar(PlayableMixin):
...     pass
```

This will work. However, with multiple aspects of instruments in general, and guitars in particular to model, we would quickly end up with a large number of mix-in classes, bloating the APIs of the sub-classes, and incurring the risk of naming conflicts. Furthermore, if we needed to model some new aspect of an instrument, we could end up having to modify a several classes to use a new mix-in. By tightly weaving a number of application-specific classes into the inheritance hierarchy, this approach also makes re-use much more difficult.

Zope 2 suffers from all of these problems. Just take a look at the number of base classes on a typical content item, using the **Doc** tab in the ZMI. These support various aspects of content items, such as local role support, persistent properties, or WebDAV publishing.

With Zope 3 programming techniques, different aspects of various objects are provided by different **adapters**, *adapting* the object to a different interface. For example:

```
>>> from zope.interface import Interface, Attribute
>>> class IGuitar(Interface):
...     """A guitar
...     """
...
...     strings = Attribute("Number of strings")
>>> class IBass(IGuitar):
...     """A bass guitar
...     """
>>> class IElectric(IGuitar):
...     """An electric guitar
...     """
>>> from zope.interface import implements
>>> class Bass(object):
```

```
...         implements(IBass)
...         strings = 4
>>> class Electric(object):
...         implements(IElectric)
...         strings = 6
>>> pbass = Bass()
>>> tele = Electric()
```

Here, we are explicitly modeling different types of guitars. We will make use of this level of granularity later, but let us first provide a simple adapter from IGuitar to IPlayable:

```
>>> from zope.component import adapts
>>> class GuitarPlayer(object):
...         implements(IPlayable)
...         adapts(IGuitar)
...
...         def __init__(self, context):
...             self.context = context
...
...         def __call__(self, tune):
...             print "Strumming along to", tune
```

The __init__() method takes a parameter conventionally called context. This is the object being adapted, in this case an IGuitar. The adapter itself provides IPlayable, and fully implements this interface by defining a __call__() method.

We now have a means of turning any IGuitar into an IPlayable. Before we can use the adapter, however, we must register it using ZCML:

```
<adapter factory=".players.GuitarPlayer" />
```

This shorthand version inspects the class for implements() and adapts() declarations. To be more explicit, or in case these were omitted or ambiguous, we could use:

```
<adapter
    provides=".interfaces.IPlayable"
    for=".interfaces.IGuitar"
    factory=".players.GuitarPlayer"
    />
```

The simplest way of looking up an adapter is by *calling* the interface we want to get an adapter to:

```
>>> tele_player = IPlayable(tele)
>>> tele_player("Toxic Girl")
Strumming along to Toxic Girl
```

When the Component Architecture is looking for an appropriate adapter from the `tele` object to an `IPlayable`, it performs a search of the registered adapters against the interfaces provided by the context object (`tele`). If the object provides the desired interface itself, it will be returned as-is (known as a null-adapter). Otherwise, the *most specific* adapter available will be instantiated and returned.

A *more specific* adapter is one registered for a more specific interface. For example, an adapter matching an interface directly implemented by the object's class is more specific than one matching an interface implemented by a base class, a parent interface of an interface provided by the object. Although this sounds complicated, the Component Architecture tends to find the adapter you would expect it to find, given a number of general and specific adapter registrations.

Let us look at an example. If we tried to adapt the `pbass` object, we would get the same general `IGuitar` adapter:

```
>>> pbass_player = IPlayable(pbass)
>>> pbass_player("Como Ves")
Strumming along to Como Ves
```

We could register a more specific adapter for `IBass`, however:

```
>>> class BassPlayer(object):
...     implements(IPlayable)
...     adapts(IBass)
...
...     def __init__(self, context):
...         self.context = context
...
...     def __call__(self, tune):
...         print "Slappin' it to", tune
```

And in ZCML:

```
<adapter factory=".players.BassPlayer" />
```

Now, we will get the new, more specific adapter for `pbass`, but not for `tele`:

```
>>> tele_player = IPlayable(tele)
>>> tele_player("Toxic Girl")
Strumming along to Toxic Girl
>>> pbass_player = IPlayable(pbass)
>>> pbass_player("Como Ves")
Slappin' it to Como Ves
```

This is a very powerful concept. For example, imagine that Plone comes with some standard functionality, written as an adapter for, say, `Products.CMFCore.interfaces.IContentish`, which applies to most if not all content items. Content types with particular needs can then provide a more specific adapter by registering it for a more specific interface. In general, if code is written to look up adapters when working with a particular aspect of an object, it will be extensible in this way.

Furthermore, recall that specific *objects* can be marked with an interface using `alsoProvides()`. An interface that is provided directly by an object is more specific still than one implemented by its class. Therefore, we could register an adapter for an interface that is conditionally applied to objects, and expect conditional behavior accordingly. Plone's staging solution, `plone.app.iterate`, uses this technique. It marks working copies with an `IWorkingCopy` marker interface when they are checked out and uses various adapters registered for this interface to override more general adapters that apply to base copies. When a working copy is checked back in again, the marker interface is removed (using `noLongerProvides()` from `zope.interface`), and the behavior reverts to normal.

The most general adapter is one registered for `Interface`. This can sometimes be useful when constructing global fallback adapters. In ZCML, we can express this with:

```
<adapter
    for="*"
    provides=".interfaces.IPlayable"
    factory=".players.FallbackPlayer"
    />
```

With no such general fallback, we would get a `TypeError` when trying to look up an adapter for which no registration is found. This can happen legitimately if, for example, we are depending on other packages to provide appropriate adapters, or if some aspect of an object is deemed optional. We can write more defensive code by using:

```
>>> possibly_playable = IPlayable(some_object, None)
```

If no adapter is found, this will return `None`, or whatever else is passed as the second parameter.

Multi-adapters

So far, we have seen adapters that vary by a single interface, adapting a single context. It is also possible to register adapters that adapt multiple objects, and thus can be specialized on any one or more of their interfaces.

Suppose we were dealing not only with guitars, but also with amplifiers:

```
>>> class IAmp(Interface):
...        """An amplifier
...        """
...
...        goes_up_to = Attribute("How far up does it go?")
>>> class ElevenAmp(object):
...        implements(IAmp)
...        goes_up_to = 11 # This one goes to eleven!
>>> vox = ElevenAmp()
```

To do a gig, we would need both a guitar and an appropriate amp. We will model this by adapting the guitar and the amp to an `IGiggable` interface. Notice how the `__init__()` method now takes two parameters, since there are two objects being adapted:

```
>>> class IGiggable(Interface):
...        """A setup which can be gigged
...        """
...
...        def __call__(stage_set):
...            """Gig a particular set
...            """
>>> class GigRig(object):
...        implements(IGiggable)
...        adapts(IElectric, IAmp)
...
...        def __init__(self, guitar, amp):
...            self.guitar = guitar
...            self.amp = amp
...
...        def __call__(self, stage_set):
...            print "Setting volume to", self.amp.goes_up_to
...            playable = IPlayable(self.guitar)
...            for song in stage_set:
...                playable(song)
```

To register this adapter, we use the same ZCML directive as before:

```
<adapter factory=".gig.GigRig" />
```

If we omitted the `adapts()` declaration, we would need to specify the two adapted interfaces in the `for` attribute, separated by whitespace:

```
<adapter
    provides=".interfaces.IGiggable"
    for=".interfaces.IElectric .interfaces.IAmp"
    factory=".gig.GigRig"
    />
```

To look up a multi-adapter, we cannot use an interface on its own, since that only takes a single context parameter. Instead, we do:

```
>>> from zope.component import getMultiAdapter
>>> gig = getMultiAdapter((tele, vox,), IGiggable)
>>> gig(["Foxxy Lady", "Voodoo Chile",])
Setting volume to 11
Strumming along to Foxxy Lady
Strumming along to Voodoo Chile
```

There is also `zope.component.queryMultiAdapter`, which will return `None` if the adapter lookup fails.

Multi-adapters are a little less common than regular adapters. If you have an adapter where most methods take the same parameter, it is normally a sign that you really want a multi-adapter. Being able to specialize based on multiple dimensions (i.e. the different interfaces being adapted) can add a lot of flexibility, possibly at the cost of additional complexity. Internally in Zope, multi-adapters are used all the time — more on that when we get to views in a moment.

Named Adapters

Like utilities, adapters can be named, with unnamed adapters really just being named adapters called `u""`. Named single-adapters are not particularly common, but can make sense if behavior needs to vary not just based on the type of object being adapted, but also based on user input or other run-time configuration.

Suppose that we wanted to let the user pick the style in which a guitar was played.

```
>>> class StyledGuitarPlayer(object):
...     implements(IPlayable)
...
...     def __init__(self, context, style):
...         self.context = context
...         self.style = style
...
...     def __call__(self, tune):
```

```
...            print self.style, "to", tune
>>> from zope.component import adapter
>>> from zope.interface import implementer
>>> @implementer(IPlayable)
... @adapter(IGuitar)
... def fingerpicked_guitar(context):
...     return StyledGuitarPlayer(context, 'Picking away')
>>> @implementer(IPlayable)
... @adapter(IGuitar)
... def strummed_guitar(context):
...     return StyledGuitarPlayer(context, 'Strumming away')
```

And in ZCML:

```
<adapter
    factory=".styles.fingerpicked_guitar"
    name="fingerpick"
    />

<adapter
    factory=".styles.strummed_guitar"
    name="strum"
    />
```

To look up a named adapter, we need to use getAdapter() or queryAdapter(), like this:

```
>>> from zope.component import getAdapter
>>> preferred_style = u"fingerpick"
>>> playable = getAdapter(tele, IPlayable, name=preferred_style)
>>> playable("Like a Hurricane")
    Picking away to Like a Hurricane
```

Adapter Factories

In the example above, we are doing something a little different to what we did in earlier examples—using a function that returns an object as the adapter factory, rather than a class. Zope only requires that factories be callables that take the appropriate number of parameters and return an object providing the desired interface. The @adapter and @implementer function decorators are analogous to using adapts() and implements() for a class.

This pattern can also be useful if you want to return an adapter that is not a class referencing the adapted object. For example, in `plone.contentrules`, there is an adapter factory that allows constructs like:

```
assignable = IRuleAssignmentManager(context)
assignable['key'] = assignment
```

Here, the `context` could be a content object, and `assignable` is a container object that stores assignments of rules to that `context`. The adapter factory, which can be found in `plone.contentrules.engine.assignments`, retrieves a persistent instance of the container that is stored in an annotation on the context.

 An annotation is a general way to store additional metadata on an object, using a dictionary-like syntax. See `zope.annotation.interfaces` for more.

The calling code, of course, does not care where the adapter came from, only that it correctly implements `IRuleAssignmentManager` and pertains to the particular context.

8. Views and Other Presentation Components

A Zope 3 **view** is simply a component that can be found during URL traversal, and that can (usually) render itself. When Zope traverses a URL such as `http://myserver.com/guitars/@@list_guitars` it will first find the `guitars` object, using the rules outlned in the description of object publishing at the beginning of this chapter, and then do something akin to:

```
view = getMultiAdapter((guitars, request), name="list_guitars")
```

That is, a view is simply a named multi-adapter of some context and the current request. The name is usually disambiguated from content objects and attributes by prefixing it with `@@`, although this is optional. To render the view object, Zope will call it. This normally results in a page template being invoked, although some views will simply construct and return a string.

In Zope 2, a view should inherit from `Products.Five.browser.BrowserView` in order to function properly with Zope 2 security. Note that unlike page templates in skin layers, views (including their templates) execute in unprotected file system code and are not subject to additional "through-the-web" security restrictions.

Plone used to have its own base class for views in Products. CMFPlone.utils, which was introduced to deal with the kind of acquisition-related problems for self.context described in this chapter. It did so not by using aq_inner, but by keeping the object in a list (which saves it from being acquisition-wrapped on retrieval). However, this base class is now deprecated, because it breaks the convention that self.context should be the context object itself. In general, the aq_inner approach is safer, and avoids a somewhat awkward dependency on Products.CMFPlone.

By convention, views are located in a browser module. For larger packages, browser is often a package with its own configure.zcml file, included from the main ZCML file using:

```
<include package=".browser" />
```

Here is an example using a page template file in the current directory. The base class __init__() method (acting as the multi-adapter's factory) will assign self.context and self.request appropriately.

```
from Products.Five.browser import BrowserView
from Products.Five.browser.pagetemplatefile import
ViewPageTemplateFile

class GuitarsListing(BrowserView):
    """List guitars found in the current context
    """

    __call__ = ViewPageTemplateFile('listguitars.pt')

    def list_guitars(self):
        ...
```

The examples in this section are not found in the optilux. codeexamples package, because views do not lend themselves to being described in doctests. However, the next chapter will contain several examples of views.

The assignment of __call__ works because ViewPageTemplateFile is callable. Inside the page template, the implicit variables context, request, and view will refer to the context object (guitars), the request, and the view instance itself, respectively. This allows us to put all the display logic inside the view class, exemplified by list_guitars(), and use simple TAL constructs like view/list_guitars in the template.

To register views, we use the `<browser:page />` ZCML directive:

```
<browser:page
    name="list_guitars"
    class=".browser.GuitarsListing"
    for=".interfaces.IGuitarsFolder"
    permission="zope2.View"
    />
```

Here, the `for` attribute refers to the type of context for which the view is available (the request part of the multi-adapter is implied). The `permission` attribute is required. `"zope.Public"` can be used to define a view that is available to all. Other standard permissions, including the CMF core permissions described in Chapter 6, are defined in `permissions.zcml` in `Products.Five`, which is normally installed in the `$SOFTWARE_HOME`. In the buildout, this would be `parts/zope2/lib/python/ Products/Five`.

We used the `__call__()` method to reference a template. You will sometimes see a `template` attribute in the `<browser:page />` directive referencing a template, which is equivalent but somewhat more magical. Conversely, the `class` attribute could be omitted if we had no need for a class to manage the display logic. In this case, `template` is mandatory.

Sometimes, we have nothing to render at all. This can be the case if we are defining a view for some shared utility functions looked up by other views or templates, but never rendered on their own. In this case, we omit both the `__call__()` method and the `template` ZCML attribute. If we had a view called `@@guitar_utils`, we could look it up in a page template with:

```
<tal:block define="utils_view context/@@guitar_utils">
```

Or, in Python from another view class:

```
context = aq_inner(self.context)
utils_view = getMultiAdapter((context, self.request,), name="guitar_
utils")
```

See the section on Acquisition Chains in this chapter for an explanation of the use of `aq_inner()`.

As we saw in Chapter 8, it is possible to register a view for a particular **browser layer**. During traversal, Zope can set a marker interface on the request to indicate the current skin. The view is a multi-adapter on the context and the request. Hence, a view for a particular browser layer is a more specific adapter on the request, compared to a view not registered for a layer. The default layer is `zope.publisher. interfaces.browser.IDefaultBrowserLayer`.

```
<browser:page
    name="list_guitars"
    class=".browser.GuitarsListing"
    for=".interfaces.IGuitarsFolder"
    layer=".interfaces.IThemeSpecific"
    permission="zope2.View"
    />
```

In the next chapter, we will see several examples of views used to render custom content types, and in Chapter 11, we will cover standalone views and auto-generated forms.

Content Providers and Viewlets

When building pages with page templates, we can use **METAL** macros to include other pages. However, you may also see statements such as:

```
<div tal:replace="structure provider:guitars.header" />
```

 See the Zope Book on `http://zope.org` or the ZPT tutorial at `http://plone.org/documentation/tutorial/zpt` for more information about TAL and METAL.

The `provider:` expression type comes from `zope.contentprovider` (with some overrides in `Products.Five.viewlet` to support Zope 2). It will perform an operation analogous to:

```
provider = getMultiAdapter((context, request, view,), name="guitars.
header")
return provider()
```

That is, the **content provider** is a named multi-adapter of the context, request, and the current view instance. For skin layer templates (which are not Zope 3 views), Plone's `main_template` will define the default view to be the `@@plone` view, which is described in the interface `Products.CMFPlone.browser.interfaces.IPlone`.

Content providers are rarely used directly, but they are the building blocks for viewlets. A **viewlet manager** is a content provider, which when rendered will locate any number of **viewlets** appropriate for the current context, request, and view registered to the particular viewlet manager. As you may have guessed, there are some named multi-adapters involved under the hood. However, unlike raw content providers, there are ZCML directives to make things easier.

To create a new viewlet manager, we must first create a marker interface for it:

```
from zope.viewlet.interfaces import IViewletManager
class IGuitarsHeader(IViewletManager):
    """A viewlet manager that is put at the head of a guitar listing
    """
```

Then we register it in ZCML with:

```
<browser:viewletManager
    name="guitars.header"
    provides=".interfaces.IGuitarsHeader"
    permission="zope2.View"
    />
```

The name should be unique. A dotted name prefixed with the package name is the convention.

It is possible to specify a custom implementation of the viewlet manager, which allows us to control the rendering of viewlets more precisely. In Plone, we normally use the implementation from `plone.app.viewletmanager`, in order to gain support for the `@@manage-viewlets` screen and viewlet re-ordering described in Chapter 8:

```
<browser:viewletManager
    name="guitars.header"
    provides=".interfaces.IGuitarsHeader"
    permission="zope2.View"
    class="plone.app.viewletmanager.manager.OrderedViewletManager"
    />
```

We can now register any number of viewlets for this viewlet manager.

```
<browser:viewlet
    name="guitars.headers.adbanner"
    manager=".interfaces.IGuitarsHeader"
    class=".ads.GuitarAds"
    permission="zope2.View"
    />
```

We can also use the attributes `layer` and `view` to reference specific interfaces for the request (browser layer) and view. The latter allows us to have a viewlet in a general viewlet manager (say, one defined in `main_template`) that is shown on one particular view but not all views.

For example, here is a viewlet that is only shown on the main view of an object, but not on any other tabs or templates. This works because `IViewView` is a marker interface applied to the view instance during page construction:

```
<browser:viewlet
    name="guitars.headers.adbanner"
    manager="plone.app.layout.viewlets.interfaces.IAboveContent"
    view="plone.app.layout.globals.interfaces.IViewView"
    class=".ads.GuitarAds"
    permission="zope2.View"
    />
```

Because viewlets are multi-adapters, the usual rules about overrides apply. We could have a general viewlet for all views, and a more specific one with the same name for a particular type of context, request, and/or view.

Unlike views, viewlets (actually content providers) are not rendered by being called. Instead, they must provide update() and render() methods. During rendering, update() is called on all the viewlets in a viewlet manager, and then render() is called on each viewlet in turn. The results of the render() calls are concatenated and then inserted into the output stream. The update() method should be used to update state from the request, potentially allowing viewlets to communicate with each other prior to final rendering.

Here is an example, again using a page template for rendering. As with views, the implicit view variable can be used in the template to reference methods on the viewlet class:

```
from zope.interface import implements
from zope.viewlet.interfaces import IViewlet
from Products.Five.browser import BrowserView
from Products.Five.browser.pagetemplatefile import
ViewPageTemplateFile
class GuitarAds(BrowserView):
    """Rotating ads for new guitars
    """
    implements(IViewlet)
    def __init__(self, context, request, view, manager):
        self.context = context
        self.request = request
        self.__parent__ = view # from IContentProvider
        self.manager = manager # from IViewlet (child of
        IContentProvider)
    def update(self):
        pass
    render = ViewPageTemplateFile("rotating_ads.pt")
```

Plone inserts a number of viewlet managers in `main_template` and the standard content type views, offering third-party components various places to plug into the general user interface. These are defined in `plone.app.layout.viewlets` and use the viewlet manager implementation from `plone.app.viewletmanager`.

9. Synchronous Events

One of the best things that Zope 3 gave Zope 2 is an **events** system. This makes it easy to emit events and register subscribers for those events from elsewhere. Events are synchronous — emitting code will block until all event handlers have completed — and unordered — there are no guarantees about the sequence in which event handlers are called.

Defining a new type of event is easy. All we need is an interface that identifies the event, and a concrete class implementing this.

```
>>> from zope.interface import Interface, Attribute
>>> class INewGigEvent(Interface):
...     """An event signaling that there's a new gig in town
...     """
...
...     band = Attribute("Name of the band")
>>> from zope.interface import implements
>>> class NewGigEvent(object):
...     implements(INewGigEvent)
...
...     def __init__(self, band):
...         self.band = band
```

Somewhere else, we would then define a subscriber for this event. This is simply a callable, which will be passed the event when invoked:

```
>>> from zope.component import adapter
>>> @adapter(INewGigEvent)
... def invite_friends(new_gig):
...     print "Hey guys, let's go see", new_gig.band
```

The `@adapter` decorator is used to identify the type of event being handled. This has to do with the fact that events are really just a special case of **subscription adapters**. Unlike regular adapters, there can be multiple subscription adapters adapting an object to a particular interface. They are not used very often, except in situations like object validation. We will see an example of using subscription adapters for object validation in the next chapter.

Event subscribers are registered with ZCML:

```
<subscriber handler=".events.invite_friends" />
```

If we did not use the `@adapter` decorator, we could specify the type of event explicitly:

```
<subscriber
    for=".interfaces.INewGigEvent"
    handler=".events.invite_friends"
    />
```

Triggering the event, and thus calling all appropriate event subscribers, is as simple as:

```
>>> from zope.event import notify
>>> notify(NewGigEvent("The Gypsy Sun and Rainbow Band"))
Hey guys, let's go see The Gypsy Sun and Rainbow Band
```

There is no need to explicitly register the event type, because event subscribers are found based on the interface(s) provided by the event object. This also means that if an event object provides an interface that has a base interface, and there is a more general subscriber for the base interface, this will be called as well.

Object Events

Zope and Plone emit a few generic events, known as **object events**, when items are added to, removed from, or moved in containers, as well as when they are first created, modified, or copied. These events all derive from `zope.component.interfaces.IObjectEvent`.

We can register subscribers for object events just like any other type of event, but most often, we are only interested in handling an object event for a particular type of object. That is, we register an event subscriber for both the object type and the event type:

```
>>> class IBand(Interface):
...     """A band
...     """
...
...     name = Attribute("The name of the band")
>>> class Band(object):
...     implements(IBand)
...
...     def __init__(self, name):
...         self.name = name
```

```
>>> from zope.lifecycleevent.interfaces import IObjectModifiedEvent
>>> @adapter(IBand, IObjectModifiedEvent)
... def band_changed(band, event):
...     assert band == event.object # At least normally, see below
...     print "Changes to the lineup in", band.name
```

And in ZCML:

```
<subscriber handler=".events.band_changed" />
```

Or, if we did not use the `@adapter` decorator, separating the interfaces by whitespace:

```
<subscriber
    for=".interfaces.IBand
          zope.lifecycleevent.interfaces.IObjectModifiedEvent"
    handler=".events.band_changed"
    />
```

There is no difference in the way that an object event is emitted, although we must ensure that we construct the object event instance properly, so that `event.object` references the right object:

```
>>> from zope.lifecycleevent import ObjectModifiedEvent
>>> beatles = Band("The Beatles")
>>> notify(ObjectModifiedEvent(beatles))
Changes to the lineup in The Beatles
```

Because we are now relying on two interfaces, the subscriber is passed two objects: the object and the event. In most cases, as asserted in the code example, the object passed as the first parameter and `event.event` will be the same.

However, container events are re-dispatched to items inside the container recursively. For example, if a folder is moved or deleted, items inside that folder will be notified with the appropriate event. In this case `event.object` will refer to the folder the event originated from, while the object passed as the first parameter will be the child object currently being processed.

Container events, found in `zope.app.container.interfaces` and emitted largely from `OFS.ObjectManager`, are a little tricky, because they all provide `IObjectMovedEvent`. This specifies attributes `oldParent`, `oldName`, `newParent`, and `newName` referring to where the object used to be, what it was called, where it is now located, and what it is now called, respectively. In an `IObjectAddedEvent`, `oldParent`, and `oldName` are both `None` — the object moved in from the great unknown. In an `IObjectRemovedEvent`, the reverse is true — the object moved away into the ether. This means that if you register a subscriber for `IObjectMovedEvent`, it will be called when objects are renamed, moved, added, or removed. In this case, you may need to explicitly check whether any of the aforementioned four variables are None if you want to react only when objects are actually moved.

Given the generic and object-centric nature of the Plone user interface, object events are quite prevalent. A few of the more commonly used types of object events are:

- The aforementioned container events in zope.app.container.interfaces.
- The life-cycle events IObjectCreatedEvent and IObjectModifiedEvent from zope.lifecycleevent.interfaces, which are emitted from view code when objects are first created and subsequently modified.
- Archetypes-specific events in Products.Archetypes.interfaces including IObjectInitializedEvent and IObjectEditedEvent, both of which inherit from IObjectModifiedEvent. These deal with the fact that Archetypes objects are created in the ZODB before they are first populated with real data.
- Workflow events like Products.CMFCore.interfaces. IActionSucceededEvent and the more low-level Products.DCWorkflow. IAfterTransitionEvent.

You can create your own object events by inheriting from and fulfilling zope. component.interfaces.IObjectEvent. If you are curious about how the re-dispatching of object events work, take a look at zope.component.event, in particular the objectEventNotify() method.

Summary

In this chapter, we have taken a high-level look at Zope programming concepts, including:

- Zope as an object publisher
- Traversal of object graphs
- Automatic ZODB persistence
- Zope 2's concept of "acquisition"
- Using the catalog to search for objects in the ZODB
- Describing components with interfaces
- Using the utility registry to look up singletons
- Using the utility registry as a general registry of homogenous components
- Aspect-oriented programming with adapters

- Zope 3 style views
- Zope's synchronous events system

Don't worry if this is all a bit too much to take in on the first reading. Take a look at the `optilux.codeexamples` package, and play with the examples there. If you want to explore the namespace at a particular point of a doctest interactively, remember that you can add this line to enter the debugger:

```
>>> import pdb; pdb.set_trace()
```

In the remainder of Part 3, we will put the concepts from this chapter to use when creating content types, building forms and interactive functionality, talking to relational databases, and managing users, groups, and workspaces. You may find it useful to come back to this chapter from time to time when you see Zope programming concepts demonstrated as part of the examples we will present later in the book.

10
Custom Content Types

Plone being a Content Management System, it is not surprising that programming for Plone usually revolves around content. Although it is possible to employ traditional web development techniques such as using standalone forms to populate a database, Plone is most powerful as a platform when problems can be modeled in terms of hierarchical, semi-structured content types.

In this chapter, we will learn how to design and implement new content types that address some of the specific requirements of the Optilux Cinema's example application. In particular, we will discuss the Archetypes framework and its role in modern Plone development. We will also demonstrate how to create a custom portlet, using Plone 3's new portlet management infrastructure.

Content-Centric Design

Let us revisit the requirements from Chapter 2 that relate to cinemas and films. We will delay considering the actual screening of a film at a particular cinema until Chapter 12, where we show how to connect to an external database. We will also delay reporting on cinemas and films until the next chapter, where we look at creating standalone forms and dynamic pages.

	Requirement	Importance
2	The site should show information about all of Optilux's cinemas.	High
3	Non-technical cinema staff should be able to update information about each cinema.	High
4	The site should allow staff to highlight promotions and special events. These may apply to one or more cinemas.	High
5	Cinema staff should be able to publish information about new films. It should be possible to update this information after publication.	High

The *nouns* in these requirements, together with the information architecture proposed in Chapter 5, suggest that we need five content types—**Cinema Folder**, **Cinema**, **Film Folder**, **Film**, and **Promotion**. These are represented in the class diagram below, which is a more detailed version of the relevant parts of the high-level initial class diagram presented in Chapter 2.

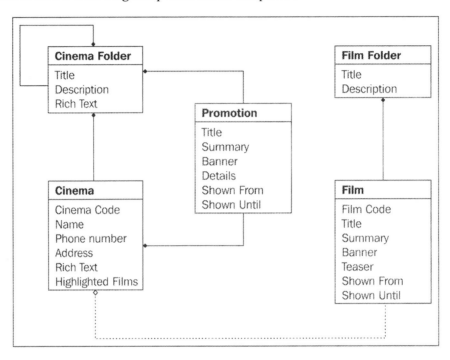

This shows that films are contained within film folders—for example to group similar films—and cinemas are created within cinema folders—for example to group cinemas by geographical location. Cinema folders may contain other cinema folders, allowing arbitrary nesting.

Promotions are permitted inside both cinema folders and cinemas, to allow promotions specific to one cinema or to a group of cinemas in the same folder. We will not show promotions in regular content listings, but rather through a custom portlet displayed when viewing a cinema folder or cinema. In addition to specific promotions, we allow the manager of a cinema to select one or more **Highlighted Films** from across the site to display next to that cinema.

Notice the inclusion of a **Film Code** and a **Cinema Code**. These will be simple strings for now and are not shown to the user. When we connect cinemas and films to the external database system manages film showings and custom bookings, these will act as keys in its tables.

There are other legitimate ways in which we could have modeled these particular requirements. For example, we could have done away with the **Cinema Folder** and **Film Folder** types, and let **Cinema** and **Film** be first-order content types, or we could have required all promotions to live in a separate *Promotion Folder*. However, some general concepts usually apply:

- Plone provides a rich user interface for managing content objects. Leveraging this by conceptualizing problems as content types with specific fields is usually a good idea.

- If you need a one-to-many relationship, it is often easiest to model the *one* as a container, and the *many* as children inside that container, as we have done with **Cinema** and **Promotion**, for example.

- If it is impractical to have the *many* part of the relationship live inside the *one*, you may want to use Archetypes reference fields instead. For *many-to-many* type relationships — such as the *related items* field found on most standard content types — you will need to use references as well. We will look at references later in this chapter.

- Use the content hierarchy to your advantage. Most users instinctively think in terms of folders and files. By allowing a **Promotion** to sit inside a **Cinema** as well as a higher-level **Cinema Folder**, we can easily and naturally manage promotions relative to specific cinemas or cinema folders at any depth.

- If possible, try to avoid the need for complicated or composite content edit forms. The edit form found on the **Edit** tabs of Plone's standard content types is generated by Archetypes. It is perfectly possible to write your own edit form if the standard one is too limiting, but it can be a laborious and error-prone process.

- If you find yourself with dozens (or even hundreds) of content types, or write types with a huge number of fields, you are probably doing something wrong. Neither Plone nor your users will be particularly pleased about having to navigate a maze of content types or lengthy edit forms.

Package Layout

Our new content types will be contained in a new package, called `optilux.cinemacontent`. As before, we will create a skeleton using Paste Script and register the new package with our project's buildout environment. In the `src/` directory, we run the following command:

```
$ paster create -t plone optilux.cinemacontent
```

As before, we use `optilux` as the namespace of the package and `cinemacontent` as the package name. We must also remember to answer `True` to the question, whether we want a Zope 2 product. This is because Archetypes' content type registration code should be run during product initialization.

We must then inform our build environment of the new package. Add the following to `buildout.cfg`:

```
[buildout]
...
develop =
    src/optilux.policy
    src/optilux.theme
    src/optilux.cinemacontent
...
eggs =
    elementtree
    optilux.policy
    optilux.theme
    optilux.cinemacontent
...
```

Do not forget to re-run buildout with:

```
$ ./bin/buildout -o
```

Unlike for the policy product, we do not add a new ZCML slug for this package. Instead, we include it as a dependency in the policy product. In the `optilux.policy` package's `configure.zcml` file, we now have:

```
<configure
    xmlns="http://namespaces.zope.org/zope"
    xmlns:five="http://namespaces.zope.org/five"
    xmlns:genericsetup="http://namespaces.zope.org/genericsetup">

    <!-- Include direct package dependencies -->
    <include package="optilux.theme" />
    <include package="optilux.cinemacontent" />

    ...

</configure>
```

This ensures that we only need to manage one ZCML slug — for our central policy product. It will also alert us immediately if the new package is not properly installed when we try to start Zope.

The complete `optilux.cinemacontent` package is part of the source code that accompanies this book. You are encouraged to browse the code as you read this chapter and to borrow from it in your own code as much as you would like.

For the sake of brevity, we will not reproduce every line of code here (especially where code for the different content types is conceptually similar). To provide additional guidance, the source code contains lots of inline comments (taken out of the code listings in this chapter). In particular, the code pertaining to the **Cinema Folder** type is explained in detail.

The package follows generally accepted conventions for code layout. Under `src/optilux.cinemacontent/optilux/cinemacontent`, you will find the following files and directories:

`__init__.py`	Registers a message factory for internationalization of strings and invokes the Archetypes machinery that registers content types with Zope.
`browser/`	Contains one Zope 3 view for each content type, consisting of a view class (e.g. `film.py`) and a template (`film.pt`). Each content type also gets an icon (`film_icon.gif`). Other resources such as custom style sheets go here as well.
`config.py`	Contains global constants, including the project name and the names of the various "add" permissions we will register, mapped to their respective content types.
`configure.zcml`	Performs component registration. The `browser/`, `content/`, and `portlets/` sub-package have their own `configure.zcml` files, included from this one.
`content/`	Contains the content type definitions. Some types depend on additional adapters and event handlers, also found in this sub-package.
`interfaces.py`	Contains the interfaces describing the content types and other components. These are implemented by the classes in the `content` sub-package.
`portlets/`	Contains the definition and registration of the promotions portlet, following the patterns demonstrated by Plone's own portlets in `plone.app.portlets.portlets`.
`profiles/`	Contains the GenericSetup extension profile used to install the product.
`README.txt`	Describes the package in the form of a doctest that exercises the main content types and other functionality.
`tests/`	Contains the test suites to set up the `README.txt` doctest, as well as other tests, including a standard set of tests for the portlet.
`version.txt`	Read by Plone when it needs to know which version this package is at.

Modeling with Interfaces

In the previous chapter, we saw how interfaces are usually the first step of detailed design and act as formal documentation of the capabilities of an object. Therefore, we define an interface for each content type as described in the class diagram earlier, all found in the `interfaces.py` file. For example, the following interfaces describe cinema folders and cinemas:

```python
from zope.interface import Interface
from zope import schema
from zope.app.container.constraints import contains

from optilux.cinemacontent import CinemaMessageFactory as _

class ICinemaFolder(Interface):
    """A folder containing cinemas
    """

    contains('optilux.cinemacontent.interfaces.ICinema',
             'optilux.cinemacontent.interfaces.IPromotion',)

    title = schema.TextLine(title=_(u"Title"), required=True)

    description = schema.TextLine(title=_(u"Description"),
                description=_(u"A short summary of this folder"))

    text = schema.SourceText(title=_(u"Descriptive text"),
                description=_(u"Descriptive text about this cinema"),
                required=True)

class ICinema(Interface):
    """A cinema
    """

    cinema_code = schema.ASCIILine(title=_(u"Cinema Code"),
            description=_(u"This should match the cinema code used by "
                        "the booking system"), required=True)

    name = schema.TextLine(title=_(u"Cinema name"),
                required=True)

    phone = schema.TextLine(title=_(u"Telephone number"),
                description=_(u"Main contact number for this cinema"),
                required=True)

    address = schema.Text(title=_(u"Address"),
                description=_(u"Address of this cinema"),
                required=True)

    text = schema.SourceText(title=_(u"Descriptive text"),
                description=_(u"Descriptive text about this cinema"),
                required=True)
```

```
highlighted_films = schema.List(title=_(u"Highlighted films"),
                description=_(u"Selected films to highlight"),
                value_type=schema.Object(title=_(u"Film"),
                                                    schema=IFilm),
            unique=True)
```

We are being quite detailed here, indicating which fields are required, and giving full titles and descriptions. Archetypes will not enforce the constraints, nor use the titles or descriptions in the user interface. However, the author finds it useful to write out the interface contract as part of the design process, and for the purposes of documentation, this level of detail is useful to someone reading the code for the first time. A sensible public interface is also the only contract a third-party developer can rely upon. Other aspects of the code may be intended as implementation detail only.

We will learn more about zope.formlib at the end of this chapter and in the next, which *does* make use of the titles, descriptions, and constraints in interfaces directly.

The contains() declaration expresses what types a cinema folder can nominally contain, using a string representation of the dotted name of the appropriate interfaces to avoid circular dependencies. Again, these are used for information only in Zope 2 and will not be enforced.

The various attributes are specified using the descriptors found in the zope.schema package. See zope.schema.interfaces for an overview of the various field types. The title and description of each property are primarily for documentation. We follow good practice and make them translatable by using a message factory, defined in the package's __init__.py file such as:

```
from zope.i18nmessageid import MessageFactory
CinemaMessageFactory = MessageFactory('optilux.cinemacontent')
```

By importing this with the special name _ (an underscore), internationalization tools will be able to extract these strings.

The schema.List declaration, used for the highlighted_films field, is a little more complex than the rest. The value_type attribute explicitly specifies what type of objects are contained within the list, in this case IFilm's.

The other content types are described in IFilmFolder, IFilm, and IPromotion, which are analogous to the two interfaces seen above. In addition, interfaces.py contains the following:

```
class IBannerProvider(Interface):
    """A component which can provide an HTML tag for a banner image
    """

    tag = schema.TextLine(title=_(u"A HTML tag to render to show "
                                "the banner image"))
```

This is used for the **Film** and **Promotion** content types, both of which contain banner images. Objects of these types will be adapted to the IBannerProvider interface in order to obtain an HTML tag suitable for rendering this banner in a page. We could of course have put this functionality into the content types themselves, but this way, we make clearer the separation between *model* components (i.e. content objects) and presentational logic.

 As a rule of thumb, content classes should contain only data. Behavior is best separated out into appropriate adapters.

Using the Archetypes Framework

Archetypes, currently at version 1.5, was once an add-on to Plone. It first shipped with Plone 2.1, when the core content types were moved from plain CMF to Archetypes. Even before that, Archetypes was the de facto way to create new content types.

We will not provide a comprehensive reference to all of Archetypes in this chapter, partially because such a guide already exists, and partially because Archetypes is changing with the times, making some older practices obsolete. Instead, we will show the key techniques of modern Archetypes development and reference other documentation where necessary.

You should take a look at the Archetypes Reference Manual found at http://plone.org/documentation/manual/archetypes. Additional examples of Archetypes-based code are abundant. For example, take a look at the RichDocument product described in Chapter 7, or Products.ATContentTypes, which houses the standard Plone content types.

 The Plone 2.1-2.5 version of this product is the subject of a detailed tutorial at http://plone.org/documentation/tutorial/richdocument. The Plone 3.0-compatible code base is a little different, but most of the lessons in that tutorial are still valid. The main differences lie in the use of GenericSetup for installation and the separation of the attachment support into a new SimpleAttachment product.

Most of Archetypes' public API is found through the convenience import Products.Archetypes.atapi. You may find it useful to inspect this file if you are looking for a particular piece of code.

Content Base Classes

Archetypes' content classes typically derive from one of the following classes, all importable form `Products.Archetypes.atapi`:

- `BaseContent` is a simple non-folderish content type. This includes the Dublin Core set of metadata (via the `ExtensibleMetadata` mix-in class).

- `BaseFolder` is a version of `BaseContent` that is folderish.

- `OrderedBaseFolder` is a version of `BaseFolder` that allows explicit ordering of contained items.

- `BaseBTreeFolder` is an unordered version of `BaseFolder` that stores its contents in a binary tree and is thus suitable for containers expecting to hold thousands of items.

These base classes are often all you need, but in our case, we want to have content that behaves as closely to Plone's standard content types as possible. This includes support for standard metadata such as the *related items* field, categorization of fields into multiple tabs on the edit form, and so on. Therefore, we extend Plone's core content types, found in `Products.ATContentTypes.content`. These types ultimately inherit from one of the base classes above.

Cinema, **Cinema Folder**, and **Film Folder** all extend `folder.ATFolder`, the implementation of Plone's *Folder* type, allowing them to act very much like folders. **Cinemas** are folders because they can contain arbitrary pages and images about that cinema, linked to the information on the main cinema view, which is provided by a rich text field in the content type itself. **Film** and **Promotion** use `base.ATCTContent`, which includes all the common, non-folderish ATContentTypes behavior.

Let us take a look at the declaration of the `Cinema` class:

```
from zope.interface import implements

from Products.Archetypes import atapi
from Products.ATContentTypes.content import folder
from Products.ATContentTypes.content.schemata import
finalizeATCTSchema

from optilux.cinemacontent.interfaces import ICinema
from optilux.cinemacontent.config import PROJECTNAME
from optilux.cinemacontent import CinemaMessageFactory as _

...
```

```
class Cinema(folder.ATFolder):
    """Describe a cinema.

    This is a folder in that it can contain further pages with
    information, or promotions.
    """

    implements(ICinema)

    portal_type = "Cinema"
    _at_rename_after_creation = True
    schema = CinemaSchema

    cinema_code = atapi.ATFieldProperty('cinemaCode')
    name = atapi.ATFieldProperty('title')
    phone = atapi.ATFieldProperty('phone')
    address = atapi.ATFieldProperty('description')
    text = atapi.ATFieldProperty('text')
    highlighted_films = atapi.ATReferenceFieldProperty(
        'highlightedFilms')

atapi.registerType(Cinema, PROJECTNAME)
```

This creates a class to encapsulate the content type, declares that it implements
`ICinema`, and specifies a portal type name. As we learned in the previous chapter,
portal types must be unique in the site. We also set `_at_rename_after_creation`
to `True`, which will cause Archetypes to rename the object based on a normalized
version of the title (which is part of the standard Dublin core metadata and pretty
much required for all Plone content types) when the object is first saved. This is
what gives Plone nice, readable URLs and normally makes sense unless you need
to manage the ID explicitly yourself. The `ATFieldProperty` declarations will be
explained shortly.

 In this case, you will need to override the `id` field in the `BaseObject`
schema so that it is not hidden by default. Note that you can also override
`generateNewId()` to provide different naming semantics.

Schemata, Fields, and Widgets

Most of the magic of Archetypes is found within a content type's **schema**. We
referenced this in the code excerpt above, assigning it to the `schema` class variable.
The `CinemaSchema` is defined just before the class in the same file, like this:

```
CinemaSchema = folder.ATFolderSchema.copy() + atapi.Schema((

    atapi.StringField('cinemaCode',
        required=True,
        searchable=True,
```

```
            storage=atapi.AnnotationStorage(),
            widget=atapi.StringWidget(label=_(u"Cinema code"),
            description=_(u"This should match the cinema code used in the "
                            "booking system."))
        ),

    atapi.StringField('phone',
        required=True,
        searchable=True,
        storage=atapi.AnnotationStorage(),
        widget=atapi.StringWidget(label=_(u"Phone number"),
                                description=_(u""))
        ),

    atapi.TextField('text',
        required=False,
        searchable=True,
        storage=atapi.AnnotationStorage(),
        validators=('isTidyHtmlWithCleanup',),
        default_output_type='text/x-html-safe',
        widget=atapi.RichWidget(label=_(u"Descriptive text"),
                                description=_(u""),
                                rows=25,
                                allow_file_upload=False),
        ),

    atapi.ReferenceField('highlightedFilms',
        relationship='isPromotingFilm',
        multiValued=True,
        storage=atapi.AnnotationStorage(),
        vocabulary_factory=u"optilux.cinemacontent.CurrentFilms",
        enforceVocabulary=True,
        widget=atapi.ReferenceWidget(label=_(u"Highlighted films"),
                                description=_(u""))
        ),

    ))

CinemaSchema['title'].storage = atapi.AnnotationStorage()
CinemaSchema['title'].widget.label = _(u"Cinema name")
CinemaSchema['title'].widget.description = _(u"")

CinemaSchema['description'].storage = atapi.AnnotationStorage()
CinemaSchema['description'].widget.label = _(u"Address")
CinemaSchema['description'].widget.description = _("")

finalizeATCTSchema(CinemaSchema, folderish=True, moveDiscussion=False)
```

First, we copy the schema from the base type, in this case ATContentTypes'
`ATFolderSchema`.

 The `copy()` bit is important — without it, you may inadvertently change
the original schema due to Python's reference semantics!

At this point, we also have the Dublin Core metadata from `ExtensibleMetadata`,
and the `'id'` field, which we always need (although it is hidden in the edit form by
default, since we use the title-to-ID mechanism).

We then append our own schema. The `atapi.Schema()` constructor
takes a sequence of fields as arguments. Notice the double brackets — we are
passing a single tuple, not a list of arguments. All the core fields are found in
`Products.Archetypes.Field`, which can be useful reading, though the Archetypes
Reference Manual also has a list of these fields and their properties. Various third
party-fields and widgets can also be found at `http://plone.org/products`.

Some of the most commonly used field types are:

Field	Appropriate widgets	Description
StringField	StringWidget, SelectionWidget, PasswordWidget	A single line of text.
TextField	TextAreaWidget, RichWidget	A multi-line text field. The `RichWidget` invokes the WYSIWYG editor.
LinesField	LinesWidget, MultiSelectionWidget, InAndOutWidget,	A list of strings.
IntegerField	IntegerWidget	An integer number.
FixedPointField	DecimalWidget	A decimal number.
BooleanField	BooleanWidget	A true/false checkbox.
FileField	FileWidget	A file upload box.
ImageField	ImageWidget	An image upload box.
DateTimeField	CalendarWidget	A date picker.
ReferenceField	ReferenceWidget, InAndOutWidget	A reference to another Archetypes object (see later in this chapter).

Fields are initialized with any number of properties, and many fields accept
specific settings. Please refer to the Archetypes Reference Manual. Some of the most
commonly used properties are:

Field Property	Description
required	Set to `True` or `False` to make a field mandatory or optional.
searchable	Set to `True` to include the contents of this field in the main `SearchableText` of this content object. This is indexed in the catalog, and is what is searched when you use the main search box or the **Advanced Search** form in Plone.
default	Supply a default value for the field.
default_method	Give the name of a method (as a string) on the object that will be called to obtain a default value. Another way of supplying a default is to register a named adapter from the content object to `Products.Archetypes.interfaces.IFieldDefaultProvider`, with a name equal to the field name.
schemata (sic)	The name of a tab of the edit field. The default "schemata" is called `"default"`. Note that the call to `finalizeATCTSchema()` will make various changes to the schema to comply with Plone's standard look and feel.
read_permission, write_permission	The name of a permission required to read or write the field, respectively. Defaults to `"View"` and `"Modify portal content"`, respectively, which is probably what you want — object-specific security is best managed with workflow.
vocabulary, vocabulary_factory, enforceVocabulary	Define a vocabulary for selection fields — more on this later in this chapter.
validators	A list of field validators — more on this later.
accessor, edit_accessor, mutator	Override the name of the accessor, edit accessor, and mutator methods — more on this later.
widget	An instance of a widget to use to render this field.
storage	The storage abstraction to use for the field — we need to set this to `AnnotationStorage` for reasons explained in the section on field properties. The default storage is `AttributeStorage`, which saves field values in attributes on the object with the same name as the field. `AnnotationStorage` stores the value in a Zope 3-style annotation, which avoids the risk of namespace clashes.

The core **widgets** are defined in `Products.Archetypes.Widget`. Each field has a default widget, but you probably want to at least update the label and description of the widget on a field-by-field basis. Like fields, widgets take a number of properties. Common widget properties include:

Widget Property	Description
`label`	A string or translatable message used as the widget label.
`description`	A string or translatable message used as widget help text.
`condition`	A TALES expression used to determine if the widget should be shown. The variables `object`, `portal`, and `folder` are available in the expression context.
`size`	Used to define the length of text boxes or height of selection boxes.
`rows`	Used to define the height of text boxes.
`default_output_type`	Used by `RichWidget` to determine how to transform input text when rendering a view template (usually to HTML). Setting this to `'text/x-html-safe'` will invoke Plone's HTML filtering policies, stripping out potentially dangerous tags. If you trust your users, you can use `'text/html'` instead.

Notice how each field has a name. You can access this later with `field.__name__`. Names are always unique within the schema. If you append a field with a name that is used by an earlier field in the schema, the new field will override the original one. However, the *position* of the field will be that of the one defined first in the sequence.

Sometimes this is quite useful, for example to override the `'title'` and `'description'` fields, but you can just as easily modify the originals (or rather, the copies of the originals), as we do at the end of the snippet to change the storage, label, and description of these very fields. This also shows how the fields in the schema can be accessed using dictionary notation.

After defining the schema, we call `finalizeATCTSchema()` on it. This method re-orders a number of fields, and assigns field *schemata* (tabs) according to Plone conventions. If you need more control, you use the `moveField()` method from `Products.Archetypes.interfaces.ISchema` to re-arrange fields after a schema has been defined.

With the schema finalized, we assign it to the content object's `schema` class-variable, as seen above:

```
class Cinema(folder.ATFolder):
    ...
    schema = CinemaSchema
    ...
```

Archetypes will now be able to generate edit forms and views from these fields and widgets. If you need to access the schema from a content object later, you can use one of:

```
content.Schema()
content.getField('someField')
```

The first statement will return the full schema of `content`. The second returns a specific field.

Vocabularies

You can specify a **vocabulary** for a field using the `vocabulary` property. If `enforceVocabulary` is `True`, Archetypes will issue a validation error when the user enters a value not in the vocabulary. Vocabularies are normally used in conjunction with a `SelectionWidget`, `MultiSelectionWidget`, or `InAndOutWidget`, in which case only those values that are in the vocabulary will be available for selection.

The simplest vocabulary is a static list of values acceptable to the field (i.e. integers for an `IntegerField` and strings for a `StringField`). If you want to have labels that differ from the field value, you can pass a list of (`value`, `label`) tuples, where the label is a string. Archetypes will convert either of these forms into a `DisplayList`, found in `Products.Archetypes.utils`. You may pass a `DisplayList` instead of a raw list if you want to save Archetypes the trouble of converting it for you.

For dynamic vocabularies, you can set `vocabulary` to a string containing the name of a method on the object (or a method on a parent object, or a script in a skin layer—it is found using standard path traversal). Archetypes will call this method to obtain a vocabulary value—either a flat list, a list of tuples, or a `DisplayList`. Here is an example, adapted from a field in the `ATTopic` type:

```
LinesField('customViewFields',
        default=('Title',),
        vocabulary='listMetaDataFields',
        enforceVocabulary=True,
        widget=InAndOutWidget(label=_(u'Table Columns'),
            description=_(u"Select which fields to display when "
                            "'Display as Table' is checked.")),
```

And then on the class itself:

```
def listMetaDataFields(self):
    tool = getToolByName(self, 'portal_atct')
    return tool.getMetadataDisplay()
```

The method calculates and returns a `DisplayList` with values and labels appropriate for this field.

Since Plone 3, we have the option of using Zope 3-style vocabularies as well. These make it easier to re-use vocabularies across multiple content types, or indeed in any code we write. There is even a set of commonly used vocabularies in the `plone.app.vocabularies` package, providing, among other things, a list of available content types and a list of installed workflow types.

In `film.py`, we define a general vocabulary of all published films, and then use it for the **Highlighted Films** field on the **Cinema** type:

```
from zope.interface import directlyProvides

from zope.schema.interfaces import IVocabularyFactory
from zope.schema.vocabulary import SimpleVocabulary

from optilux.cinemacontent.interfaces import IFilm
from Products.CMFCore.utils import getToolByName

def CurrentFilmsVocabularyFactory(context):
    """Vocabulary factory for currently published films
    """
    catalog = getToolByName(context, 'portal_catalog')
    items = [(r.Title, r.UID) for r in
                catalog(object_provides=IFilm.__identifier__,
                    review_state="published",
                    sort_on='sortable_title')]

    # This turns a list of title->id pairs into a Zope 3 style
    vocabulary return SimpleVocabulary.fromItems(items)
    directlyProvides(CurrentFilmsVocabularyFactory, IVocabularyFactory)
```

To create a new vocabulary, we define a **vocabulary factory**, which constructs the vocabulary when requested, using the `SimpleVocabulary` helper class to turn (`label`, `value`) pairs into a vocabulary (note how this is the other way around to Archetypes' `DisplayList`, which expects (`value`, `label`) pairs). The factory is just a callable (in this case a function) taking the current context as an argument. It must provide the `IVocabularyFactory` interface, which we declare using `directlyProvides()`. The factory is registered as a named utility in `configure.zcml`:

```
<utility
    component=".film.CurrentFilmsVocabularyFactory"
    name="optilux.cinemacontent.CurrentFilms"
    />
```

We can now use the `vocabulary_factory` property of any field to reference this vocabulary:

```
atapi.ReferenceField('highlightedFilms',
    relationship='isPromotingFilm',
    multiValued=True,
    storage=atapi.AnnotationStorage(),
    vocabulary_factory=u"optilux.cinemacontent.CurrentFilms",
    enforceVocabulary=True,
    vocabulary_display_path_bound=-1, # Avoid silly paths in the UI
    widget=atapi.ReferenceWidget(label=_(u"Highlighted films"),
                                 description=_(u"")),
    ),
```

Reference Fields

The preceding example also serves to demonstrate reference fields. Notice how the values are **UIDs** (unique, system-generated identifiers), in this case retrieved from catalog metadata. A reference field just stores UIDs. Two special catalogs, the `uid_catalog` and the `reference_catalog`, maintain the connections between UIDs and actual objects, though you should rarely, if ever, need to use these directly.

References only work between Archetypes objects, or rather those objects providing `Products.Archetypes.interfaces.IReferenceable`. This defines methods for inspecting references and back-references.

The reference engine is quite powerful, for example supporting custom reference type implementations. The `IReferenceable` API also supports distinguishing between different semantic *relationships* — string names that indicate the *type* of relationship being expressed. We set the `relationship` on the field above for this reason, making it easier to query for a particular type of back reference later.

Unless you need to inspect back-references or associate some custom metadata with the reference itself, however, the regular field API is usually the most convenient:

```
>>> film1_uid = film1.UID()
>>> cinema1.setHighlightedFilms([film1_uid])
>>> cinema1.getHighlightedFilms() == [film1]
True
```

Notice that we *set* a list of UIDs (here, `multiValued` is `True` — otherwise we set a single UID string), but the return value from the normal field *get* method is a list of objects (or a single object for single-valued fields). The `getRawHighlightedFilms()` method, also known as the edit accessor, would return the UIDs without a transformation.

An object's UID is indexed in the catalog, so if you have a list of UIDs you can use it for catalog searches.

Field and Object Validation

When the user submits an Archetypes edit form, `BaseObject`'s `validate()` method will be called. All fields provide basic validation, such as ensuring a value is entered if the field is required, or checking that the value for a numeric field does not contain letters.

It is also possible to write generic validators that can be applied to specific fields. For example:

```
atapi.TextField('text',
    ...
    validators=('isTidyHtmlWithCleanup',),
    ...
    ),
```

This will apply one or more validators with the given name(s), looked up in the validator registry. It is not very hard to register your own generic validators — see `Products.ATContentTypes.validators` for several examples — but this is only necessary if you need to re-use the same validator for multiple fields and content types.

To make a field-specific validator, we can add a method called `validate_fieldName()` to the content class, where `fieldName` is the name of the field to validate, taking the submitted value as a parameter. This should return an error message if there is a problem, or `None` if the value is valid:

```
def validate_text(self, value):
    if "!" in value:
        return _(u"Please do not shout")
    return None
```

This is very convenient, but it does cause some namespace pollution on the content type class and does not allow more detailed inspection of the submitted request.

For more flexibility, we can use a subscription adapter to perform validation. For example, in `cinema.py`, we have:

```
from zope.interface import implements
from zope.component import adapts, getUtility

from Products.CMFCore.interfaces import ICatalogTool
```

```
from Products.Archetypes.interfaces import IObjectPostValidation

from optilux.cinemacontent.interfaces import ICinema
from optilux.cinemacontent import CinemaMessageFactory as _

...

class ValidateCinemaCodeUniqueness(object):
    """Validate site-wide uniqueness of cinema codes.
    """
    implements(IObjectPostValidation)
    adapts(ICinema)

    field_name = 'cinemaCode'

    def __init__(self, context):
        self.context = context

    def __call__(self, request):
        value = request.form.get(self.field_name,
                                 request.get(self.field_name, None))
        if value is not None:
            catalog = getToolByName(self.context, 'portal_catalog')
            results = catalog(cinema_code=value,
                              object_provides=ICinema.__identifier__)
            if len(results) == 0:
                return None
            elif len(results) == 1 and results[0].UID ==
                self.context.UID():
                return None
            else:
                return {self.field_name :
                        _(u"The cinema code is already in use")}
        # Returning None means no error
        return None
```

And in `configure.zcml`:

```
<subscriber
    provides="Products.Archetypes.interfaces.IObjectPostValidation"
    factory=".cinema.ValidateCinemaCodeUniqueness"
    />
```

All subscription adapters providing `IObjectPostValidation` will be called during object validation, after the main schema validation has taken place. There is also `IObjectPreValidation`, which executes before schema validation.

The subscription adapter takes as its context the object being validated and does its work in the __call__() method, inspecting the request directly. It returns a dictionary mapping the name(s) of one or more erroneous fields to error messages, or None if there were no errors.

The Class Generator

Recall this line, immediately after the content type class definition:

```
atapi.registerType(Cinema, PROJECTNAME)
```

In addition to making Archetypes aware of the content object, this invokes the Class Generator, which will add (at run time only) three methods to the Cinema class for each (read/write mode) field — an **accessor** (*getter*), an **edit accessor** (for the cases where the main accessor performs a transformation, and the edit field needs another way of reading the raw value to edit), and a **mutator** (*setter*).

Take the cinemaCode field. The Class Generator will generate the methods getCinemaCode(), getRawCinemaCode(), and setCinemaCode() as accessor, edit accessor, and mutator, respectively. (This naming convention is the reason why Archetypes field names tend to be in *mixedCase*.) The following snippet shows what Archetypes' generated code might look like if we were to write it ourselves:

```
from AccessControl import ClassSecurityInfo

...

class Cinema(folder.ATFolder):
    ...
    security = ClassSecurityInfo()

    security.declareProtected('View', 'getCinemaCode')
    def getCinemaCode(self):
        return self.getField('cinemaCode').get(self)

    security.declareProtected('View', 'getRawCinemaCode')
    def getRawCinemaCode(self):
        return self.getField('cinemaCode').getRaw(self)

    security.declareProtected('Modify portal content',
                                           'setCinemaCode')
    def setCinemaCode(self, value):
        self.getField('cinemaCode').set(self, value)
```

The ClassSecurityInfo declarations apply security as per the read_permission and write_permission settings, giving the name of a permission and the name of the method to protect. This is the traditional way to protect methods in Zope 2. It is also possible to use ZCML for this, as we shall see later.

Sometimes, it is necessary to write custom accessors and mutators that perform additional processing (you may also consider writing a new generic field type). If you define a method with a name matching that of an accessor or mutator, Archetypes will assume you want to use that and not generate a method.

It is possible to override these names using the `accessor`, `edit_accessor`, and `mutator` field properties. For example, the `ExtensibleMetadata` mix-in class schema defines several custom accessor names to comply with Dublin Core naming conventions, such as `Title` and `Description` for the title and description fields:

```
TextField(
    'description',
    default='',
    searchable=1,
    accessor="Description",
    default_content_type = 'text/plain',
    allowable_content_types = ('text/plain',),
    widget=TextAreaWidget(
        label=_(u'label_description', default=u'Description'),
        description=_(u'help_description',
                     default=u'A short summary of the content.'),
        ),
```

Field Properties

The generated accessor and mutator are the standard way to get and set field values using Archetypes. You may have noticed, however, that these alone do not comply with the `ICinema` interface. This interface assumes fields are accessed not as a pair of get/set methods but as Python properties, which is the more *Pythonic*, Zope 3-like way of defining fields on objects. Unfortunately, Python did not have properties when Archetypes was invented.

> Also note that acquisition does not work properly inside a Python property *get* or *set* method. In practice, this is not usually a problem, but there may be situations where you need a custom accessor/mutator that depends on acquisition, in which case you will need to use regular methods.

There are three possible courses of action:

1. Rewrite the interface to use *get* and *set* methods instead of properties and `zope.schema` field descriptors. In some cases, we can ignore the *set* methods, and define a read-only interface, essentially declaring that setting of values should be left to Archetypes' generated forms and nothing else. The edit accessor is best left out of the interface, being an Archetypes implementation detail.

2. Use a bridge from Archetypes fields to Python properties so that non-generated code that uses the object can access the fields in this arguably more natural way.

3. Ignore the problem safe in the knowledge that there will only ever be a single, Archetypes-based implementation of this interface: either live with the inaccuracy (bad), or remove the detail, turning the interface into a simple marker interface (not as bad, but not as useful either).

Many developers prefer the first or the last option, because the second option involves some duplication, both between the interface and the Archetypes schema, and between the generated methods and explicitly defined properties. The author prefers to explicitly define *bridge* properties to make code using objects of the class from other code feel more natural, but will not take offense if the reader disagrees.

Creating the *bridge* properties is relatively easy, using the property definition class in `Products.Archetypes.fieldproperty.ATFieldProperty`.

```
class Cinema(folder.ATFolder):
    """Describe a cinema.

    This is a folder in that it can contain further pages with
information,
    or promotions.
    """
    implements(ICinema)

    portal_type = "Cinema"
    _at_rename_after_creation = True

    schema = CinemaSchema

    cinema_code = atapi.ATFieldProperty('cinemaCode')
    name = atapi.ATFieldProperty('title')
    phone = atapi.ATFieldProperty('phone')
    address = atapi.ATFieldProperty('description')
    text = atapi.ATFieldProperty('text')
    highlighted_films = atapi.ATReferenceFieldProperty(
                        'highlightedFilms')
```

The property factory takes the name of the field to manage as an argument. Notice how Archetypes prefers mixed-case field names while the properties generally use underscores. There is no need for the two to match, except to avoid confusion. Of course, the generated accessors and mutators continue to work.

There is, however, one important thing to watch out for—by default, Archetypes uses `AttributeStorage` for its fields, which means that field values are stored in attributes directly on the content object. The field name is used as the attribute name. This can cause namespace clashes, especially if the Archetypes field name and the property name are the same (in this case, you may even get infinite recursion).

The solution is either to use a different storage—such as `AnnotationStorage`, which stores the field value in a Zope 3-style annotation on the object—or to make sure field names are different from property names, for example by suffixing an underscore. The author prefers the first option, since `AttributeStorage` can cause clashes with other things anyway, and can make it easier to inadvertently circumvent the Archetypes field logic by accessing attributes directly.

Behind the scenes, the property get and set methods will use the low-level field accessors shown in the last section. Any custom mutators or accessors will not be called. If you need custom logic, you can write your own property get/set methods. It is also possible to define *input* and *output* transformations between fields and property values—see the documentation in the `fieldproperty` module. Finally, there is an `ATDateTimeFieldProperty` class, which takes care of conversion from the Zope 2 `DateTime` type to Python's newer `datetime` type (which again did not exist when DateTime was introduced eons ago), and an `ATReferenceFieldProperty`, which is needed to deal with the special semantics of `ReferenceField`s.

With field properties in place, we can use syntax like the following:

```
cinema.cinema_code = "C1"
current_cinema_code = cinema.cinema_code
```

Which is of course equivalent to:

```
cinema.setCinemaCode("C1")
current_cinema_code = cinema.getCinemaCode()
```

Content Security

As indicated earlier, the Class Generator will automatically apply appropriate permissions to the methods it generates. The Archetypes base classes have proper security declarations as well. However, we have not yet protected the field properties. Without any explicit security declarations, untrusted code would be able to find and read the contents of these variables.

We could use the old `ClassSecurityInfo` approach outlined earlier to protect each attribute. However, it is generally preferable to use ZCML for security declarations, keeping implementation and configuration separate. This also allows us to save some typing by using the content interfaces from `interfaces.py` to specify which attributes we want to protect.

In `content/configure.zcml`, we have added declarations such as:

```
<class class=".cinema.Cinema">
    <require
        permission="zope2.View"
        interface="..interfaces.ICinema"
        />
    <require
        permission="cmf.ModifyPortalContent"
        set_schema="..interfaces.ICinema"
        />
</class>
```

This specifies that the *View* permission (as indicated by `zope2.View`—see Chapter 6 for more on Zope 3-style permission names) is required to read the properties and call any methods from the `ICinema` interface on an object of the `Cinema` class. Similarly, *Modify portal content* is required to set any of the field properties as described in schema attributes in the same interface.

In general, we would try to avoid having additional methods in the content class, using adapters to provide additional functionality and keeping the class concerned with persistence only. However, it is sometimes convenient or necessary to have some additional methods or public attributes on a content type. For example, in the `Promotion` and `Film` classes, we have borrowed a method called `tag()` from the *News Item* type:

```
def tag(self, **kwargs):
    return self.getField('image').tag(self, **kwargs)
```

Various standard folder listings will use this to display a thumbnail image. To protect the method, we have added an additional `<require />` directive for this class in `configure.zcml`:

```
<class class=".film.Film">
    <require
        permission="zope2.View"
        interface="..interfaces.IFilm"
        />
    <require
        permission="cmf.ModifyPortalContent"
```

```
            set_schema="..interfaces.IFilm"
            />
    <require
        permission="zope2.View"
        attributes="tag"
        />
</class>
```

This means that the *View* permission is required to access the `tag` attribute, which in this case happens to be a method. Additional attributes protected by the same permission may be specified, separated with whitespace.

 Recall from Chapter 6 that methods or properties with names beginning with an underscore are not accessible from protected code. Therefore, they do not require explicit security declarations.

Views and Browser Resources

Having created the content types and their schemata, we will now turn to the user interface. This code is found in the `browser` sub-package. We will depend entirely on Zope 3 views and browser resources, as opposed to registering a new skin layer with `portal_skins` (although Archetypes' auto-generated forms are still skin templates).

Icons and Style Sheets

We define an icon for each content type in `browser/configure.zcml`, referencing image files in that same directory. For example:

```
<browser:resource
    name="cinema_icon.gif"
    image="cinema_icon.gif"
    />
```

This icon can be referenced as `++resource++cinema_icon.gif`. We use this in the GenericSetup files registering our content types, for example. To get the icon in a template, we could write:

```
<img tal:attributes="src context/++resource++cinema_icon.gif" />
```

There is also a style sheet shared by the various views, defined with:

```
<browser:resource
    name="optilux-cinemacontent.css"
    file="cinemacontent.css"
    />
```

Because this is only needed in a handful of templates, we include it explicitly in each one, using:

```
<metal:css fill-slot="css_slot">
    <style type="text/css" media="all"
            tal:content="string: @import url(${context/
++resource++optilux-cinemacontent.css});"></style>
</metal:css>
```

Main Content Views

The views for the various content types are registered in `browser/configure.zcml` with declarations such as:

```
<browser:page
    for="..interfaces.ICinema"
    name="view"
    class=".cinema.CinemaView"
    permission="zope2.View"
    />
```

By convention, the default view of a type is called `@@view`. Because we register it for a particular content type's interface, there are no clashes even though several content types use the same name.

> In Zope 3, you will often see names such as `index.html`. However, using suffixes for view names like this goes against Plone's URL conventions, where the standard view is called `/view`, the edit form is called `/edit` and so on.

We will also allow content authors to choose between various views of some of the content types, using Plone's **display** menu. The list of available views will be specified with GenericSetup below. However, we should provide a user-friendly title and description of the newly registered view:

```
<browser:menuItem
    for="..interfaces.ICinema"
    menu="plone_displayviews"
    title="Cinema view"
    action="@@view"
    description="Default representation of a cinema"
    />
```

The `action` attribute refers to the name of the view, and we make sure the menu item is registered only for the desired content type. Because of the processing order, we need to add this at the beginning of `configure.zcml`:

```
<include package="plone.app.contentmenu" />
```

The view class itself contains two methods, both relating to the **Highlighted Films** field:

```
from Acquisition import aq_inner

from Products.Five.browser import BrowserView
from Products.Five.browser.pagetemplatefile import
ViewPageTemplateFile

from plone.memoize.instance import memoize
from optilux.cinemacontent.interfaces import IBannerProvider

class CinemaView(BrowserView):
    """Default view of a cinema
    """

    __call__ = ViewPageTemplateFile('cinema.pt')

    def have_highlighted_films(self):
        return len(self.highlighted_films()) > 0

    @memoize
    def highlighted_films(self):
        context = aq_inner(self.context)
        return [dict(url=film.absolute_url(),
                     title=film.title,
                     summary=film.summary,
                     banner_tag=IBannerProvider(film).tag,)
                for film in context.highlighted_films]
```

Recall from the previous chapter the idiom of letting the `__call__` attribute refer specifically to the (callable) page template, which is initialized with a relative path to a file containing the template code. When executed, the template will be passed an implicit variable called `view` referring to an instance of the view class.

The `highlighted_films()` method finds any referenced *Films* and invokes the `IBannerProvider` adapter on each one to obtain a suitable `<img />` tag for its banner. It returns a list of dictionaries in order to make the template contain as little logic as possible.

Notice the use of the `@memoize` decorator. This ensures that no matter how many times `highlighted_films()` is called on this instance (during this request), it will only be executed once — the return value is cached (keyed by method arguments, but in this case there are no arguments). We do this so that if the template calls `have_highlighted_films()` first and then subsequently invokes `highlighted_films()`, the list is constructed only once.

This pattern is often used in views to avoid a performance penalty when templates may need to call the same method multiple times. Of course, the template could store the return value in a variable, but this would complicate it. As a rule of thumb, all non-trivial logic should go in the view class, not the template.

The template is found in `cinema.pt`:

```
<html xmlns="http://www.w3.org/1999/xhtml" xml:lang="en"
      xmlns:tal="http://xml.zope.org/namespaces/tal"
      xmlns:metal="http://xml.zope.org/namespaces/metal"
      xmlns:i18n="http://xml.zope.org/namespaces/i18n"
      lang="en"
      metal:use-macro="context/main_template/macros/master"
      i18n:domain="optilux.cinemacontent">
<body>

<metal:css fill-slot="css_slot">
    <style type="text/css" media="all"
           tal:content="string: @import url(${context/
++resource++optilux-cinemacontent.css});"></style>
</metal:css>

<metal:main fill-slot="main">
<tal:main-macro metal:define-macro="main"
       tal:define="text context/text;">

    <div tal:replace="structure provider:plone.abovecontenttitle" />

    <h1 class="documentFirstHeading">
<span metal:use-macro="python:context.widget('title', mode='view')" />
    </h1>

    <div tal:replace="structure provider:plone.belowcontenttitle" />

    <div class="documentDescription">
        <span metal:use-macro="python:context.widget(
        'description', mode='view')" />
    </div>
    <label for="parent-fieldname-phone"
```

```
    i18n:translate="label_cinema_phone_number">Phone number:</label>
      <div metal:use-macro="python:context.widget('phone', mode='view')" />

        <div tal:replace="structure provider:plone.abovecontentbody" />

        <div class="highlighted-films"
             tal:condition="view/have_highlighted_films">
           <h3 i18n:translate="heading_featured_films">
                               Featured films:</h3>
           <div tal:repeat="film view/highlighted_films">
              <a tal:attributes="href film/url; title film/summary">
                 <img tal:replace="structure film/banner_tag" />
                 <div tal:content="film/title" />
              </a>
           </div>
        </div>

        <p tal:condition="python: not text and is_editable"
           i18n:translate="no_body_text"
           class="discreet">
          This item does not have any body text,
          click the edit tab to change it.
        </p>

        <div tal:condition="text"
             metal:use-macro="python:context.widget('text', mode='view')" />

        <div metal:use-macro="context/document_relateditems/
                              macros/relatedItems">
           show related items if they exist
        </div>

        <div tal:replace="structure provider:plone.belowcontentbody" />
    </tal:main-macro>
    </metal:main>

    </body>
    </html>
```

This was originally adapted from Plone's `document_view.pt`.

Notice the various viewlet managers that are included with statements such as:

```
<div tal:replace="structure provider:plone.abovecontenttitle" />
```

Plone uses to these insert common UI elements such as common document actions or various messages. You should include them in your view templates unless you have a good reason not to.

Inline Editing

With this template, we will get *inline* editing of the title, description, phone number, and body text fields. That is, a user with edit privileges can click on the any of these fields on the **View** tab to change its value, without having to go to the **Edit** tab first.

To enable inline editing, we need only make use of Archetypes' widget *view* mode. For example:

```
<div metal:use-macro="python:context.widget('phone', mode='view')" />
```

Here, `'phone'` is the name of the field in the Archetypes schema. If we did not care about inline editing, we could have used a slightly simpler construct, calling the field accessor directly:

```
<div tal:content="context/phone" />
```

We will learn more about KSS and dynamic JavaScript-driven functionality in Chapter 14.

Edit Forms, Add Forms, and Events

Archetypes' standard edit form is called `base_edit`. When using ATContentTypes' base classes, we use a wrapper called `atct_edit`, but the two are essentially the same. This form iterates over the fields of its context content type and renders their widgets using standard layout. The vast majority of content types use `base_edit`.

The edit form also doubles as an *add form* when creating new objects. With Archetypes, as with the CMF types before it, objects have to be created in the ZODB before they can be edited. This is because various validators and vocabularies depend on having a full object, with a proper acquisition context. Such **premature object creation** can be troublesome. For example, if the user creates an object but never saves it, there will be a stale object left in the parent folder.

The `portal_factory` tool is used to mitigate against this problem. It lets objects be created in a temporary folder and then moved to the intended destination only when they are properly saved for the first time. It is not a perfect solution, but works well for most content types. New content types need to be explicitly registered with `portal_factory`, either in the ZMI, or using the `factorytool.xml` GenericSetup import step, shown in the next section.

Premature object creation also has implications for event handlers. If you write an event handler for IObjectCreatedEvent, you will get an object that is not yet initialized, possibly living in the portal_factory tool, which is probably not very useful. You may also get several IObjectModifiedEvents during initialization, and several IObjectMovedEvents as the object is added to, and then moves out of, the factory's temporary storage.

To make it easier to distinguish between events for premature objects and events for proper content, Archetypes provides two events (both found in Products.Archetypes.interfaces) that extend IObjectModified. IObjectInitializedEvent is fired when the object is first saved and moved out of the factory. IObjectEditedEvent is sent each time the object is saved thereafter.

Installing and Registering Types

With the content types and their views created, all that remains is to write the installation code. We do this with a GenericSetup extension profile in the optilux. cinemacontent product. In the package's main configure.zcml file, we have:

```
<genericsetup:registerProfile
  name="default"
  title="Optilux Cinema Content Types"
  directory="profiles/default"
  description="Content types to describe Optilux Cinemas"
  provides="Products.GenericSetup.interfaces.EXTENSION"
  />
```

The import step profiles/default/types.xml registers the content types:

```
<object name="portal_types" meta_type="Plone Types Tool">
 <object name="Cinema Folder"
    meta_type="Factory-based Type Information with dynamic views"/>
 <object name="Cinema"
    meta_type="Factory-based Type Information with dynamic views"/>
 <object name="Film Folder"
    meta_type="Factory-based Type Information with dynamic views"/>
 <object name="Film"
    meta_type="Factory-based Type Information with dynamic views"/>
 <object name="Promotion"
    meta_type="Factory-based Type Information with dynamic views"/>
</object>
```

This will cause various factory-based type information objects (**FTIs**) to be created in the portal_types tool. We use *dynamic view* FTIs, as found in Products. CMFDynamicViewFTI, which powers the selectable views in the **display** menu.

We must also derive from `Products.CMFDynamicViewFTI.`
`browserdefault.BrowserDefaultMixin`, which all the
ATContentTypes base classes do.

Each FTI is configured in more detail in the corresponding file in
`profiles/default/types/`. The file name must match the portal type name,
but spaces are converted to underscores, as in `types/Cinema_Folder.xml`.

Before GenericSetup configuration became standard, developers would
set a number of the FTI properties as class variables directly on a content
type. A helper method called `installTypes()` was then used to extract
this information and construct an FTI. This is why you will sometimes see
class variables like `global_allow` or `filter_content_types` in older
Archetypes content types.

Let us go through the configuration for *Cinema*, found in `types/Cinema.xml`:

```xml
<?xml version="1.0"?>
<object name="Cinema"
    meta_type="Factory-based Type Information with dynamic views"
    i18n:domain="optilux.cinemacontent"
    xmlns:i18n="http://xml.zope.org/namespaces/i18n">
  <property name="title" i18n:translate="">Cinema</property>
  <property name="description"
      i18n:translate="">A description of a cinema</property>
  <property name="content_icon">++resource++cinema_icon.gif</property>
```

These first few lines give the content type a name, description, and icon, which
will be shown in the Plone user interface. The icon references the browser resource
described earlier.

```xml
  <property name="content_meta_type">Cinema</property>
  <property name="product">optilux.cinemacontent</property>
  <property name="factory">addCinema</property>
  <property name="immediate_view">atct_edit</property>
```

Here, we set the meta-type of the content type, which is usually the same as the
portal type name, which, in turn, is the same as the ID of the FTI object in the
`portal_types` tool. We then specify a factory that will create and initialize a new
content object of this type, and the product the factory is associated with. The
factory is generated and registered by Archetypes—more on that in a moment.
The `immediate_view` property is supposed to define the view that will be shown
immediately after the object is created, but it is not used in Plone at the time
of writing.

```
<property name="global_allow">False</property>
<property name="filter_content_types">True</property>
<property name="allowed_content_types">
    <element value="RichDocument" />
    <element value="Image" />
    <element value="Promotion" />
</property>
```

These properties control the relationship between containers and their children. We set `filter_content_types` to `True`, and specify a list of types allowable inside **Cinemas** with `allowed_content_types`. Similarly, **Cinema Folder** specifies **Cinema** as an allowed type. Generic folder types would set `filter_content_types` to `False`. In this case, all types that are *globally addable* — those (unlike **Cinema**) that have `global_allow` set to `True` — would be allowed in these containers.

```
<property name="allow_discussion">False</property>
```

This property determines whether or not comments are allowed by default on content of this type.

```
<property name="default_view">view</property>
<property name="view_methods">
 <element value="view"/>
</property>
```

These properties relate to Plone's **display** menu and are particular to *dynamic views* FTIs. They specify which view is used by default, and the full list of available **view methods** for objects of this type. **Cinema Folder** and **Film Folder** both allow a few of the standard Plone folder listings to be selected as alternatives to their own standard views. In fact, **Film Folder** does not define a custom view at all, offering only generic folder listing templates from Plone.

```
<alias from="(Default)" to="(dynamic view)"/>
<alias from="edit" to="atct_edit"/>
<alias from="sharing" to="@@sharing"/>
<alias from="view" to="(selected layout)"/>
```

These specify the method aliases for our content type. By convention, most Plone content types use these four aliases. If you are not using a *dynamic views* FTI, you must specify the name of a view or template to use for the `(Default)` and `view` aliases (which would normally be the same). Here, we use the special targets `(dynamic view)` and `(selected layout)` from `CMFDynamicViewFTI`. These both relate to the currently selected view method, but the former also supports a *default page* content item selection. This should never be used for the `view` alias, because the user should always be able to append `/view` to a URL, and see the exact object at this location, regardless of any default page.

```
<action title="View" action_id="view" category="object"
  condition_expr=""
    url_expr="string:${folder_url}/" visible="True">
 <permission value="View"/>
</action>
<action title="Edit" action_id="edit" category="object" condition_
expr=""
    url_expr="string:${object_url}/edit" visible="True">
 <permission value="Modify portal content"/>
</action>
</object>
```

Finally, we register several type-specific actions, which, by virtue of being in
the `object` category, are displayed as tabs on the content item. Notice how they
reference the method aliases shown previously. For the sake of URL consistency
across content types, they are almost always the two shown above—**view** and
edit, pointing to their respective method aliases. Note that folderish types will use
`string:${folder_url}/` as the view action, whereas non-folderish items such as
Film or **Promotion** use `string:${object_url}` (note the lack of a trailing slash).

Factories and Add Permissions

When setting up the FTI earlier, we saw a reference to a *factory* called `addCinema`.
The factory is generated by Archetypes when the product is initialized, in the root
`__init__.py`, which also registers the add permissions for each content type. For the
most part, this is boilerplate, which can be copied into your own products.

```
from Products.Archetypes import atapi
from Products.CMFCore import utils
from optilux.cinemacontent import config

...

def initialize(context):
    from content import cinemafolder, cinema, filmfolder,
    film, promotion
    content_types, constructors, ftis = atapi.process_types(
        atapi.listTypes(config.PROJECTNAME),
        config.PROJECTNAME)

    for atype, constructor in zip(content_types, constructors):
        utils.ContentInit("%s: %s" % (config.PROJECTNAME,
            atype.portal_type),
            content_types  = (atype,),
            permission     = config.ADD_PERMISSIONS[atype.portal_type],
            extra_constructors = (constructor,),
            ).initialize(context)
```

This references two variables in `config.py`:

```
PROJECTNAME = "optilux.cinemacontent"
ADD_PERMISSIONS = {
    "Cinema Folder" : "Optilux: Add Cinema Folder",
    "Cinema"        : "Optilux: Add Cinema",
    "Film Folder"   : "Optilux: Add Film Folder",
    "Film"          : "Optilux: Add Film",
    "Promotion"     : "Optilux: Add Promotion",
}
```

The first line of `initialize()` imports the modules containing Archetypes content types. This has the effect of invoking the various `atapi.registerType()` calls, which in turn tell Archetypes about the types and run the Class Generator.

The next few lines call `process_types()`, which will create the factory. If you are curious, the generated code looks something like this:

```
def addCinema(self, id, **kwargs):
    from zope.event import notify
    from zope.lifecycleevent import ObjectCreatedEvent,
ObjectModifiedEvent
    obj = Cinema(id)
    notify(ObjectCreatedEvent(obj))
    self._setObject(id, obj)
    obj = self._getOb(id)
    obj.initializeArchetype(**kwargs)
    notify(ObjectModifiedEvent(obj))
    return obj.getId()
```

Finally, we initialize the content types with their respective add permissions. This idiom allows the creation of each content type to be controlled by a different permission, for maximum flexibility.

We also have to set the roles for each of the new permissions. As before, we use a `rolemap.xml` import step:

```
<rolemap>
  <permissions>
    <permission name="Optilux: Add Cinema Folder" acquire="False">
        <role name="Manager" />
    </permission>
    <permission name="Optilux: Add Cinema" acquire="False">
        <role name="Manager" />
        <role name="Owner" />
        <role name="Contributor" />
```

```
        </permission>
        <permission name="Optilux: Add Film Folder" acquire="False">
            <role name="Manager" />
        </permission>
        <permission name="Optilux: Add Film" acquire="False">
            <role name="Manager" />
            <role name="Owner" />
            <role name="Contributor" />
        </permission>
        <permission name="Optilux: Add Promotion" acquire="False">
            <role name="Manager" />
            <role name="Owner" />
            <role name="Contributor" />
        </permission>
      </permissions>
    </rolemap>
```

Notice that we do not use the StaffMember role here. This is because StaffMember is a feature of our site policy product, and depending on it in the more general optilux.cinemacontent product would make it harder to re-use and test the latter. Therefore, we let optilux.policy make the necessary adjustments for the StaffMember role after it has installed optilux.cinemacontent, as shown in a moment.

Registering Content Types with the Factory Tool

All our new content types should use the portal_factory tool to mitigate against stale content items caused by premature object creation. Most user-facing content types based on Archetypes will use the factory tool.

The factory-aware types are configured using the factorytool.xml import step:

```
<?xml version="1.0"?>
<object name="portal_factory" meta_type="Plone Factory Tool">
 <factorytypes>
  <type portal_type="Cinema Folder"/>
  <type portal_type="Cinema"/>
  <type portal_type="Film Folder"/>
  <type portal_type="Film"/>
  <type portal_type="Promotion"/>
 </factorytypes>
</object>
```

Adding Catalog Indexes and Metadata Columns

When we defined validators for film and cinema codes, we made use of two new catalog indexes, `film_code` and `cinema_code`. These are configured with the `catalog.xml` import step:

```
<object name="portal_catalog" meta_type="Plone Catalog Tool">
    <index name="film_code" meta_type="FieldIndex">
        <indexed_attr value="film_code"/>
    </index>
    <index name="cinema_code" meta_type="FieldIndex">
        <indexed_attr value="cinema_code"/>
    </index>

    <column value="film_code"/>
    <column value="cinema_code"/>
</object>
```

 It used to be possible to define a new index for an Archetypes field by using the `index` property on that field, which was read by `installTypes()`, as described earlier. This API was slightly awkward, however, and could not be made to work with GenericSetup.

Installation and Configuration in the Policy Product

Finally, we will amend the `optilux.policy` product to install and configure `optilux.cinemacontent` in accordance with our other policy decisions. We already saw how the `optilux.cinemacontent` package is included from `optilux.policy`'s main `configure.zcml` file:

```
<include package="optilux.cinemacontent" />
```

We also make sure the new product gets installed when the policy product itself is installed. In `Extensions/Install.py`, we now have:

```
PRODUCT_DEPENDENCIES = ('RichDocument',
                        'optilux.theme',
                        'optilux.cinemacontent',)
```

Adjusting the Security Policy

Most of the cinema-related content types will use the default workflow. To keep things simple, we turn off workflow for **Cinema Folder** and **Film Folder**, under the assumption that they will only be set up by site administrators as part of the creation of the initial structure of the site. In `workflow.xml`:

```
<?xml version="1.0"?>
<object name="portal_workflow" meta_type="Plone Workflow Tool">
 ...
 <bindings>
  ...
  <type type_id="Cinema Folder" />
  <type type_id="Film Folder" />
 </bindings>
</object>
```

We also want to allow staff members to add promotions by default. Therefore, we amend `rolemap.xml` as follows:

```
<rolemap>
  ...
  <permissions>
    ...
    <permission name="Optilux: Add Promotion" acquire="False">
        <role name="Manager" />
        <role name="Owner" />
        <role name="Editor" />
        <role name="StaffMember" />
    </permission>
  </permissions>
</rolemap>
```

Adjusting Navigation Tree Properties

Because promotions are intended to be shown using the promotions portlet, we do not want them to show up in the navigation tree under cinemas and cinema folders. Thus, we hide the **Promotion** type from the navigation tree by adding it to the `metaTypesNotToList` property in the `navtree_properties` property sheet, found in the `portal_properties` tool in the ZMI. This property sheet stores several of the settings managed through Plone's **Navigation** control panel.

The `propertiestool.xml` import step can be used to add or change properties in the `portal_properties` tool. For our purposes, it looks like this:

```
<?xml version="1.0"?>
<object name="portal_properties">
    <object name="navtree_properties">
        <property name="metaTypesNotToList" type="lines"
purge="False">
            <element value="Promotion"/>
        </property>
    </object>
</object>
```

Notice the `purge="False"` attribute on the `<property />` directive. Without this, we would be replacing the list under the `metaTypesNotToList`, rather than appending to it.

Enabling Content Object Versioning

Finally, we want to make sure certain content types can be versioned. The administrator can configure this in Plone's **Types** control panel, but we provide defaults by adding a method to `setuphandlers.py` that calls the appropriate API from the `portal_repository` tool:

```
from Products.CMFCore.utils import getToolByName
from Products.CMFEditions.setuphandlers import DEFAULT_POLICIES

...

def setVersionedTypes(portal):
    portal_repository = getToolByName(portal, 'portal_repository')
    versionable_types = list(portal_repository.
    getVersionableContentTypes())
    for type_id in ('RichDocument', 'Film', 'Cinema', 'Promotion',):
        if type_id not in versionable_types:
            versionable_types.append(type_id)
            # Add default versioning policies to the versioned type
            for policy_id in DEFAULT_POLICIES:
                portal_repository.addPolicyForContentType(type_id,
                policy_id)
    portal_repository.setVersionableContentTypes(versionable_types)

def importVarious(context):
    ...
    portal = context.getSite()
    ...
    setVersionedTypes(portal)
```

The DEFAULT_POLICIES here refer to Plone's default versioning policies, which will cause content to be versioned when it is edited and/or just before being rolled back to a previous version.

Site Policy Tests

Of course, we must not forget the tests. First, we need to tell tests/base.py about the new product:

```
from Products.Five import zcml
from Products.Five import fiveconfigure

from Testing import ZopeTestCase as ztc

from Products.PloneTestCase import PloneTestCase as ptc
from Products.PloneTestCase.layer import onsetup

ztc.installProduct('SimpleAttachment')
ztc.installProduct('RichDocument')

@onsetup
def setup_optilux_policy():

    fiveconfigure.debug_mode = True
    import optilux.policy
    zcml.load_config('configure.zcml', optilux.policy)
    fiveconfigure.debug_mode = False

    ztc.installPackage('optilux.theme')
    ztc.installPackage('optilux.cinemacontent')
    ztc.installPackage('optilux.policy')

setup_optilux_policy()
ptc.setupPloneSite(products=['optilux.policy'])

class OptiluxPolicyTestCase(ptc.PloneTestCase):
    """We use this base class for all the tests in this package.
    If necessary, we can put common utility or setup code in here.
    """
```

There are also a few new tests in test_setup.py:

```
def test_types_versioned(self):
    repository = getToolByName(self.portal, 'portal_repository')
    versionable_types = repository.getVersionableContentTypes()
    for type_id in ('RichDocument', 'Film',
    'Cinema', 'Promotion',):
        self.failUnless(type_id in versionable_types)

def test_promotions_not_in_navtree(self):
    self.failIf('Promotion' not in
```

```
            self.portal.portal_properties.navtree_properties.
        metaTypesNotToList)

    def test_cinemacontent_installed(self):
        self.failUnless('Cinema' in self.types.objectIds())

    def test_cinemafolder_filmfolder_have_no_workflow(self):
        for portal_type, chain in self.workflow.listChainOverrides():
            if portal_type in ('Cinema Folder', 'Film Folder'):
                self.assertEquals((), chain)


    def test_add_promotion_permission_for_staffmember(self):
        self.failUnless('Optilux: Add Promotion' in [r['name'] for r
        in self.portal.permissionsOfRole('StaffMember')
                            if r['selected']])
```

Functional Tests

When creating new content types, it is important to test in the browser, to make sure the user experience is correct and the content types' look and feel is consistent with the rest of the site. However, that does not mean we should not perform automated testing. As the number of content types and their interdependencies grow, it becomes harder to manually test the various ways in which content interacts.

For this package, we have opted to write a README.txt file, which contains a zope. testbrowser functional test, exercising all the content types and showing a quasi-realistic example of how they relate to each other. Test-browser tests simulate the user's interaction with the system through a web browser (without JavaScript support). There is a relatively simple API for filling in form fields, *clicking* on links and buttons, and inspecting the contents of the rendered page. To learn more about test-browser tests, see the README.txt file in the zope.testbrowser package, or the Plone testing tutorial at http://plone.org/documentation/tutorial/testing.

Test-browser tests can take a little longer to write than regular integration tests, mostly because they take longer to run and are sometimes less intuitive to debug. However, they can help ensure that your content continues to work as you make changes, because they test the end-to-end processes of managing content: finding a content type in Plone's **add** menu, filling in its fields, dealing with validation failures, invoking events at the appropriate time, exercising custom view templates, and so on.

As before, we add a common test case base class and set setup code to
`tests/base.py`:

```
from Products.Five import zcml
from Products.Five import fiveconfigure

from Testing import ZopeTestCase as ztc

from Products.PloneTestCase import PloneTestCase as ptc
from Products.PloneTestCase.layer import onsetup

@onsetup
def setup_optilux_cinemacontent():
    fiveconfigure.debug_mode = True
    import optilux.cinemacontent
    zcml.load_config('configure.zcml', optilux.cinemacontent)
    fiveconfigure.debug_mode = False

    ztc.installPackage('optilux.cinemacontent')

setup_optilux_cinemacontent()
ptc.setupPloneSite(products=['optilux.cinemacontent'])

...

class CinemaContentFunctionalTestCase(ptc.FunctionalTestCase):
    """Test case class used for functional (doc-)tests
    """
```

Notice the use of `ptc.FunctionalTestCase` as a base class, as opposed to
`ptc.PloneTestCase`. To set up the functional test, we have the following in
`tests/test_doctest.py`:

```
import unittest
import doctest

from zope.testing import doctestunit
from zope.component import testing, eventtesting

from Testing import ZopeTestCase as ztc

from optilux.cinemacontent.tests import base

def test_suite():
    return unittest.TestSuite([
        ztc.ZopeDocFileSuite(
            'README.txt', package='optilux.cinemacontent',
            test_class=base.CinemaContentFunctionalTestCase,
            optionflags=doctest.REPORT_ONLY_FIRST_FAILURE |
                    doctest.NORMALIZE_WHITESPACE | doctest.ELLIPSIS),
        ])
```

This ensures that the full setup code and helper methods of `PloneTestCase` are available inside the doctest. We also pass a few configuration options to simplify debugging and matching of expected results to test output.

The `README.txt` file itself is much too long to reproduce here, but it begins with some initial configuration of the test-browser control object.

```
>>> from Products.Five.testbrowser import Browser
>>> browser = Browser()
>>> browser.handleErrors = False
>>> self.portal.error_log._ignored_exceptions = ()
```

To make it easier to check for specific strings in the HTML output after various actions, we then turn off all of Plone's standard portlets.

```
>>> from zope.component import getUtility, getMultiAdapter
>>> from plone.portlets.interfaces import IPortletManager
>>> from plone.portlets.interfaces import IPortletAssignmentMapping
>>> left_column = getUtility(IPortletManager, name=u"plone.
leftcolumn")
>>> left_assignable = getMultiAdapter((self.portal, left_column),
...                                    IPortletAssignmentMapping)
>>> for name in left_assignable.keys():
...     del left_assignable[name]
>>> right_column = getUtility(IPortletManager,
...     name=u"plone.rightcolumn")
>>> right_assignable = getMultiAdapter((self.portal, right_column),
...                                     IPortletAssignmentMapping)
>>> for name in right_assignable.keys():
...     del right_assignable[name]
```

We then log into the portal as the portal owner:

```
>>> from Products.PloneTestCase.setup import portal_owner from
>>> Products.PloneTestCase.setup import default_password
>>> portal_url = self.portal.absolute_url()
>>> browser.open(portal_url + '/login')
>>> browser.getControl(name='__ac_name').value = portal_owner
>>> browser.getControl(name='__ac_password').value = default_password
>>> browser.getControl(name='submit').click()
```

You are encouraged to read through the rest of the file, and examine the patterns being used to create content and verify output. You may also want to put a break point at any line when running the tests, to inspect the state of the `browser` object.

```
>>> import pdb; pdb.set_trace()
```

The property `browser.url` is the current URL; `browser.contents` is the rendered HTML of the current page. Because reading raw HTML in the console can be a little cumbersome, the author sometimes uses this trick during debugging:

```
>>> open('/tmp/test-output.html', 'w').write(browser.contents)
```

This can be run equally from the `pdb` prompt. When executed, this statement will write the current contents of the test-browser to `/tmp/test-output.html`. Images and style sheets will not work, but the text in the page is normally enough to understand why some output is not as expected.

Creating a New Portlet

With the content types in place, we now have a flexible system for managing cinema content. The site administrator can create the basic site structure with standard folders and pages as well as the more specific **Cinema Folder** and **Film Folder** types. Inside these, staff can describe **Cinemas** and **Films** in some detail, and add promotions for cinemas and groups of cinemas. However, we have not yet explained how promotions are shown to the user, which we will do using a new type of portlet.

The portlet is found in the `portlets` sub-package. The files here follow the conventions established in `plone.app.portlets`. For the promotions portlet, there is a page template called `promotions.pt` and a Python module called `promotions.py`.

Starting with the template, it looks like this:

```
<dl class="portlet portletPromotions"
    i18n:domain="optilux.cinemacontent">
    <dt class="portletHeader">
        <span class="portletTopLeft"></span>
        Promotions
        <span class="portletTopRight"></span>
    </dt>
    <tal:items tal:repeat="promotion view/promotions">
        <dd class="portletItem"
            tal:define="oddrow repeat/promotion/odd;"
            tal:attributes="class python:oddrow and 'portletItem even'
            or 'portletItem odd'">
        <a href=""
            tal:attributes="href promotion/url;
                            title promotion/title;">
            <img tal:replace="structure promotion/image_tag" />
            <tal:title content="promotion/title">
                Title
            </tal:title>
```

```
                    <span class="portletItemDetails"
                        tal:content="promotion/summary"
                        >Promotion summary</span>
                </a>
            </dd>
        </tal:items>
        <dd class="portletFooter">
            <span class="portletBottomLeft"></span>
            <span class="portletBottomRight"></span>
        </dd>
    </dl>
```

This employs the styling used by most of the standard Plone portlets. As is good practice, all the logic for determining which promotions to show is delegated to a view — or rather, a portlet renderer — found in promotions.py.

Let us now look at promotions.py. Again, this follows the conventions and structure of Plone's standard portlets. First, a few imports:

```
import random

from zope import schema
from zope.component import getMultiAdapter
from zope.formlib import form
from zope.interface import implements

from plone.app.portlets.portlets import base
from plone.memoize.instance import memoize
from plone.portlets.interfaces import IPortletDataProvider

from DateTime import DateTime
from Acquisition import aq_inner
from Products.CMFCore.interfaces import ICatalogTool
from Products.Five.browser.pagetemplatefile import \
    ViewPageTemplateFile

from Products.CMFCore.utils import getToolByName

from optilux.cinemacontent.interfaces import IPromotion
from optilux.cinemacontent.interfaces import IBannerProvider
from optilux.cinemacontent import CinemaMessageFactory as _
```

Notice the base module imported from plone.app.portlets. This contains various base classes, which make the task of creating new portlet components easier.

```
class IPromotionsPortlet(IPortletDataProvider):

    count = schema.Int(title=_(u'Number of promotions to display'),
            description=_(u'Maximum number of promotions to be shown'),
```

```
                 required=True,
                 default=5)

    randomize = schema.Bool(title=_(u"Randomize promotions"),
            description=_(u"If enabled, promotions to show will be "
            "picked randomly. If disabled, newer promotions will be "
            " preferred."),
            default=False)
    sitewide = schema.Bool(title=_(u"Sitewide promotions"),
            description=_(u"If enabled, promotions from across the "
            "site will be found. If disabled, only promotions in this "
            "folder and its subfolders are eligible."),
            default=False)
```

This interface defines the configurable aspects of the portlet type. Again, we use the fields in `zope.schema` to specify the various attributes, but unlike before, we will use these directly to create add and edit forms for the portlet, complete with validation. The interface is implemented by the following class:

```
    class Assignment(base.Assignment):
        implements(IPromotionsPortlet)

        def __init__(self, count=5, randomize=False, sitewide=False):
            self.count = count
            self.randomize = randomize
            self.sitewide = sitewide

        @property
        def title(self):
            return _(u"Promotions")
```

This—the **portlet assignment** type—is a persistent object that manages the *configuration* of an instance of this portlet. The title property is defined in `plone.portlets.interfaces.IPortletAssignment`, declared by `base.Assignment`. It will be shown in Plone's portlet management user interface. We could of course have used a simple string class variable here, but in other cases you may wish the title to be a dynamic property.

Most of the logic of the portlet is found in the **portlet renderer**. This class is akin to a view, except that it only renders part of a page. It is initialized with various parameters. In the base class, you will find:

```
    def __init__(self, context, request, view, manager, data):
        self.context = context
        self.request = request
        self.view = view
        self.manager = manager
        self.data = data
```

The `context` and `request` are passed in as they are for regular views. The current `view` within which the portlet is being rendered is also provided. The variable `manager` is the **portlet manager** (such as the left column or right column), which is just a named utility providing `plone.portlets.interfaces.IPortletManager`. Finally, `data` is the **portlet data provider**, which in most cases is the same object as the portlet assignment (notice how we derived `IPromotionsPortlet` from `IPortletDataProvider`). Thus, we can access the configuration properties of the `Assignment` through `self.data`:

```
class Renderer(base.Renderer):

    render = ViewPageTemplateFile('promotions.pt')

    @property
    def available(self):
        return len(self._data()) > 0

    def promotions(self):
        for brain in self._data():
            promotion = brain.getObject()
            banner_provider = IBannerProvider(promotion)
            yield dict(title=promotion.title,
                       summary=promotion.summary,
                       url=brain.getURL(),
                       image_tag=banner_provider.tag)

    @memoize
    def _data(self):
        context = aq_inner(self.context)
        limit = self.data.count

        query = dict(object_provides = IPromotion.__identifier__)

        if not self.data.sitewide:
            query['path'] = '/'.join(context.getPhysicalPath())
        if not self.data.randomize:
            query['sort_on'] = 'modified'
            query['sort_order'] = 'reverse'
            query['sort_limit'] = limit

        query['effectiveRange'] = DateTime()

        catalog = getToolByName(context, 'portal_catalog')
        results = catalog(query)

        promotions = []
        if self.data.randomize:
            promotions = list(results)
            promotions.sort(lambda x,y: cmp(random.
            randint(0,200),100))
```

```
            promotions = promotions[:limit]
        else:
            promotions = results[:limit]
    return promotions
```

Portlet renderers, being cousins of viewlets, are a special kind of content provider. Therefore, they have update() and render() methods. An empty update() method is defined in the base class, and the render callable is set to the page template shown earlier. We also define the available property. If this is False, the portlet will not be displayed. If all portlets in a column are unavailable, the entire column will be hidden (as opposed to showing an empty column).

The rest of the class is providing display logic specific to the promotions portlet. It searches for promotions in the current context (a **Cinema Folder** or **Cinema**), using the settings in the portlet assignment to control how the list is constructed. It returns a simplified list of dicts for the template to loop over and render.

Finally, we must declare the add forms and edit forms for this new portlet type, which allow the user to create and modify promotions portlet assignments.

```
class AddForm(base.AddForm):
    form_fields = form.Fields(IPromotionsPortlet)
    label = _(u"Add Promotions portlet")
    description = _(u"This portlet displays cinema promotions.")

    def create(self, data):
        assignment = Assignment()
        form.applyChanges(assignment, self.form_fields, data)
        return assignment
class EditForm(base.EditForm):
    form_fields = form.Fields(IPromotionsPortlet)
    label = _(u"Edit Promotions portlet")
    description = _(u"This portlet displays cinema promotions.")
```

These classes use zope.formlib to generate a series of form widgets (held in the form_fields class variable) from the interface defined at the beginning of the file. The add form additionally implements a create() method, which is required to construct a new assignment instance and apply the submitted form data to it. We will learn more about zope.formlib in the next chapter.

Configuring and Registering New Portlet Types

To configure the new portlet type, we add the following to `portlets/configure. zcml`:

```
<configure
    xmlns="http://namespaces.zope.org/zope"
    xmlns:plone="http://namespaces.plone.org/plone">

    <include package="plone.app.portlets" />

    <plone:portlet
        name="optilux.Promotions"
        interface=".promotions.IPromotionsPortlet"
        assignment=".promotions.Assignment"
        renderer=".promotions.Renderer"
        addview=".promotions.AddForm"
        editview=".promotions.EditForm"
        />

</configure>
```

Behind the scenes, this statement registers a few utilities, adapters, and browser views. Note that if there is nothing to edit, you can skip the `editview` attribute. In this case, you may also want to use `plone.app.portlets.portlets.base. NullAddForm` as a base class for the add form class.

Finally, we must register the new portlet type when the product is installed, so that it may be added from the portlet management screen. This is done using GenericSetup, with the `portlets.xml` import step.

```
<portlets>
    <portlet
        addview="optilux.Promotions"
        title="Promotions"
        description="A portlet which can show current promotions."
        />
</portlets>
```

The `addview` defined here must match the `name` of the portlet as defined in `portlets/configure.zcml`.

Naturally, we have also written tests for the portlet—`plone.app.portlets.`
`tests` establishes a convention for portlet tests. Please see `tests/test_portlet_`
`promotions.py`; this contains two test cases: `TestPortlet`, which ensures the portlet
is properly registered and installed and is mostly boilerplate, and `TestRenderer`,
which exercises view logic in the `Renderer` class above.

Assigning Portlets Automatically

Because our new portlet is the primary way in which promotions are viewed,
we will ensure that it is added to all new top-level **Cinema Folders**. In `content/`
`cinemafolder.py`, we have:

```
from zope.component import adapter, getUtility, getMultiAdapter
from zope.app.container.interfaces import INameChooser
from Acquisition import aq_inner, aq_parent
from Products.Archetypes.interfaces import IObjectInitializedEvent
from optilux.cinemacontent.interfaces import ICinemaFolder
from optilux.cinemacontent.config import PROMOTIONS_PORTLET_COLUMN

...

@adapter(ICinemaFolder, IObjectInitializedEvent)
def add_promotions_portlet(obj, event):
    parent = aq_parent(aq_inner(obj))
    if ICinemaFolder.providedBy(parent):
        return

    column = getUtility(IPortletManager,
    name=PROMOTIONS_PORTLET_COLUMN)
    manager = getMultiAdapter((obj, column,),
IPortletAssignmentMapping)

    assignment = promotions.Assignment()
    chooser = INameChooser(manager)
    manager[chooser.chooseName(None, assignment)] = assignment
```

This event handler will be invoked when a **Cinema Folder** is first saved. First, we
make sure the portlet is only added to a top-level **Cinema Folder**, since children
will by default acquire the portlet from their parent. Then, we look up the portlet
manager (column) we wish to modify—in this case Plone's right column. This is
multi-adapted (together with the context object) to `IPortletAssignmentMapping`,
which provides an ordered container of portlet assignments for the given context
and portlet manager. It has a dict-like interface, with string keys. To make sure we
get a unique and proper key, we rely upon a name chooser adapter.

The event handler is registered in `content/configure.zcml` like so:

```
<subscriber handler=".cinemafolder.add_promotions_portlet" />
```

Zope 3, Formlib, and the Role of Archetypes

Archetypes has been enormously beneficial to Plone developers' productivity, and in this chapter, we have aimed to show its most modern side. At the same time, some aspects of its design are showing their age. For example, it would be nice if Archetypes schemata did not overlap with interfaces using fields from `zope.schema`. Some developers also frown at the Class Generator, and the use of separate accessor and mutator methods for each field. Perhaps more importantly, it would be very useful to be able to support proper add forms, and avoid premature object creation.

All of this is of course part of the same type of evolution that Plone, CMF, and Zope are experiencing in light of Zope 3. Given the incredible prevalence of Archetypes in modern Plone development (not at least as the framework underpinning all the core content types), there are absolutely no plans to abandon it. However, in the future, more of Archetypes' internals may be built upon a more general architecture shared with Zope 3 and other aspects of Plone. For example, there is ongoing work to separate out functionality such as the reference and transformation engines into generic components not tied to Archetypes and its notion of a schema.

With Plone 3, it is already possible to create content types based entirely on interfaces and `zope.formlib` forms. However, formlib widgets cannot yet quite match Archetypes widgets in richness. More advanced functionality such as inline editing, text transformation, and references do not yet have canonical equivalents outside of Archetypes. Over time, it is likely that these gaps will be filled with new components, of which Archetypes will merely be one of several users.

Even today, non-Archetypes content may be attractive if you need simple, lightweight content types. The relevant integration code can be found in `plone.app.content` and is explained in `basecontent.txt` in that package. For examples of how to set up FTIs and factories for non-Archetypes content, you may want to look at `Products.CMFCore`, in particular `content.zcml` and `profiles/default`. However, if in doubt, use Archetypes.

Summary

In this chapter, we have seen:

- How to express requirements in terms of content types
- How to model these content types using interfaces
- How to use Archetypes to create new content types
- How to create custom views for our content types
- How to install and configure the new content types
- How to create and install a new type of portlet

We have also considered the role Archetypes plays in Plone programming, and alluded to some of the forces that may see its role change in the future.

You are encouraged to read the source code of the `optilux.cinemacontent` package and borrow from it freely. The code contains copious comments to explain what is going on at each step. To save repetition, the code pertaining to the **Cinema Folder** type is described in the most detail.

In the next chapter, we will move on to create a few pages that are not connected to content types directly, and learn more about generating forms with `zope.formlib`.

11

Standalone Views and Forms

In the previous chapter, we learned how to create content types with custom views. When rendering a view, the current content item was accessed through the `context` variable. Because of the way in which the views were registered in ZCML, they could make the assumption that their context provided a particular interface, through which it could be inspected or modified.

Not all pages in an application will be tied to a specific content type, however. In this chapter, we will consider templates and forms more generally, and learn how to create views that are not registered for a particular type of context. We will also consider how to deal with form submission, and how to auto-generate forms using `zope.formlib`.

Pages Without a Specific Context

As it happens, there is no such thing as a truly context-less template or view. In Chapter 9, we learned how Zope 3 views are always passed as a `context` and a `request`, and we have seen that templates in skin layers have an implicit variable `context` (also available under the older name `here`). Even though the view may not directly access properties of its context, it may still use the context as the starting point for looking up other views or CMF tools. At the very least, Zope's security machinery needs to know the context to determine the user's current roles.

Templates in Skin Layers

Chapter 4 introduced templates in skin layers in the `portal_skins` tool. Unlike Zope 3-style views, these can be invoked on any context. Take for example the `document_view` template in the `plone_content` layer. This assumes its context is a *Page* (internally called *Document*), but Zope will still attempt to invoke the template if you call it on a different type of object, for example with a URL like:

```
http://mysite.com/news/some-news-item/document_view
```

Of course, you may get an `AttributeError` if the context does not provide an attribute that the view is expecting to find.

Some templates are intended to be generic. For example, the `content_status_history` template, found in the `plone_forms` layer and linked to from the workflow **state** drop-down menu, works on all workflow-aware content types.

Finally, consider the `search` template, also found in `plone_forms`. It is invoked when a user performs a search from the quick-search box found on every page. It is always invoked in the context of the portal root—in `CMFPlone/skins/plone_templates/global_searchbox.pt` you will find:

```
<form name="searchform"
      ...
         tal:attributes="action string:${portal_url}/search">
```

There is no reason why it cannot be invoked in other contexts, but no reason why we should do that either; it behaves the same regardless of the context. In this case, it is better for web spiders and cache servers if the URL is always the same.

Views Available on All Objects

With Zope 3 views, we can be a little more formal. In the previous chapter, we registered the main view for each new content type, using the name `@@view` and tying it to a type-specific interface:

```
<browser:page
    for="..interfaces.IFilm"
    name="view"
    class=".film.FilmView"
    permission="zope2.View"
    />
```

Sometimes, we may want a general view available for all content types. In this case, we could register it for a generic interface such as `Products.CMFCore.interfaces.IContentish`. However, it may be more appropriate to specify that a view is simply available for any type of context. For example, in `plone.app.workflow`, we have:

```
<browser:page
    name="sharing"
    for="*"
    class=".sharing.SharingView"
    permission="cmf.ChangeLocalRoles"
    />
```

Recall from Chapter 9 that views are multi-adapters on a context and a request. The `for` attribute is actually specifying of what type the `context` must be for the adapter lookup to succeed, and the `for="*"` idiom is equivalent to saying `for="zope.interface.Interface"` —in other words, this view is registered for the most general of all interfaces.

Generic views can also be useful as a default option when there are more specific registrations available. For example, here is a pair of registrations from `Products.CMFPlone.browser`:

```
<browser:page
    for="*"
    name="breadcrumbs_view"
    class=".navigation.PhysicalNavigationBreadcrumbs"
    permission="zope.Public"
    allowed_attributes="breadcrumbs"
    />
<browser:page
    for="plone.app.layout.navigation.interfaces.INavigationRoot"
    name="breadcrumbs_view"
    class=".navigation.RootPhysicalNavigationBreadcrumbs"
    permission="zope.Public"
    allowed_attributes="breadcrumbs"
    />
```

The `breadcrumbs_view` is used to construct the *you are here* bread crumbs across the top of the site.

 Note that it is not being *called* in the same way as the full-page views are to render HTML. Instead, it exposes methods, which are used by Plone's `main_template`.

The former, more general view will look up the `breadcrumbs_view` recursively on its parent. When it reaches the navigation root (normally the portal root), it will find the latter view, which is responsible for rendering the first element in the bread crumb list and does not try to look further up the chain.

Views on the Portal Root

For views that do not make direct use of their context, the **portal root** is normally the most appropriate context. Avoid using `for="*"` unless there is a compelling reason to do so, in order to avoid namespace pollution.

In the `optilux.cinemacontent` package, we have added a view that allows site administrators to view recently modified *Cinema*s and *Film*s. In the case study, this falls under the requirement to produce site reports. The view is registered in `browser/configure.zcml`:

```
<browser:page
    for="Products.CMFCore.interfaces.ISiteRoot"
    name="recent-cinema-film-activity"
    class=".activityreport.ActivityReportView"
    permission="cmf.ManagePortal"
    />
```

This ensures that if we try to traverse to `/@@recent-cinema-film-activity` anywhere other than the site root, we will get a `NotFound` exception and a 404 error message.

The code in `activityreport.py` is similar to thaat of the other views in the `browser` sub-package:

```
from Products.Five.browser import BrowserView
from Products.Five.browser.pagetemplatefile import
ViewPageTemplateFile
...
class ActivityReportView(BrowserView):
    """View for showing recent cinema and film modifications
    """

    template = ViewPageTemplateFile('activityreport.pt')

    def __call__(self):
        # Hide the edtiable-object border
        self.request.set('disable_border', True)


        ...


        return self.template()


    ...
```

> Notice how we define `__call__()` explicitly to set the `disable_border` request variable, before rendering and returning the template. This trick will cause Plone to hide the *editable border* — the tabs around the current content item.

Without disabling the border, the template would appear, a little awkwardly, under the **View** tab of the portal root object. Another way of achieving this would be to put the logic in the template itself:

```
<metal:block fill-slot="top_slot"
        tal:define="dummy python:request.set('disable_border',1)" />
```

This is the only way to set a variable in skin layer templates, which do not have a backing Python class. For Zope 3 views, it is more appropriate to set the request variable in the view class as we have done above.

The `activityreport.pt` template is no different from other templates we have seen. It uses the implicit `view` variable to query the view class for items to display. Of course, it does not attempt to extract the title or description from the current context object (the portal):

```
<html xmlns="http://www.w3.org/1999/xhtml" xml:lang="en"
      xmlns:tal="http://xml.zope.org/namespaces/tal"
      xmlns:metal="http://xml.zope.org/namespaces/metal"
      xmlns:i18n="http://xml.zope.org/namespaces/i18n"
      lang="en"
      metal:use-macro="context/main_template/macros/master"
      i18n:domain="optilux.cinemacontent">
<body>
<metal:css fill-slot="css_slot">
<style type="text/css" media="all"
tal:content="string: @import
url(${context/++resource++optilux-cinemacontent.css});">
</style>
</metal:css>

<metal:main fill-slot="main">
    <tal:main-macro metal:define-macro="main"
          tal:define="films view/recently_modified_films;
                      cinemas view/recently_modified_cinemas">
        <h1 class="documentFirstHeading"
            i18n:translate="header_recent_activity_report">
          Recent activity
        </h1>
        <p i18n:translate="description_recent_activity_report">
            This report shows recently modified films and cinemas.
        </p>
        ...
</body>
</html>
```

Please refer to the book's accompanying source code for the full code of this template.

Invoking Standalone Pages

When we created views for content types in the previous chapter, we made use of actions and aliases in the FTI that we installed in the `portal_types` tool. Plone renders the actions in the `object` category as tabs on the object (so long as the *editable border* is visible), making it easy to assign a custom view to the **View** tab of a content type.

When we create standalone pages such as the cinema and film activity report earlier, we need to decide how they will be invoked. Some developers assume that they should be shown in the navigation tree, but this is really about navigating site content, and templates are definitely not content.

One option is to render a link from another template. For example, we could have a statement like this in the view of a *Cinema Folder* or a template forming part of our custom theme:

```
<a
tal:attributes="href string:${portal_url}/@@recent-cinema-film-activity"
   tal:condition="python:checkPermission('Manage portal', context)">
  View recent activity report
</a>
```

Another option would be to use an action in a category that is displayed independently of the context. For example, the `site_actions` category refers to the **Site Map**, **Site Setup**, and the related links normally found across the very top of the site. The `portal_tabs` category can be used to add additional static tabs next to **Home** in the main site navigation.

 The other tabs are constructed from the folders in the root of the site. It is possible to turn this automatic tab generation off in the **Navigation** control panel and manage all folders explicitly as actions.

To see the full list of available actions and their contents, take a look at the `portal_actions` tool in the ZMI or the GenericSetup import step that creates them in `CMFPlone/profiles/default/actions.xml`.

For the purposes of our case study, we have opted to add another link in the `site_actions` category. Since this is a policy decision, we do this in the GenericSetup profile of the `optilux.policy` product. The file `profiles/default/actions.xml` contains:

```
<?xml version="1.0"?>
<object name="portal_actions"
   xmlns:i18n="http://xml.zope.org/namespaces/i18n">
 <object name="site_actions">
```

```
<object name="activity-report" meta_type="CMF Action"
        i18n:domain="optilux.cinemacontent">
 <property name="title" i18n:translate="">Activity report</property>
 <property name="description" i18n:translate=""></property>
 <property name="url_expr">string:$portal_url/
                 @@recent-cinema-film-activity</property>
 <property name="icon_expr"></property>
 <property name="available_expr"></property>
 <property name="permissions">
  <element value="Modify portal content"/>
 </property>
 <property name="visible">True</property>
</object>
</object>
</object>
```

There are plenty of other examples in Plone's own `actions.xml` file. The associated test in `tests/test_setup.py` reads:

```
def test_activity_report_action_installed(self):
    self.failUnless('activity-report' in
            self.portal.portal_actions.site_actions.objectIds())
```

Here is how it looks:

Writing Custom Forms

So far, we have only created views to present information already in the ZODB and the only forms we needed were taken care of by Archetypes. Now, letting Archetypes provide edit forms and validation for content objects is a good idea, but we often need ad hoc forms as well, and Archetypes is not much help there.

 There is, however, a popular third-party product called **PloneFormGen**, which can be used to create ad hoc forms via a Plone GUI.

There is nothing magic about forms in Zope. Form submit targets resolve to views, page templates, or scripts that may inspect the request and take some action. A fairly common pattern is to create *self-submitting* forms—those where a page has a form that submits to the same page again. In fact, the report view we saw on the previous page contains such a form, in `activityreport.pt`:

```
<form method="get"
tal:attributes="action string:${context/absolute_url}/${view/__name__}">
    <div i18n:translate="activity_report_days_searched">
        Show changes in the last
        <input type="text" size="2" name="days"
            tal:attributes="value view/days"
            i18n:name="num_days" />
        days.
        <input type="submit" class="context"
                name="form.button.UpdateDays"
            value="Refresh"
            i18n:name="submit_button"
            i18n:attributes="value" />
    </div>
</form>
```

Notice how the `action` attribute is dynamically constructed to ensure that the form will submit to the same view, in the same context. Of course, you can construct a URL referring to a different view, template, or script, just as easily.

 In a skin template, you cannot use ${view/__name__}, but ${template/getId} will work instead. See the section on CMFFormController later

We process the form when the view in `activityreport.py` is invoked, using its
`__call__()` method:

```
template = ViewPageTemplateFile('activityreport.pt')

def __call__(self):
 # Hide the editable-object border
 self.request.set('disable_border', True)

 # Ensure we have a sensible number for days; since this is a non-
 # critical field, we fall silent back on the default if the input
 # is invalid
   try:
       self.days = int(self.request.get('days', 7))
   except ValueError:
       self.days = 7

   return self.template()
```

The other methods of the view inspect `self.days` to construct search parameters:

```
def recently_modified_films(self):
    context = aq_inner(self.context)
    catalog = getToolByName(context, 'portal_catalog')
    results = []
    for r in catalog(object_provides=IFilm.__identifier__,
                    modified=dict(query=self.modified_after(),
                                  range='min'),
                    sort_on='modified',
                    sort_order='reverse',):
        results.append(dict(url=r.getURL(),
                            title=r.Title,
                            description=r.Description,
                            modified=self.localize(r.modified)))
    return results

    ...

def localize(self, time):
    return self._time_localizer()(time, None, aq_inner(
                            self.context), domain='plonelocales')

def modified_after(self):
    return DateTime() - self.days
```

```
@memoize
def _time_localizer(self):
    context = aq_inner(self.context)
    translation_service = getToolByName(context,
                            'translation_service')
    return translation_service.ulocalized_time
```

In this example, we access the request parameter directly from `self.request`, using dict-like syntax.

 In templates, you can use the implicit request variable. If you have legacy code that needs to access the request outside a view, you may need to acquire the request, using `request = context.REQUEST`.

This is appropriate for HTTP GET requests and parameters passed on the query string as part of the URL. For POST requests, you can also use `self.request.form`, which is a dictionary of submitted form fields. Using this ensures that you do not accidentally accept variables passed on the query string when you were expecting a form submission.

Of course, the first time the template is invoked, we would not expect the `"days"` request variable to have been set. Therefore, we fall back on a default of 7 days.

Checking Form Submit Buttons

Sometimes, it may be important to check whether a particular button was pressed, and take different actions depending on which button, if any, is present in the request. Browsers will only send the button that was clicked as a request parameter (the value of that parameter is the button's label, which is not all that useful). Here is an example from `plone.app.workflow.browser.sharing`:

```
class SharingView(BrowserView):

    # Actions

    template = ViewPageTemplateFile('sharing.pt')

    def __call__(self):
        """Perform the update and redirect if necessary,
        or render the page
        """

        postback = True

        form = self.request.form

        # Make sure we had a proper form submit, not just a GET request
        submitted = form.get('form.submitted', False)
```

```
save_button = form.get('form.button.Save', None) is not None
cancel_button = form.get('form.button.Cancel',
                    None) is not None

if submitted and not cancel_button:
    # Update the acquire-roles setting
    ...

# Other buttons return to the sharing page
if save_button or cancel_button:
    postback = False

if postback:
    return self.template()
else:
    self.request.response.redirect(self.context.absolute_url())
    return ''
```

Notice how we check for the save and cancel buttons in the request. In the `sharing.pt` template, you will find these buttons again:

```
<input class="context" type="submit" name="form.button.Save"
value="Save" />
<input class="standalone" type="submit" name="form.button.Cancel"
value="Cancel" />
```

Form Input Converters

The `sharing.pt` template also demonstrates marshaling of form fields into Python types other than strings. It contains form fields such as:

```
<input
    type="hidden"
    name="entries.id:records"
    tal:attributes="value entry/id"
    />
<input
    type="hidden"
    name="entries.type:records"
    tal:attributes="value entry/type"
    />
```

These are being rendered inside a `tal:repeat` loop. Notice the `:records` part of the name. When the form is submitted, the view will receive a single form variable called `entries`, containing a list of dictionaries, with keys `"id"` and `"type"`. Here are the various types of marshaling directives available:

Converter	Example	Result
`boolean`, `int`, `long`, `float`, `string`, `date`	`<input type="hidden" name="limit:int" value="10" />`	Cast the variable to the appropriate Python type. `date` results in a Zope `DateTime`. `string` is the default and therefore, a little superfluous. Note that these are normally only useful in hidden fields; if the user enters a value that cannot be converted, the resulting error message is not very friendly.
`text`	`<textarea name="message: text" />`	Convert to a string with normalized line breaks appropriate for the server platform.

`list`, `tuple`	`<input type="checkbox" name="selection:list" value="1"/>`
	
	 `<input type="checkbox" name="selection:list" value="2"/>`
		Produce a list or a tuple from multiple fields with the same name, or from a multi-selection list box. This can be combined with other converters. e.g., `:int:list` will result in a list of integers.

`tokens`, `lines`	`<input type="text" name="keywords:tokens" />`	Turn a space-separated (`tokens`) or a newline-separated (`lines`) string into a list.

`record`, `records`	`<input type="text" name="data.id:record" />`
	
	 `<input type="text" name="data.val:record" />`
		Produce a dictionary (`record`) or list of dictionaries (`records`). The name before the `.` is the variable name, and the name after the `.` is the key. In the example, we would get `data['id']` and `data['val']`.

`required`	`<input type="text" name="name:required" />`	Raise an exception if the field is not filled in. Again, this is rarely used because the error message is not very friendly.
`ignore_empty`	`<input type="text" name="id:ignore_empty" />`	Omit the variable from the request if no value was entered. Can be combined with other converters.

Converter	Example	Result

`default`	`<input type="hidden" name="accept:boolean: default" value="True" />`
	
	`<input type="checkbox" name="accept:boolean: default" value="False" />`
		Give a default value if no other field with the same name was submitted. This is very useful for checkboxes, which are omitted from the request unless they were checked. Can be combined with other converters.

Performing Redirects

In certain circumstances, the view in `sharing.py` will call:

```
self.request.response.redirect(self.context.absolute_url())
```

This instructs the browser to perform a redirect, here returning to the default view of the context, leaving the current template.

Redirects are the easiest way to control the flow between pages in response to form input or other conditions. When performing a redirect, the view does not need to return any content. In fact, it would be a waste of server resources to do so, since the browser is not going to render the page anyway. It should, however, return an empty string.

Alternatively, if you need to abort and cause a redirect at the same time, you can raise a `Redirect` exception:

```
from zExceptions import Redirect
...
if bad_thing_happened:
    raise Redirect(fallback_url)
```

The Zope Publisher will catch this exception, abort the current transaction, and issue a redirect to the browser using the URL passed as an argument to the exception constructor.

Automatically Generating Forms

It is not terribly difficult to create manual forms, even if you want basic validation and a standardized look and feel. For example, `CMFPlone/skins/plone_forms/ search_form.pt` contains a good example of the usual form markup and patterns. However, creating forms from scratch can be quite time-consuming. Luckily, there are ways to automatically create forms.

In the previous chapter, we saw how to use zope.formlib to create portlet *add* and *edit* forms from an interface describing the configurable aspects of that portlet. These are just special cases of the forms that can be created using the tools in the formlib package.

To demonstrate formlib more generally, we will use a *page form* to create an enquiries page for the Optilux website. For the sake of convenience, we will keep this in the optilux.cinemacontent package. Forms are just views, so the registration in browser/configure.zcml is simply:

```
<browser:page
    for="Products.CMFCore.interfaces.ISiteRoot"
    name="make-an-enquiry"
    class=".enquiry.EnquiryForm"
    permission="zope2.View"
    />
```

The entire form is found in browser/enquiry.py — there is no corresponding template, since formlib takes care of the visuals for us. First we define an interface that describes the form fields:

```
import re

from zope.interface import Interface

from zope import schema

from zope.formlib import form
from Products.Five.formlib import formbase
from Products.Five.browser.pagetemplatefile import \
    ViewPageTemplateFile

from Products.CMFCore.interfaces import IURLTool
from Products.MailHost.interfaces import IMailHost
from Products.statusmessages.interfaces import IStatusMessage

from Acquisition import aq_inner
from Products.CMFCore.utils import getToolByName

from optilux.cinemacontent import CinemaMessageFactory as _

# Define a validation method for email addresses
class NotAnEmailAddress(schema.ValidationError):
    __doc__ = _(u"Invalid email address")

check_email = re.compile(
        r"[a-zA-Z0-9._%-]+@([a-zA-Z0-9-]+\.)*[a-zA-Z]{2,4}").match
def validate_email(value):
    if not check_email(value):
        raise NotAnEmailAddress(value)
    return True
```

```
MESSAGE_TEMPLATE = """\
Enquiry from: %(name)s <%(email_address)s>

%(message)s
"""

class IEnquiryForm(Interface):
    """Define the fields of our form
    """

    subject = schema.TextLine(title=_(u"Subject"),
            required=True)
    name = schema.TextLine(title=_(u"Your name"),
            required=True)
    email_address = schema.ASCIILine(title=_(u"Your email address"),
    description=_(u"We will use this to contact you if you request it"),
            required=True,
            constraint=validate_email)
    message = schema.Text(title=_(u"Message"),
            description=_(u"Please keep to 1,000 characters"),
            required=True,
            max_length=1000)
```

 This code is adapted from Philipp von Weitershausen's book *Web Component Development with Zope 3*, where you will also find further explanation of zope.formlib.

See the interfaces in zope.schema for more information about which fields and options are available.

Take note of the constraint property of the email_address field. This is a callable, which should return True if the value entered is valid. When it is not, we raise an exception deriving from ValidationError. The docstring (__doc__) of this exception will be presented to the user as an error message.

The form view class itself derives from zope.formlib's base classes. However, we must use an intermediary class from Products.Five.formlib.formbase to keep Zope 2 happy.

```
class EnquiryForm(formbase.PageForm):
    form_fields = form.FormFields(IEnquiryForm)
    label = _(u"Make an enquiry")
    description = _(u"Got a question or comment? Please submit it
    using the form below!")
```

The form_fields variable contains the fields to be rendered. It is possible to assign custom widgets or to add or omit fields from this list. See the IFormFields and IFormField interfaces in zope.formlib.interfaces. The label and description will be rendered at the top of the page.

Next, we make use of the same trick as before to hide the editable border when the form is displayed:

```
# This trick hides the editable border and tabs in Plone
def __call__(self):
    self.request.set('disable_border', True)
    return super(EnquiryForm, self).__call__()
```

Then, we define the form's only button. When clicked, the decorated function will be called, with the submitted values passed in the data dict.

```
@form.action(_(u"Send"))
def action_send(self, action, data):
    """Send the email to the site administrator and redirect to the
    front page, showing a status message to say the message
    was received.
    """
```

The body of this function sends the email, and then redirects to the portal front page with a status message. The status message is queued up by adapting the request to IStatusMessage from Products.statusmessages.interfaces, and calling the adapter's addStatusMessage() method.

```
context = aq_inner(self.context)
mailhost = getToolByName(context, 'MailHost')
urltool = getToolByName(context, 'portal_url')
portal = urltool.getPortalObject()
email_charset = portal.getProperty('email_charset')
# Construct and send a message
to_address = portal.getProperty('email_from_address')
source = "%s <%s>" % (data['name'], data['email_address'])
subject = data['subject']
message = MESSAGE_TEMPLATE % data
mailhost.secureSend(message, to_address, str(source),
                    subject=subject, subtype='plain',
                    charset=email_charset, debug=False,
                    From=source)
# Issue a status message
confirm = _(u"Thank you! Your enquiry has been received and we "
            "will respond as soon as possible")
```

```
IStatusMessage(self.request).addStatusMessage(
                                    confirm, type='info')
# Redirect to the portal front page. Return an empty string as
# the page body - we are redirecting anyway!
self.request.response.redirect(portal.absolute_url())
return ''
```

Do not forget to configure a mail host in Plone's control panel! Here is how the form will look:

As before, we will add this as a site action, using `actions.xml` in `optilux.policy`:

```
<object name="contact" meta_type="CMF Action"
        i18n:domain="optilux.cinemacontent">
  <property name="title" i18n:translate="">Contact us</property>
```

```
        <property name="description" i18n:translate=""></property>
    <property name="url_expr">string:$portal_url/@@make-an-enquiry</property>
        <property name="icon_expr"></property>
        <property name="available_expr"></property>
        <property name="permissions">
         <element value="View"/>
        </property>
        <property name="visible">True</property>
    </object>
```

The name `"contact"` is not accidental. It will cause this action to override the standard Plone action with the same name.

To learn more about `zope.formlib`, take a look at the interfaces and the `forms.txt` doctest in that package.

The Form Controller Tool

Plone ships with the **CMFFormController** product, which can be used to manage the flow of control between forms and scripts, optionally taking into account which button was pressed or invoking validators. It can be quite useful for complex page flows, but is becoming less important since it does not work with Zope 3 views. It can also be a little cumbersome because it spreads the form logic across multiple files. Still, a lot of products and a number of forms in Plone itself use it. Note that form controller templates and scripts can only be defined in skin layers.

Let us look at an example. Plone's **Send this page to someone** form is defined in `CMFPlone/skins/plone_forms/sendto_form.cpt` — the `.cpt` extension declaring it as a *Controller Page Template*. The form is like any other form, except that it submits to itself, defines a hidden `"form.submitted"` field, and uses names beginning with `form.button` for its buttons. It also accesses the `options/state` variable, which CMFFormController provides, to find out if there were any validation errors:

```
<div metal:fill-slot="main"
     tal:define="errors options/state/getErrors;">

  ...

  <form name="sendto_form"
        method="post"
        tal:attributes="action string:$here_url/$template_id">

    ...

      <div class="field"
           tal:define="error errors/send_to_address|nothing;"
```

```
                 tal:attributes="class python:test(error, 'field error',
                                                   'field')">

       <label for="send_to_address"
              i18n:translate="label_send_to_mail">Send to</label>
       <span class="fieldRequired" title="Required"
             i18n:attributes="title title_required;"
             i18n:translate="label_required">(Required)</span>
             <div class="formHelp"
                   i18n:translate="help_send_to_mail">
               The e-mail address to send this link to.
             </div>
             <div tal:content="error">Validation error output</div>
             <input type="text"
               id="send_to_address"
               name="send_to_address"
               size="25"
               tabindex=""
               tal:attributes="value request/send_to_address | nothing;
                               tabindex tabindex/next;"
                   />
       </div>
         ...
       <div class="formControls">
         <input class="context"
                tabindex=""
                type="submit"
                name="form.button.Send"
                value="Send"
                i18n:attributes="value label_send;"
                tal:attributes="tabindex tabindex/next;"
                />
       </div>
       <input type="hidden" name="form.submitted" value="1" />
     </fieldset>
   </form>
</div>
```

In the same directory, there is a corresponding `sendto_form.cpt.metadata` file, which the form controller uses to determine which validators (if any) to invoke and where to go next if they succeed:

```
[default]
title=Send this page to somebody

[validators]
validators=validate_sendto

[actions]
action.success=traverse_to:string:sendto
action.failure=traverse_to:string:sendto_form
```

Here, `success` and `failure` refer to the state that the validator gives. The default state is `success`. It is possible to specify different outcomes for different buttons, too, using syntax like:

```
[actions]
action.success=traverse_to:string:folder_constraintypes_form
action.success..Cancel=redirect_to_action:string:view
action.success..Save=traverse_to:string:setConstrainTypes
action.failure=traverse_to:string:folder_constraintypes_form
```

This example is taken from `folder_constraintypes_form.cpt.metadata`.

An action can be one of `redirect_to`, `redirect_to_action`, `traverse_to`, or `traverse_to_action`, followed by a TALES expression resulting in the name of a template or script (for `traverse_to` and `redirect_to`) or the name of an action on the context (for `traverse_to_action` or `redirect_to_action`).

The difference between a *traverse* and a *redirect* is that the former will traverse to and invoke a template or script directly on the server, whereas the latter will ask the browser to redirect to the given template or script. Normally, intermediary form processing steps will use `traverse_to`, so that request variables are carried forward between each script or template, and the final step will use `redirect_to` so that the URL in the browser reflects the current page.

Here is the validator script — `validate_sendto.vpy` — from the `plone_form_scipts` skin layer. It was referenced in the `[validators]` section of the previous item in the chain as seen above in `sendto_form.cpt.metadata`. This is like a normal Script (Python) in a skin layer, except that it is passed a controller `state`, which it may manipulate, and must return:

```
## Controller Script Python "validate_sendto"
##bind container=container
##bind context=context
##bind namespace=
```

```
##bind script=script
##bind state=state
##bind subpath=traverse_subpath
##parameters=send_to_address='',send_from_address=''
##title=validates the email adresses

from Products.CMFPlone import PloneMessageFactory as _
plone_utils=context.plone_utils

if not send_to_address:
    state.setError('send_to_address',
        _(u'Please submit an email address.'), 'email_required')

...

if state.getErrors():
    context.plone_utils.addPortalMessage(_(u'Please correct the
indicated errors.'), 'error')
    return state.set(status='failure')
else:
    return state
```

If validation is successful, the controller will continue to the sendto.cpy script
(again, note the special extension), as specified in the sendto_form.cpt.metadata
file. As with the validator, this is passed, and must return, the controller state:

```
## Controller Python Script "sendto"
##bind container=container
##bind context=context
##bind namespace=
##bind script=script
##bind state=state
##bind subpath=traverse_subpath
##parameters=
##title=Send an URL to a friend
##

# send the message
...

if not mtool.checkPermission(AllowSendto, context):
    context.plone_utils.addPortalMessage(
            _(u'You are not allowed to send this link.'), 'error')
    return state.set(status='failure')

...

context.plone_utils.addPortalMessage(_(u'Mail sent.'))
return state
```

Finally, this script needs a corresponding `sendto.cpy.metadata` in the same directory telling the form controller where to go next:

```
[validators]
validators=validate_sendto

[actions]
action.success = redirect_to_action:string:view
action.failure = redirect_to_action:string:view
```

For more information about the form controller, refer to the **Documentation** tab of the `portal_form_controller` tool in the ZMI.

Forms in Viewlets

Finally, let us consider how to use forms in a generic viewlet. In Chapter 2, we presented the requirement to allow users to rate films. To manage film ratings, we have added an `IRatings` interface to `interfaces.py` in `optilux.cinemacontent`:

```
class IRatings(Interface):
    """An object which can be rated
    """

    score = schema.Int(title=_(u"A score from 1-100"),
                       readonly=True)

    def available(user_token):
        """Whether or not rating is available for the given user
        """

    def rate(user_token, positive):
        """Give a positive (True) or negative (False) vote.
        """
```

In `ratings.py`, there is an adapter from `IFilm` to `IRatings`, which stores ratings in annotations on a *Film* object. We will not reproduce that code here, but take a look at the class and its doctest to understand how it works. This is a perfect example of adding new behavior to an existing object using an adapter!

The viewlet itself is registered in `browser/configure.zcml` with:

```
<browser:viewlet
    name="optilux.cinemacontent.ratings"
    for="optilux.cinemacontent.interfaces.IFilm"
    view="plone.app.layout.globals.interfaces.IViewView"
    manager="plone.app.layout.viewlets.interfaces.IBelowContentTitle"
    class=".ratings.RatingsViewlet"
    permission="zope2.View"
    />
```

We choose to render it below the title. See `plone.app.layout.viewlets` for other possible viewlet managers. We also choose to only show the viewlet on the canonical *view* (i.e. the **View** tab) of an `IFilm` object, as formalized by the `IViewView` marker interface. This marker interface is applied to the *view* automatically during traversal, if appropriate.

The viewlet template can be found in `browser/ratings.pt`. It defines a simple form with two buttons, and outputs the current rating:

```
<dl class="portalMessage info" i18n:domain="optilux.cinemacontent">
    <dt i18n:translate="">
        Ratings
    </dt>
    <dd>
        <div i18n:translate="info_film_rating"
            tal:condition="view/have_score">
            <span i18n:name="rating" tal:replace=
            "view/score" />% of those who voted liked this film.
        </div>
        <form method="get"
            tal:condition="view/available"
            tal:attributes="action context/absolute_url">
            <div i18n:translate="vote_film_rating">
                Did you like this film?
                <input
                    type="submit"
                    name="optilux.cinemacontent.ratings.VotePositive"
                    value="Yes"
                    i18n:attributes="value"
                    />
                <input
                    type="submit"
                    name="optilux.cinemacontent.ratings.VoteNegative"
                    value="No"
                    i18n:attributes="value"
                    />
            </div>
        </form>
    </dd>
</dl>
```

Notice the fairly long names for the form buttons. We have opted to let the form submit to the current context's default view, as part of which the viewlet will be rendered. However, we cannot be sure what that is, or what it would do with a particular request parameter. By using a very specific name, we reduce the risk that it could be interpreted incorrectly by the view or another viewlet.

When submitted, the form will be processed in the `update()` method of the viewlet. This is guaranteed to be called before the `render()` method — indeed before any viewlet in this viewlet manager is rendered.

```python
from zope.interface import implements
from zope.component import getMultiAdapter
from zope.viewlet.interfaces import IViewlet

from Acquisition import aq_inner
from Products.Five.browser import BrowserView
from Products.Five.browser.pagetemplatefile import
ViewPageTemplateFile

from optilux.cinemacontent.interfaces import IRatings
class RatingsViewlet(BrowserView):
    """Viewlet for allowing users to rate a film
    """
    implements(IViewlet)

    render = ViewPageTemplateFile('ratings.pt')

    def __init__(self, context, request, view, manager):
        super(RatingsViewlet, self).__init__(context, request)
        self.__parent__ = view
        self.view = view
        self.manager = manager
        self.ratings = IRatings(self.context)
        self.portal_state = getMultiAdapter((context, self.request),
                            name=u"plone_portal_state")

    def update(self):
        vote = None
        if self.request.has_key(
                    'optilux.cinemacontent.ratings.VotePositive'):
            vote = True
        elif self.request.has_key(
                    'optilux.cinemacontent.ratings.VoteNegative'):
            vote = False
        if vote is None or self.portal_state.anonymous():
            return
        user_token = self.portal_state.member().getId()
```

```
        if user_token is not None and self.ratings.available(
                                               user_token):
            self.ratings.rate(user_token, vote)
    def have_score(self):
        return self.score() is not None
    def available(self):
        if self.portal_state.anonymous():
            return False
        return self.ratings.available(
                          self.portal_state.member().getId())
    def score(self):
        return self.ratings.score
```

Here is how the viewlet looks when looking at a *Film*:

Global Template Variables and Helper Views

You may have noticed a few template variables that we did not define explicitly, such as `portal_url` or `checkPermission`. These are global variables (in templates only), pulled into `main_template` via `global_defines`. You can see a list of these variables in the docstring for `globalize()` in the interface `Products.CMFPlone.browser.interfaces.IPlone`.

Some of these global variables may eventually be deprecated, because they are being calculated on every page whether they are actually used or not. However, a few of the most useful (and least inefficient) ones are:

Global template variable	Purpose
portal	The Plone site root object
portal_url	The URL of the Plone site root
member	The currently authenticated member
checkPermission	A function used to check whether the current user has a permission in the current context, e.g. used as `python: checkPermission('Modify portal content', context)`
isAnon	`True` if the current user is not logged in
is_editable	`True` if the current user can edit the current context
isLocked	`True` if the current object is locked for editing

In addition, there are three *helper* views in `plone.app.layout.globals`, which can be used to access commonly used information. These are:

- `@@plone_portal_state`, which contains information about the portal in general, such as the portal root URL, the current user (member), and whether or not that user is anonymous

- `@@plone_context_state`, which contains information specific to the current context, such as its URL, its path, whether or not it is a folder, its workflow state, and whether it is editable

- `@@plone_tools`, which gives access to the most commonly used CMF tools

In all of these views, the various methods are cached so that, for a given request, they will only calculate their return values the first time they are called. Unlike the globals from `global_defines`, the values are not calculated at all if they are not needed, and they can be looked up in Python code, not just in templates. In fact, we saw this in the viewlet earlier:

```
self.portal_state = getMultiAdapter((context, self.request),
                          name=u"plone_portal_state")
...
if self.portal_state.anonymous():
    return False
```

In a template, you could do something like:

```
<div tal:define="context_state context/@@plone_context_state">
    ...
    <div tal:condition="context_state/is_view_template"> ... </div>
</div>
```

You should aim to use these views in your own views and templates if possible, rather than perform potentially expensive calculations that may already have been performed and cached. Take a look at `plone.app.layout.globals.interfaces` to see the full list of methods available.

Summary

In this chapter, we have shown:

- That no view or template in Zope is entirely context-free
- How to register views available on all types of context
- How to register a general view to only be available at the portal root
- A few suggestions for how the user may be directed to a standalone view
- Techniques for processing forms submitted by the user
- The pattern of letting views have forms that submit to the view itself
- How to create forms with a standard layout automatically from an interface, using `zope.formlib`
- How the CMFFormController tool works
- How forms may be used in viewlets
- An overview of standard helper views and global template variables, which may be useful in your own views

In the next chapter, we will create some more advanced forms and views, this time linked to an external relational database.

12

Relational Databases

Until now, all our content and persistent configuration have been managed in the ZODB. This is appropriate for almost all Plone installations. However, many organizations have existing relational databases that they want to integrate into a Plone website. Furthermore, certain kinds of data may be more appropriately managed using an RDBMS.

In this chapter, we will demonstrate techniques for interacting with relational databases, using the example of connecting an existing screenings and ticket-reservations database to the Optilux website.

Relational Databases vs. the ZODB

Some customers are frightened by the ZODB. It feels opaque and unfamiliar. They worry about performance and resilience. And surely, it cannot integrate into their existing data environment, can it?

In fact, the ZODB is a proven data store, which scales well. It is well-documented and provides low-level tools to extract data if necessary. As we learned in Chapter 9, it also largely frees developers from worrying about persistence, improving their productivity.

 For example, run `./bin/instance debug` in the buildout directory to enter the Zope debugger, from which you can traverse the ZODB.

Relational databases, relying on normalized database schemata, are not terribly good at storing hierarchical, semi-structured content, possibly with binary attachments and unpredictable field lengths—precisely the kind of thing users may create in a CMS. On the other hand, relational databases are hard to beat for storing large amounts of homogenous data, such as payment or customer records. Such data is typically easier to query using SQL than the Zope catalog and custom Python scripts.

When developing with Plone, the default position should always be to use the ZODB. Certainly, you cannot do without it completely, nor would you want to. However, you should know when to consider moving aspects of your application to a relational database, and how to use existing databases when appropriate.

Modeling Screenings and Reservations

In our example application, we have used Plone content types to represent *Films* and *Cinemas*. However, we have not yet connected the two. We could have modeled a *Screening* of a particular film at a particular cinema as a content type, but given that screenings recur frequently over time and could cover lots of different combinations of films and cinemas, we would end up with a large number of *Screening* objects. The ZODB could handle this without problem, but we would probably need to develop a custom user interface to populate and manage them, since Plone's UI paradigms are not really geared towards managing lots of similar objects in bulk.

A *Screening* is just a relationship (between a *Cinema* and a *Film*) with a single piece of metadata—the scheduled date/time. We will almost certainly need to perform queries across different dimensions on this relationship, such as finding all films showing at a given cinema, or all screenings of a particular film in a particular time period. With many cinemas and films, there will likely be a large number of scheduled screenings. Thus, screenings appear to be a good candidate for a relational model. Besides, the requirements in Chapter 2 already hinted that this data was to be found in an existing SQL database.

We will use the same relational database to hold ticket *Reservations*. To keep things simple, we will not concern ourselves with taking payments, but merely allow customers to reserve a number of tickets in their name. The database schema will be restricted to two tables:

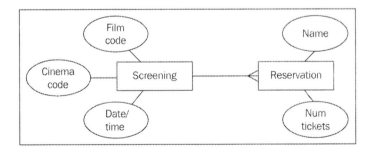

Recall from Chapter 10 that the *Film* and *Cinema* content types have `film_code` and `cinema_code` fields, respectively, and that we index these in the catalog. They are used as database keys, linking the ZODB content hierarchy to the relational data model.

Although they are not stored in the ZODB, we will use *Screening* and *Reservation* entities in Python code. Therefore, we define interfaces for them, in optilux. cinemacontent.interfaces:

```
class IScreening(Interface):
    """A screening of a film at a particular cinema
    """

    screening_id = schema.Int(title=_(u"Screening identifier"),
                    description=_(u"A unique id for this screening"),
                    required=True,
                    readonly=True)

    cinema = schema.Object(title=_(u"Cinema"),
                    schema=ICinema,
                    required=True,
                    readonly=True)

    film = schema.Object(title=_(u"Film"),
                    schema=IFilm,
                    required=True,
                    readonly=True)

    show_time = schema.Date(title=_(u"Date/time"),
                    required=True,
                    readonly=True)

    remaining_tickets = schema.Int(title=_(u"Remaining tickets"),
     description=_(u"Number of tickets available for this screening"))

class IReservation(Interface):
    """A ticket reservation for a particular screening
    """

    customer_name = schema.TextLine(title=_(u"Customer name"),
        description=_(u"The name of the customer making the
                    reservation"),
                    required=True)

    num_tickets = schema.Int(title=_(u"Number of tickets"),
                    description=_(u"Number of tickets to reserve"),
                    required=True,
                    min=1)

    screening = schema.Object(title=_(u"Screening"),
                    description=_(u"Film screening to book for"),
                    schema=IScreening,
                    required=True)
```

These interfaces are implemented by simple **domain classes**, which we will map to the database tables later. In `screening.py`:

```
class Screening(object):
    """A screening of a film at a particular cinema
    """

    implements(IScreening)

    screening_id = None
    cinema = None
    film = None
    show_time = None
    remaining_tickets = 0
```

And in `reservation.py`:

```
class Reservation(object):
    """A ticket reservation for a particular screening
    """

    implements(IReservation)

    customer_name = u""
    num_tickets = 0
    screening = None
```

Notice how, unlike the content classes from Chapter 10, these do not derive (directly or indirectly) from `persistence.Persistent`, making them ineligible for persistence in the ZODB. We will not attempt to connect them to the object graph by storing them as attributes on a persistent object or adding them to a folder.

Screening Query and Reservation Services

Later in this chapter, we will add listings of *Screenings* to the views of the *Cinema* and *Film* content types. Logged-in users will be able to click on a particular screening and make a ticket reservation.

This suggests that we need tools to query the database for screenings by cinema, film, and time. We will also need a way to make a reservation. However, we do not want the view code to deal with the database directly.

Database operations should be abstracted into plain-Python domain classes and general utilities in order to isolate other code from a hard dependency on the storage mechanism. This makes future provision of alternative storage modes possible. Importantly, it also makes it possible to write tests that do not depend on a live database, by providing mock implementations of database-centric components.

With this in mind, we will add interfaces describing two new utilities to
`interfaces.py`:

```
class IScreeningLocator(Interface):
    """A utility used to locate appropriate screenings based on search
       criteria
    """

    def films_at_cinema(cinema, from_date, to_date):
        """Return a list of all films screening at the particular
        ICinema between the specified dates.

        Returns a list of dictionaries with keys 'film_code', 'url',
        'title' and 'summary'.
        """

    def cinemas_for_film(film, from_date, to_date):
        """Return a list of all cinemas screening the given film
        between the specified dates.

        Returns a list of dictionaries with keys 'cinema_code', 'url',
        'name' and 'address'.
        """

    def screenings(film, cinema, from_date, to_date):
        """Return all screenings of the given film, at the given
        cinema,between the given dates

        Returns a list of IScreening objects.
        """

    def screening_by_id(screening_id):
        """Get an IScreening from a screening id
        """

class ITicketReservations(Interface):
    """A utility capable of making reservations
    """

    def __call__(reservation):
        """Make a reservation
        """
```

We will spend the rest of this chapter implementing these utilities and the views that
use them.

Setting Up the Database

The examples in this book use MySQL 5.0, with InnoDB tables, but the concepts we describe should apply equally to other databases.

 Unlike tables using the MyISAM engine, InnoDB tables properly support foreign key constraints. We will make use of these to infer relationships between tables.

We chose MySQL because it is free and relatively easy to set up. You can download it from `http://mysql.org`.

The table definitions, as well as some sample data, are provided with the book, in the `extra` folder. The scripts create two database instances: `optilux`, the main database, and `optilux_test`, a blank database used for testing. Here is the code that sets up the main database:

```
create database if not exists optilux;
use optilux;

-- Screenings
create table if not exists screening (
    screening_id integer unsigned not null auto_increment primary key,
    cinema_code char(4) not null,
    film_code char(4) not null,
    show_time datetime not null,
    remaining_tickets integer unsigned not null,
    index showing_cinema_code(cinema_code),
    index showing_film_code(film_code),
    index showing_show_time(show_time),
    index showing_remaining_tickets(remaining_tickets)
) engine=InnoDB;

-- Reservations
create table if not exists reservation (
    reservation_id integer unsigned not null auto_increment primary
key,
    screening_id integer unsigned not null,
    num_tickets tinyint unsigned not null,
    customer_name varchar(64) not null,
    index reservation_num_tickets(num_tickets),
    foreign key(screening_id)
        references screening(screening_id)
            on update restrict
            on delete restrict
) engine=InnoDB;
```

We will refer to this database as a whole as the *reservations database*.

You will also need to set up an appropriate database user. For testing purposes, the default super-user account in MySQL, called *root* with no password will suffice, but obviously this is not a good idea for production systems.

SQLAlchemy—Turning SQL Lead into Python Gold

Over the years, the Zope community has created several approaches for integrating Zope 2 and relational databases. Let us briefly look at the most important ones:

- **ZSQL methods** are akin to *Script (Python)*'s or DTML templates and can be created through the Web or in a skin layer. Essentially, they provide a way to parameterize SQL queries and retrieve the results for processing in a page template. ZSQL methods are quite simple, but can be a little awkward to use with component-based program designs because they are used through skin layers only.

- **Archetypes SQLStorage** and its derivatives are a valiant attempt to let Archetypes content objects store their actual data in a relational database. A ZODB stub is still required. Unfortunately, it is difficult to map Archetypes schemata onto existing (or even well-normalized) data models using this storage, and there are intrinsic performance issues related to the way Archetypes uses its storage abstraction layer.

- **PGStorage** is a low-level ZODB back end that stores binary *pickles* in a *PostgreSQL* database, rather than on the file system. This may give some performance and resilience benefits, but has nothing to do with accessing relational data models.

- **APE**, the Adaptable Persistence Engine, was an experiment in bridging the ZODB with other storage media, including relational databases, which is now largely abandoned.

More recently, attention has shifted away from Zope-specific solutions to third-party Python libraries dedicated to relational database integration. The most promising of these is **SQLAlchemy**—a powerful, flexible, well-supported, and well-documented package that supports a multitude of databases. It offers low-level connection management, a Python API for constructing SQL queries, and advanced Object/Relational Mapping (**ORM**) functionality.

We will use SQLAlchemy to implement our two database utilities, demonstrating ORM mapping as well as query building. We will also make use of a package called collective.lead to manage shared database connections and tie SQL transactions into Zope's transaction machinery.

> The code in this chapter uses SQLAlchemy 0.3 and collective.lead version 1.0. As the book went to press, SQLAlchemy 0.4, which features a revised query syntax among other improvements, was entering beta. If you are using a later version of SQLAlchemy, you may want to use the newer query syntax as shown in the SQLAlchemy documentation, and look out for a newer version of collective.lead. The general integration patterns should be the same, however.

When dealing with SQLAlchemy, there are some key terms that you should be familiar with:

Component	Purpose
Engine	Manages database connections and various database-specific details. In our case, the Engine will be managed by a named utility providing collective.lead.interfaces.IDatabase.
Table	Represents a table in the database. A Table must be bound to the Metadata of an Engine for SQLAlchemy to be aware of it.
Metadata	Binds a collection of Tables to a specific Engine.
Mapper	Represents an entity in the database (as described by a Table) as a Python class.
Session	Manages instances of Mapper classes. The Session can load new instances from the database, save changes to objects, or add new objects as records in the database.
Connection	Allows the execution of SQL queries, either constructed with Python statements or passed as strings.

We will not cover SQLAlchemy itself in great detail in this book. We will concentrate only on what we need to support the case study, and show how the Zope integration works. To learn more, you should consult http://sqlalchemy.org, where you will find SQLAlchemy's excellent documentation, including several in-depth tutorials and an API reference.

Managing Database Connections

SQLAlchemy provides a standard interaction pattern for creating engines, metadata, tables, and mappers. However, in the context of a Plone application, we have some particular requirements:

- Different products may want to manage their own database connections, meaning that we need to be able to manage multiple Engines simultaneously.

- Zope is a multi-threaded server. We need to ensure that any shared database resources are thread-safe.

- Database transactions need to be synchronized with Zope transactions. If one fails and rolls back, so should the other.

- Data source names (DSNs) may not be known until run time, for example if they are stored in the ZODB and exposed as configuration settings to the site administrator.

Luckily, all of this is taken care of by the `collective.lead` package. It provides a base class for creating named utilities encapsulating connection settings, tables, and mappers. We will create such a utility for the reservations database, naming it `"optilux.reservations"`.

We declare `collective.lead` as a dependency in `optilux.cinemacontent`'s `setup.py` file:

```
install_requires=[
    # -*- Extra requirements: -*-
    'setuptools',
    'MySQL-python',
    'collective.lead>=1.0b3,<2.0dev',
    ],
```

Now, if we re-run `./bin/buildout`, it should install `collective.lead`, which in turn will install the latest supported version of SQLAlchemy. We also require the MySQL-python package, which provides MySQL drivers for Python.

The database utility itself is found in `db.py`. This file also contains the implementation of a persistent, local utility providing `IDatabaseSettings`, which we will use to store connection settings:

```
from persistent import Persistent

from zope.interface import implements
from zope.component import getUtility

from collective.lead import Database
from optilux.cinemacontent.interfaces import IDatabaseSettings

from sqlalchemy.engine.url import URL
from sqlalchemy import Table, mapper, relation

from optilux.cinemacontent.screening import Screening
from optilux.cinemacontent.reservation import Reservation

class ReservationsDatabaseSettings(Persistent):
```

```
        implements(IDatabaseSettings)
        drivername = 'mysql'
        hostname = 'localhost'
        port = None
        username = ''
        password = None
        database = ''

    class ReservationsDatabase(Database):

        @property
        def _url(self):
            settings = getUtility(IDatabaseSettings)
            return URL(drivername=settings.drivername,
            username=settings.username,
                        password=settings.password, host=settings.hostname,
                        port=settings.port, database=settings.database)

        def _setup_tables(self, metadata, tables):
            tables['screening'] = Table('screening',
            metadata, autoload=True)
            tables['reservation'] = Table('reservation',
            metadata, autoload=True)

        def _setup_mappers(self, tables, mappers):
            mappers['screening'] = mapper(Screening, tables['screening'])
            mappers['reservation'] = mapper(Reservation,
            tables['reservation'],
                                    properties = {
                                    'screening' : relation(Screening),
                                        })
```

The `collective.lead.Database` superclass does all the hard work for us. It only
asks that we provide the `_url` property to return a database connection string, and
that we implement the `_setup_tables()` and `_setup_mappers()` methods. These
are used to construct tables and mappers, which we must store in the provided
`tables` and `mappers` dictionaries.

Notice how the mappers *map* the database tables onto the `Screening` and
`Reservation` domain classes we saw earlier. Thus, instances of these classes will
be able to participate in ORM sessions, with SQL column names and foreign key
relationships translated into object properties.

 Please consult the SQLAlchemy documentation to learn more about the
various options available when constructing database metadata and
ORM mappers.

The global IDatabase named utility is registered in the main configure.zcml for the package:

```
<utility
    provides="collective.lead.interfaces.IDatabase"
    factory=".db.ReservationsDatabase"
    name="optilux.reservations"
    />
```

The local IDatabaseSettings utility must be set up when the product is installed. This can be done with a GenericSetup import step, found in profiles/default/componentregistry.xml:

```
<componentregistry>
 <utilities>
  <utility
     interface="optilux.cinemacontent.interfaces.IDatabaseSettings"
     factory="optilux.cinemacontent.db.ReservationsDatabaseSettings"
     />
 </utilities>
</componentregistry>
```

With these pieces in place, we can access the database from any code within the site, like this:

```
>>> from zope.component import getUtility
>>> from collective.lead.interfaces import IDatabase
>>> db = getUtility(IDatabase, name='optilux.reservations')
```

The db object will have the properties of collective.lead.interfaces.IDatabase, notably session, a managed instance of an ORM session, and connection, which can be used to execute SQL statements constructed with SQLAlchemy's Python helper classes or passed in as strings. collective.lead ensures that these participate properly in a Zope transaction, and that each request uses at most one database connection from the connection pool.

Making a New Plone Control Panel

We would like to make the database settings configurable from a control panel in Plone's **Site Settings**. To do this, we will use zope.formlib and the interface describing the local utility that holds the settings. This is found in interfaces.py:

```
class IDatabaseSettings(Interface):
    """Database connection settings.
    """
```

```
drivername = schema.ASCIILine(title=_(u"Driver name"),
                description=_(u"The database driver name"),
                default='mysql',
                required=True)
hostname = schema.ASCIILine(title=_(u"Host name"),
                description=_(u"The database host name"),
                default='localhost',
                required=True)

port = schema.Int(title=_(u"Port number"),
                description=_(u"The database port number. "
                            "Leave blank to use the default."),
                required=False)
username = schema.ASCIILine(title=_(u"User name"),
                description=_(u"The database user name"),
                required=True)
password = schema.Password(title=_(u"Password"),
                description=_(u"The database password"),
                required=False)
database = schema.ASCIILine(title=_(u"Database name"),
                description=_(u"The name of the database on this
                            server"), required=True)
```

The form itself will use the general control panel infrastructure from `plone.app.`
`controlpanel`. Here is the code, in `browser/dbsettings.py`:

```
from zope.component import getUtility
from zope.formlib import form

from plone.app.controlpanel.form import ControlPanelForm

from collective.lead.interfaces import IDatabase

from optilux.cinemacontent.interfaces import IDatabaseSettings
from optilux.cinemacontent import CinemaMessageFactory as _

def reservations_database_settings(context):
    return getUtility(IDatabaseSettings)

class ReservationsDatabaseControlPanel(ControlPanelForm):

    form_fields = form.FormFields(IDatabaseSettings)

    form_name = _(u"Reservations Database settings")
    label = _(u"Reservations Database settings")
    description = _(u"Please enter the appropriate connection settings"
                    "for the database")
```

```
def _on_save(self):
    db = getUtility(IDatabase, name='optilux.reservations')
    db.invalidate()
```

And in `browser/configure.zcml`:

```
<browser:resource
    name="optilux_dbsettings_icon.gif"
    image="dbsettings_icon.gif"
    />

<browser:page
    name="reservations-database-controlpanel"
    for="Products.CMFPlone.interfaces.IPloneSiteRoot"
    class=".dbsettings.ReservationsDatabaseControlPanel"
    permission="cmf.ManagePortal"
    />

<adapter
    for="Products.CMFPlone.interfaces.IPloneSiteRoot"
    provides="optilux.cinemacontent.interfaces.IDatabaseSettings"
    factory=".dbsettings.reservations_database_settings"
    />
```

This form deserves some explanation. Apart from the icon, which we will use in a moment, there are two components that play a part in the new control panel:

- A `zope.formlib` form, which has the Plone site root as its context and uses a base class from `plone.app.controlpanel` to gain the standard control panel buttons and look and feel.

- An adapter from the form's context (which is the Plone site root, although it is not really important what it is) to the form's interface, `IDatabaseSettings`.

When the form is saved, the base class will call `zope.formlib.form.applyChanges` in the action (button) handler to process the user input. This will attempt to adapt the context (the Plone site root) to the form interface (`IDatabaseSettings`) and set properties corresponding to form fields on that adapter. Similarly, when the form is rendered, formlib will read default values for the various form fields from the adapter.

If the context provides the form interface directly, this will be a null-adapter accessing properties directly on the context object. We saw this in Chapter 10, when we wrote an edit form for our custom portlet. However, for the purposes of a control panel, we are not storing the properties on the context (the Plone site root) directly.

Instead, we implement a specific adapter, which retrieves and saves form values to wherever they need to go. This means that by providing an appropriate adapter, we can let the data being read and set by the form come from anywhere.

In our case, the form values need to go to the local `IDatabaseSettings` utility. We could have written a custom adapter that implemented all the properties of this interface (so that we could have a form field for each) and delegated each property getter and setter to the utility (so that they would be saved), but this would be cumbersome. Instead, we rely on the fact that the utility already provides the interface we need. We only require an adapter factory that looks up and returns the utility object, causing `applyChanges` to manipulate the local utility directly. This is precisely the role played by the `reservations_database_settings()` function.

 If that all made sense, congratulate yourself on mastering the Component Architecture. If not, do not worry. Take a look at the other control panels in the `plone.app.controlpanel` package to see more (simpler) examples of control panels. The `site.py` module contains a good example of a control panel form managing settings from various sources.

The `_onSave()` function is called by the base class when the save action has been processed. Here, we call the `invalidate()` method on the `IDatabase` utility, which will clear its internal caches, allowing the new database settings to take effect.

For the control panel page to show up under **Site Settings**, we need a `controlpanel.xml` import step:

```
<object name="portal_controlpanel" meta_type="Plone Control Panel Tool">
  <configlet title="Reservations Database"
             action_id="ReservationsDatabase"
             appId="ReservationsDatabase"
             category="Products" condition_expr=""
  url_expr="string:${portal_url}/@@reservations-database-controlpanel"
             visible="True">
    <permission>Manage portal</permission>
  </configlet>
</object>
```

We also need to register a corresponding icon, in `actionicons.xml`:

```
<action-icons>
  <action-icon category="controlpanel"
             action_id="ReservationsDatabase"
             title="Reservations Database"
             priority="0"
             icon_expr="++resource++optilux_dbsettings_icon.gif"/>
</action-icons>
```

Notice how the `action_id` attributes of the two registrations are the same. Here is how it looks, once the product is re-installed:

Reservations Database settings

⟵ Up to Site Setup

Please enter the appropriate connection settings for the database

┌─── Reservations Database settings ──────────────────────────────

Driver name ∗
The database driver name

`mysql`

Host name ∗
The database host name

`localhost`

Port number
The database port number. Leave blank to use the default.

User name ∗
The database user name

`root`

Password
The database password

Database name ∗
The name of the database on this server

`optilux`

`save` `cancel`

The control panel is tested via a test-browser test, in `tests/db_controlpanel.txt`. This simply ensures that values are written to the local utility when the form is submitted and is modeled on similar tests in the `plone.app.controlpanel` package. It also makes use of a test case base class from that package, which is set up in `tests/test_doctest.py`:

```
ztc.ZopeDocFileSuite(
    'tests/db_controlpanel.txt', package='optilux.cinemacontent',
    test_class=base.CinemaControlPanelTestCase,
    optionflags=doctest.REPORT_ONLY_FIRST_FAILURE |
                doctest.NORMALIZE_WHITESPACE | doctest.ELLIPSIS),
```

The test case class, in `tests/base.py` mixes `ControlPanelTestCase` from `plone.app.controlpanel.tests` into the `CinemaContentFunctionalTestCase` class we used for the functional tests described in Chapter 10.

Writing the Database Utilities

Now that we have the means to access the database, and the full power of SQLAlchemy at our fingertips, implementing the utilities that perform database operations is easy.

Database Tests

Of course, we should start with the tests. We have opted to use a doctest to demonstrate the database interaction pattern, found in `tests/database.txt`, and invoked with the following lines in `tests/test_doctest.py`:

```
ztc.ZopeDocFileSuite(
    'tests/database.txt', package='optilux.cinemacontent',
    test_class=base.CinemaContentFunctionalTestCase,
    optionflags=doctest.REPORT_ONLY_FIRST_FAILURE |
                doctest.NORMALIZE_WHITESPACE | doctest.ELLIPSIS),
```

These tests create some sample content, populate a few records in the database, and then exercise the utilities. As with all automated tests, the transaction is rolled back at the end of the test case, so they should never actually write to the database. To stay safe, however, we rely on a test database, which the tests expect to be empty:

```
>>> from zope.component import getUtility
>>> from optilux.cinemacontent.interfaces import IDatabaseSettings

>>> settings = getUtility(IDatabaseSettings)

>>> settings.drivername = 'mysql'
>>> settings.username = 'root'
>>> settings.hostname = 'localhost'
>>> settings.database = 'optilux_test'
```

We should now be able to make a connection.

```
>>> from collective.lead.interfaces import IDatabase
>>> db = getUtility(IDatabase, name='optilux.reservations')
```

Please see the book's accompanying source code for the rest of the file.

Of course, if this database does not exist, or there is no MySQL instance running on localhost, we will get test failures. For the database tests, that is fine, but for other tests, particularly the functional tests of the main optilux.cinemacontent content types, we would rather not have this dependency. Therefore, we provide mock implementations of the IScreeningLocator utility, which will be called by the *Cinema* and *Film* views, in the README.txt doctest:

```
>>> from zope.interface import implements
>>> from optilux.cinemacontent.interfaces import IScreeningLocator
>>> class DummyScreeningLocator(object):
...     implements(IScreeningLocator)
...
...     _films_at_cinema = []
...     _cinemas_for_film = []
...     _showings = []
...
...     def films_at_cinema(self, cinema, from_date, to_date):
...         return self._films_at_cinema
...
...     def cinemas_for_film(self, film, from_date, to_date):
...         return self._cinemas_for_film
...
...     def screenings(film, cinema, from_date, to_date):
...         return self._showings
>>> from zope.component import provideUtility
>>> _old_screening_locator = getUtility(IScreeningLocator)
>>> provideUtility(DummyScreeningLocator())
```

The remainder of the file is unchanged. However, at the very end of the test, we must return the component registrations to normal in order to avoid influencing other tests:

```
>>> provideUtility(_old_screening_locator)
```

This pattern of using mock utilities is of course not limited to cases where we have external dependencies. It can be equally useful in other situations where you need fine-grained control over test fixtures.

Querying the Database

The real IScreeningLocator utility, found in screening.py, is a little more interesting:

```
from zope.interface import implements
from zope.component import getUtility
from zope.app.component.hooks import getSite
```

```
from Products.CMFCore.interfaces import ISiteRoot
from Products.CMFCore.utils import getToolByName

from optilux.cinemacontent.interfaces import IFilm
from optilux.cinemacontent.interfaces import ICinema
from optilux.cinemacontent.interfaces import IScreeningLocator

import sqlalchemy as sql
from collective.lead.interfaces import IDatabase

...

class ScreeningLocator(object):
    """Find screenings of films at cinemas
    """

    implements(IScreeningLocator)

    def films_at_cinema(self, cinema, from_date, to_date):
        """Return a list of all films showing at the particular
        ICinema between the specified dates.

        Returns a list of dictionaries with keys 'film_code', 'url',
        'title' and 'summary'.
        """
        db = getUtility(IDatabase, name='optilux.reservations')
        connection = db.connection

        statement = sql.select([Screening.c.film_code],
                        sql.and_(
                Screening.c.cinema_code == cinema.cinema_code,
                Screening.c.show_time.between(from_date, to_date)
                        ),
                        distinct=True)

        results = connection.execute(statement).fetchall()

        film_codes = [row['film_code'] for row in results]

        site = getSite()
        catalog = getToolByName(site, 'portal_catalog')

        return [ dict(film_code=film.film_code,
                    url=film.getURL(),
                    title=film.Title,
                    summary=film.Description,)
                for film in
                    catalog(object_provides=IFilm.__identifier__,
                        film_code=film_codes,
                        sort_on='sortable_title')
                ]
```

First, we obtain a database connection as shown earlier in this chapter. Then we use various SQLAlchemy constructs to build a database query interrogating the screening table. The Screening.c.film_code syntax means "the film_code column of the table mapped to the Screening class". Please consult the SQLAlchemy documentation for a comprehensive guide to this syntax.

Finally, we construct a Plone catalog query that looks for the *Film* objects with the film_codes we found in the database. These are then packed into a list of dicts, as specified by the IScreeningLocator interface.

The reciprocal cinemas_for_film() method is similar.

The screenings() method, by contrast, uses SQLAlchemy's ORM API to locate screenings. In the method shown earlier, we were interested only in a particular field—the film_code. Now, we are interested in Screening objects. We have already told SQLAlchemy how to map these to the screening database table.

```
def screenings(self, film, cinema, from_date, to_date):
    """Return all screenings of the given film, at the given
    cinema, between the given dates.

    Returns a list of IScreening objects.
    """

    db = getUtility(IDatabase, name='optilux.reservations')
    session = db.session

    screenings = session.query(Screening).select(sql.and_(
            Screening.c.film_code==film.film_code,
            Screening.c.cinema_code==cinema.cinema_code,
            Screening.c.show_time.between(from_date, to_date)),
            order_by=[Screening.c.show_time])

    # Now set the 'film' and 'cinema' properties

    for screening in screenings:
        screening.film = film
        screening.cinema = cinema

    return screenings
```

Of course, since the Film and Cinema classes are not mapped to the database, SQLAlchemy cannot load and return them. Therefore, we set the film and cinema attributes on the loaded object directly, to comply with the IScreening interface.

The final method of the utility, screening_by_id(), is similar. It uses the ORM session to load a Screening by ID, and performs catalog searches to find and attach the appropriate *Film* and *Cinema* objects.

The utility itself is registered in `configure.zcml` like this:

```
<utility factory=".screening.ScreeningLocator" />
```

Updating and Inserting Records

Whereas the `IScreeningLocator` utility is only querying the database, the `ITicketReservations` utility needs to insert new records. In `reservation.py`, we have:

```python
from zope.interface import implements
from zope.component import getUtility

from optilux.cinemacontent.interfaces import ITicketReservations
from optilux.cinemacontent.interfaces import ReservationError

from optilux.cinemacontent.screening import Screening
from optilux.cinemacontent import CinemaMessageFactory as _

import sqlalchemy as sql
from collective.lead.interfaces import IDatabase

class TicketReservations(object):
    """Make reservations in the reservations database
    """

    implements(ITicketReservations)

    def __call__(self, reservation):
        """Make a reservation
        """

        db = getUtility(IDatabase, name='optilux.reservations')
        session = db.session

        # Make sure there are still seats available
        screening = reservation.screening
        session.refresh(screening)

        if screening.remaining_tickets <= 0:
            raise ReservationError(_(u"This screening is sold out!"))
        elif screening.remaining_tickets < reservation.num_tickets:
            raise ReservationError(_(u"Not enough tickets
            remaining!"))

        # Otherwise, we can save the reservation
        screening.remaining_tickets -= reservation.num_tickets
        session.update(screening)
        session.save(reservation)
        session.flush()
```

This is a perfect example of the natural flow of the SQLAlchemy ORM API. We first refresh the `Screening` the reservation is being made for, in case a concurrent transaction may have grabbed the remaining tickets. Then we update the count of remaining tickets, and insert a new reservation. We immediately flush the session to ensure database changes are saved.

If the requested screening is full, we raise a `ReservationError`. This is defined in `interfaces.py`:

```
class ReservationError(Exception):
    """Exception raised if there is an error making a reservation
    """

    def __init__(self, message):
        Exception.__init__(self, message)
        self.error_message = message
```

We will see in a moment how this is caught in the user interface in order to display a sensible error message to the user.

Adding the User Interface

All that remains now is to add the view code that uses these utilities to present information to the user. Before trying to access any of the updated views through the Web, do not forget to go to **Site Settings** and configure the database using our new control panel.

Updating the Film and Cinema Views

The changes to `browser/film.py` and `browser/film.pt` are simple. In the `FilmView` class:

```
@memoize
def cinemas(self, days=14):
    context = aq_inner(self.context)
    locator = getUtility(IScreeningLocator)
    from_date = datetime.now()
    to_date = from_date + timedelta(days)
    return locator.cinemas_for_film(context, from_date, to_date)
```

And in the template:

```
<h2 i18n:translate="title_film_showing_at">Now showing at</h2>
<dl>
    <tal:block repeat="cinema view/cinemas">
        <dt>
```

```
                <a tal:attributes="href cinema/url" tal:content=
                                              "cinema/name" />
            </dt>
            <dd tal:content="cinema/address" />
        </tal:block>
</dl>
```

The view in `browser/cinema.py` contains very similar code for listing the films shown at a cinema. In the `browser/cinema.pt` template, we also link to a new view, `@@screenings`, which shows a listing of all dates and times at which a particular film is screened at a particular cinema:

```
<h2 i18n:translate="title_cinema_now_showing">Now showing</h2>
<dl>
<tal:block repeat="film view/films">
 <dt>
 <a tal:attributes="href film/url"
     tal:content="film/title" />
 <a tal:attributes="href
 string:${context/absolute_url}/@@screenings?film_code=${film/film_code}"
    i18n:translate="label_view_screenings">
    (show times)
 </a>
 </dt>
 <dd tal:content="film/summary" />
</tal:block>
</dl>
```

Here is what the updated *Cinema* view looks like:

Screenings and Bookings

The new `@@screenings` view is registered in `browser/configure.zcml`:

```
<browser:page
    for="..interfaces.ICinema"
    name="screenings"
    class=".screenings.CinemaScreeningsView"
    permission="zope2.View"
    />
```

The template, in `screenings.pt`, simply renders a table, backed by the following method:

```
@memoize
def upcoming_screenings(self, days=14):
    cinema = aq_inner(self.context)
    locator = getUtility(IScreeningLocator)

    from_date = datetime.now()
    to_date = from_date + timedelta(days)

    can_reserve = getSecurityManager().checkPermission(
                    config.MAKE_RESERVATION_PERMISSION, cinema)

    film = self.film()
    return [dict(screening_id=screening.screening_id,
                show_time=self.localize(screening.show_time),
                remaining_tickets=screening.remaining_tickets,
                can_reserve=(can_reserve and
                    screening.remaining_tickets > 0))
            for screening in
        locator.screenings(film, cinema, from_date, to_date)]
```

In addition to asking the `IScreeningLocator` utility for screenings to show, it also checks whether the user has permission to make a reservation. This permission is defined in `config.py` as:

```
MAKE_RESERVATION_PERMISSION = "Optilux: Make reservation"
```

In the installation step in `profiles/default/rolemap.xml`, we permit logged-in users to make reservations:

```
<permission name="Optilux: Make reservation" acquire="True">
    <role name="Manager" />
    <role name="Member" />
</permission>
```

We also map this to a Zope 3-style permission in `configure.zcml`:

```
<permission
    id="optilux.MakeReservation"
    title="Optilux: Make reservation"
    />
```

With this, we can register the `@@reserve` view, making sure it is only available to users with permission to make reservations:

```
<adapter
    for=".reserve.ReserveScreeningView"
    factory=".reserve.reserve_screening_formview"
    name="default"
    provides="zope.formlib.namedtemplate.INamedTemplate"
    />

<browser:page
    for="..interfaces.ICinema"
    name="reserve"
    class=".reserve.ReserveScreeningView"
    permission="optilux.MakeReservation"
    />
```

The view itself uses `zope.formlib` with the `IReservation` interface to construct form fields. However, to make it more user friendly, we want to put some information about the screening next to the form itself. Therefore, we register a **named template** for the form — an adapter from the form's view class itself to `INamedTemplate`. Formlib will look this up and use it when rendering the form.

Here is the view, from `browser/reserve.py`:

```
from zope.component import getUtility
from zope.formlib import form

from Acquisition import aq_inner

from Products.Five.browser.pagetemplatefile import \
    ViewPageTemplateFile
from Products.Five.formlib import formbase

from Products.statusmessages.interfaces import IStatusMessage

from plone.app.form import named_template_adapter
from plone.app.form.validators import null_validator

from plone.memoize.instance import memoize

from optilux.cinemacontent.interfaces import IReservation
from optilux.cinemacontent.interfaces import ReservationError
```

```
from optilux.cinemacontent.interfaces import IScreeningLocator
from optilux.cinemacontent.interfaces import ITicketReservations

from optilux.cinemacontent import CinemaMessageFactory as _
from optilux.cinemacontent.reservation import Reservation

# This is registered as an adapter factory. When formlib renders the #
page,
it will look up this adapter to work out which template to use.

reserve_screening_formview = named_template_adapter(
                              ViewPageTemplateFile('reserve.pt'))

class ReserveScreeningView(formbase.PageForm):
    """Reserve tickets for a screening
    """

    label = _(u"Reserve tickets")
    form_fields = form.FormFields(IReservation).omit('screening')

    @form.action(_(u"Reserve"))
    def action_reserve(self, action, data):
        """Reserve tickets
        """
        context = aq_inner(self.context)
        screening = self.screening()
        reservations = getUtility(ITicketReservations)

        try:
            reservations(Reservation(data['customer_name'],
                                     data['num_tickets'],
                                     screening))
        except ReservationError, e:
            IStatusMessage(self.request).addStatusMessage(
                                    e.error_message, type='error')
        else:
            confirm = _(u"Thank you! Your tickets will be ready for "
                        "collection at the front desk.")
            IStatusMessage(self.request).addStatusMessage(confirm,
                                                    type='info')
            self.request.response.redirect(context.absolute_url())
            return ''

    # The null_validator ensures that we can cancel the form even if
    # some required fields are not entered
    @form.action(_(u"Cancel"), validator=null_validator)
    def action_cancel(self, action, data):
        """Cancel the reservation operation
        """
```

```
        context = aq_inner(self.context)
        confirm = _(u"Reservation cancelled.")
        IStatusMessage(self.request).addStatusMessage(
                                        confirm, type='info')
        self.request.response.redirect(context.absolute_url())
        return ''

    @memoize
    def screening(self):
        screening_id = self.request['screening_id']
        locator = getUtility(IScreeningLocator)
        return locator.screening_by_id(screening_id)
```

The screening, retrieved from the database and keyed in the `screening_id` request parameter, is output in the template, found in `browser/reserve.pt`:

```
    ...
    <metal:main fill-slot="main">
        <tal:main-macro metal:define-macro="main"
                    tal:define="screening view/screening">

            <form action="."
                tal:attributes="action request/URL" method="post"
                class="edit-form" enctype="multipart/form-data"
                id="zc.page.browser_form">

                <input type="hidden"
                    name="screening_id"
                    tal:attributes="value request/screening_id" />

        <div metal:use-macro="context/@@base-pageform.html/macros/form">
                <div metal:fill-slot="extra_info">

                    <table class="listing vertical reservation-info">
                        <tr>
                          <th i18n:translate="label_reservation_cinema">
                              Cinema
                          </th>
                          <td tal:content="context/Title" />
                        </tr>
                        <tr>
                            <th i18n:translate="label_reservation_film">
                                Film
                            </th>
                            <td tal:content="screening/film/Title" />
```

```
                    </tr>
                    ...
                </table>

                ...

            </div>
        </div>
    </form>
    </tal:main-macro>
</metal:main>
```

This template uses a macro in the default form template, `@@base-pageform.html`, which in turn takes care of all the form fields, actions, and validation. Notice how we pass the screening ID along as a hidden form field — without it, the `action_reserve()` handler would not be able to work out which `Screening` to construct a `Reservation` for, and we would lose the screening information if the form was reloaded after an error.

Here is a screenshot of the finished form:

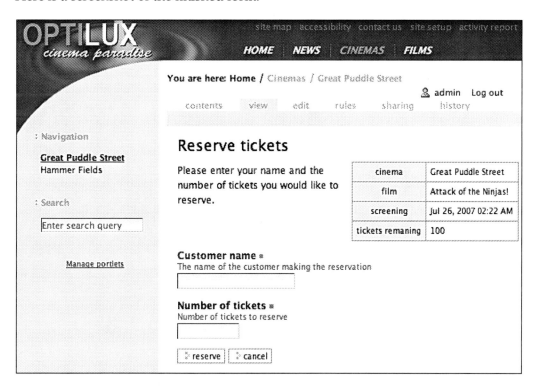

Summary

In this chapter, we have covered:

- Some rules of thumb about when to consider using a relational database instead of the ZODB
- How to connect to a relational database using the SQLAlchemy library
- How to create and register a new Plone control panel page
- Some design principles for abstracting database operations into utilities
- A few tips for testing database operations
- Some examples of how to integrate database-backed views and forms into the Plone user interface

Of course, we have just scratched the surface of what SQLAlchemy can do. You are encouraged to read its documentation, found at `http://sqlalchemy.org`.

In the next chapter, we enable members of the public to make ticket reservations using the views created in this chapter, when we design the user management policy of the site.

13

Users and Their Permissions

So far, we have focused on building functionality. Although we have introduced new permissions where appropriate, we have not yet considered user and role management in detail. It is now time to define exactly who can do what, when.

We will begin this chapter by defining a membership policy for our application. We will also show how to attach additional metadata to a user and look at configuring an area of a Plone site to support collaboration. Finally, we will point to a few more advanced technologies that may be appropriate if the built-in infrastructure cannot meet your needs.

Defining a Membership Policy

Let us take a look at the requirements from Chapter 2 that have an impact on how users are managed.

11	Customers should not need to log in to use the site, but a username and password should be required when they wish to reserve tickets.	Medium
12	Logged-in customers should have easy access to their preferred cinema or cinemas, e.g. those in their area.	Medium
15	The site should support cinema staff in developing future programming and promotions through a private collaborative workspace.	Low

In addition, other requirements make it clear that staff members will need to be represented as users distinct from customers. These users may have elevated permissions in certain parts of the site, for example to update *Cinema* information or add new *Film*s and *Promotion*s.

As usual, the best place to start is Plone's built-in functionality. Through the **Users and Groups** control panel, we can define new groups, create new users (also known as *members*), assign users to groups, and give roles to individuals and groups.

When they are first created, users are given the global *Member* role. Through the **Sharing** tab, which is available on most content objects, we can give **local roles**— those that apply only to a particular folder of the site — to specific users groups. These roles include *Editor* (can edit content), *Reader* (can view private content) and *Contributor* (can add new items to folders).

By default, users must be added by administrators, and passwords are generated and emailed for newly created accounts. Both of these policies can be changed in the **Security** control panel.

In Chapter 6, we anticipated the need to separate staff users from users representing members of the public. Thus, we created the *StaffMember* role and granted it to a new group called *Staff*. We can use this pair in two different ways:

- By granting permissions to the *StaffMember* role, either site-wide or as part of a workflow, we can let staff users perform tasks that regular members cannot.

- By assigning local roles to the *Staff* group, we can give staff special privileges in a particular area of the site. For example, a private folder could be invisible to regular users, but made available to all staff by granting the *Reader* local role to the *Staff* group.

We can refine this policy by adding additional groups. For example, the site administrator could decide to delegate responsibility for managing all cinemas in some *northern region* to a particular group of employees. The administrator could hence create a new group called *Northern Region* and grant this group the *Editor* local role, using the **Sharing** tab, in a particular *Cinema Folder* containing all northern region cinemas.

While staff users can be managed explicitly, members of the public are likely to want to sign up to the site themselves. They will not be given the chance to add any content, but will be granted permissions for activities such as rating movies and reserving tickets. Since these are the most common type of *user* (or perhaps, the least controllable), it makes sense to manage them using the default *Member* role.

 Note that unlike in previous versions, member home folders are disabled by default in Plone 3. Granting local roles such as *Contributor* (*can add*) in specific folders often makes more sense than distributing content into folders owned by different users. You can enable user folders in the **Security** control panel if you need them, though.

Updating the Site Policy Product

To support our use case, we need to make only minor changes to Plone's out-of-the-box membership functionality:

- Add the *StaffMember* role and *Staff* group.
- Disable the personal **Dashboard** for regular members. They should not need to have personalized portlets.
- Ensure that anonymous users can register themselves as site members.

We have already added the *StaffMember* role and *Staff* group, in Chapter 6. The last two points can be achieved by adding the following to `profiles/default/rolemap.xml` in the `optilux.policy` product:

```
<permissions>
    ...
    <!-- This disables the dashboard for regular members -->
    <permission name="Portlets: Manage own portlets" acquire="False">
        <role name="Manager" />
        <role name="StaffMember" />
    </permission>
    <!-- This allows anonymous visitors to register for the site -->
    <permission name="Add portal member" acquire="False">
        <role name="Manager" />
        <role name="Anonymous" />
    </permission>
</permissions>
```

The first stanza ensures that the *Member* role does not have the ability to manage personal portlets, which in turn disables the dashboard. The second allows *Anonymous* users to create new members for themselves, which enables the **Register** link. The **Security** control panel actually alters this permission when you change the appropriate setting there.

Of course, there are corresponding tests in `tests/test_setup.py`:

```
def test_manage_own_portlets_permission(self):
    permissions = [r['name'] for r in
      self.portal.rolesOfPermission('Portlets: Manage own portlets')
          if r['selected']]
    self.failUnless('StaffMember' in permissions)
    self.failIf('Member' in permissions)

def test_add_portal_members_permission(self):
    permissions = [r['name'] for r in
```

```
                    self.portal.rolesOfPermission('Add portal member')
                        if r['selected']]
            self.failUnless('Anonymous' in permissions)
            self.failUnless('Manager' in permissions)
```

We will not encode other policy decisions relating to specific content items, users, or local roles in the policy product. These are better left to site administrators, who may use techniques such as those just outlined to achieve an appropriate site structure.

Of course, we have been implying other aspects of the member policy throughout the book. For example, when we built the ticket reservation functionality in the previous chapter, we ensured that the relevant permissions were only granted to the *Member* role. When we built an administrator's report in Chapter 11, we restricted it to the *Manager* role. The choices here were mostly obvious from the requirements and easily implemented by relying on Plone's standard roles.

 Always protect views and other functionality with appropriate permissions, and create new permissions when none of the standard ones are a good match. Assign sensible default roles to new permissions, and attempt to model your site membership policy as much as possible on standard roles such as *Member*, *Reviewer*, and *Manager*.

Managing Member Metadata

In addition to considering the permissions we grant to different types of members in the site, we often want to manage some additional metadata about each user. Plone's standard member profile information, which can be accessed from the **Personal Preferences** form, covers the basics.

It is not difficult to add new member properties, however. In this case, we want to store one or more *home* cinemas for each site user.

The `portal_memberdata` tool keeps track of which user properties are available. We can use GenericSetup to add a new property. In `optilux.cinemacontent`'s `profiles/default` folder, we have a new file called `memberdata_properties.xml`:

```
<?xml version="1.0"?>
<object name="portal_memberdata" meta_type="Plone Memberdata Tool">
 <property name="home_cinemas" type="lines"></property>
</object>
```

As with all Zope property sheets, a `lines` property contains a list of strings, delimited by newlines when it is input. You can set a default value inside the `<property />` tag, though in this case we want the default to be an empty list.

To allow users to add or remove cinemas on this list, we will register a new viewlet on the main view of a *Cinema*. This is similar to the film ratings viewlet we added in Chapter 11. It can be found in `browser/mycinema.py`:

```python
from zope.interface import implements
from zope.viewlet.interfaces import IViewlet

from Acquisition import aq_inner
from Products.Five.browser import BrowserView
from Products.Five.browser.pagetemplatefile import
ViewPageTemplateFile
from Products.CMFCore.utils import getToolByName

from optilux.cinemacontent.interfaces import IRatings

class MyCinemaViewlet(BrowserView):
    """Viewlet for allowing users to set a "home" cinema
    """

    implements(IViewlet)

    template = ViewPageTemplateFile('mycinema.pt')

    def render(self):
        if self.available():
            return self.template()
        else:
            return ''

    def __init__(self, context, request, view, manager):
        super(MyCinemaViewlet, self).__init__(context, request)
        self.__parent__ = view
        self.view = view
        self.manager = manager
        self.membership = getToolByName(context, 'portal_membership')

    def update(self):

        if not self.available():
            self.is_home = False
        else:
            cinema = aq_inner(self.context)
            member = self.membership.getAuthenticatedMember()

            cinema_code = cinema.cinema_code
            home_cinemas = list(member.getProperty('home_cinemas', []))

            if self.request.has_key('optilux.cinemacontent.mycinema.
            Toggle'):
                if cinema_code in home_cinemas:
```

```
                                home_cinemas.remove(cinema_code)
                        else:
                                home_cinemas.append(cinema_code)
                        member.setProperties(home_cinemas=home_cinemas)

                self.is_home = (cinema_code in home_cinemas)

        def available(self):
                return not self.membership.isAnonymousUser()
```

Here, we obtain a member object using the `portal_membership` tool.

 An alternative would have been to use the `getUserById()` method on the `acl_users` user folder object. This is because member properties are set on the underlying user object, not the CMF member data wrapper that is applied to the user returned from `portal_membership`'s `getAuthenticatedMember()` and `getMemberById()`.

You can use `getProperty()` to read a property and `setProperties()` to set one or more properties.

Everything else in the code listing above is just logic to determine how to render the viewlet. The template in `browser/mycinema.pt` is trivial, containing only a toggle button. Naturally, there is also a registration for the viewlet in `browser/configure.zcml`.

To give the user quick access to their *home* cinema or cinemas, we will add a new portlet. This is similar to the portlet we created for promotions in Chapter 10. In `portlets/mycinema.py`, we have:

```
from zope.component import getMultiAdapter
from zope.interface import implements

from plone.app.portlets.portlets import base
from plone.memoize.instance import memoize
from plone.portlets.interfaces import IPortletDataProvider

from Products.Five.browser.pagetemplatefile import
ViewPageTemplateFile

from Acquisition import aq_inner
from Products.CMFCore.utils import getToolByName

from optilux.cinemacontent.interfaces import ICinema
from optilux.cinemacontent import CinemaMessageFactory as _

class IMyCinemaPortlet(IPortletDataProvider):
    pass
```

```
class Assignment(base.Assignment):
    implements(IMyCinemaPortlet)

    @property
    def title(self):
        return _(u"My cinema")

class Renderer(base.Renderer):

    # render() will be called to render the portlet

    render = ViewPageTemplateFile('mycinema.pt')

    @property
    def available(self):
        return len(self._cinema_codes()) > 0

    def cinemas(self):
        context = aq_inner(self.context)
        cinema_codes = self._cinema_codes()
        catalog = getToolByName(context, 'portal_catalog')
        for brain in catalog(cinema_code = cinema_codes,
                             object_provides = ICinema.__identifier__):
            yield dict(title=brain.Title,
                       address=brain.Description,
                       url=brain.getURL())

    @memoize
    def _cinema_codes(self):
        context = aq_inner(self.context)
        portal_state = getMultiAdapter((context, self.request),
                                       name="plone_portal_state")
        if portal_state.anonymous():
            return []
        return portal_state.member().getProperty('home_cinemas', [])

class AddForm(base.NullAddForm):
    def create(self):
        return Assignment()
```

Again, we use getProperty() to access member data.

> The member() function of the plone_portal_state view returns a
> cached copy of the current member. This is the same object as the one
> obtained from portal_membership.getAuthenticatedMember(),
> but it is only looked up once per request.

There are also an associated template in `portlets/mycinema.pt`, the appropriate component registration in `portlets/configure.zcml`, installation instructions in `profiles/default/portlets.xml`, and tests in `tests/test_portlet_mycinema.py`.

Here is a screenshot showing both the viewlet and the portlet:

Of course, these are just two examples of how to use custom member data. Another interesting option may be to create a form to make a particular set of member properties editable. This could use `zope.formlib` as we learned in Chapter 11. An interface representing the member schema could be used to create form fields. The action handler would use the syntax we have seen in this chapter to set member properties for the currently authenticated member, perhaps via a context adapter as we used for the control panel in Chapter 12. The form itself could be made available via an action, installed with an `actions.xml` import step as we did with the two custom forms in Chapter 11.

Collaborative Workspaces

Many sites demand some form of collaboration and sharing of content among a subset of users. For example, you could want to set up a *workspace* for a particular project or team.

Collaborative workspaces in Plone can be as simple as appropriately configured folders:

- A workspace folder could be private and thus invisible to regular members.
- A particular group could be given the local role *Reader* on the **Sharing** tab. They would thus be able to view the folder's contents.

- The same group could be given the local role *Contributor*, allowing them to create new content items.

- The **Restrict...** option in the **Add** menu could be used to restrict which content types these users would be allowed to add.

- If applicable, a local workflow policy could be installed, using CMFPlacefulWorkflow, which ships with Plone, but is not installed by default.

There are various products available to make it easier to set up all of this. Teamspace (`http://plone.org/products/teamspace`) is one of the most established and powerful ones, though it is aimed mostly at integrators and developers who wish to extend it.

Therefore, we will show how to use `borg.project`, which wraps the functionality outlined above up into a simple folderish content type called a *Project Workspace*. To install it, we must declare it as a dependency of `optilux.policy`. In the latter's `setup.py` file, we have:

```
install_requires=[
  # -*- Extra requirements: -*-
  "borg.project>=1.0b1,<2.0",
],
```

Since `borg.project` is in the Cheese Shop, this will cause it to be downloaded and installed when we re-run buildout, with:

$ ./bin/buildout

We also need to make sure its components are registered, by adding the following to `optilux.policy`'s main `configure.zcml`:

```
<include package="borg.project" />
```

To install this new product automatically when the policy product is installed, we amend `Extensions/Install.py` to contain:

```
PRODUCT_DEPENDENCIES = ('RichDocument',
                        'optilux.cinemacontent',
                        'borg.project',)
```

 `borg.project` is also interesting because it is written for Plone 3 only, using `zope.formlib` and various Plone 3 features, such as add forms and content types based on `plone.app.content` instead of Archetypes. See `http://cheeseshop.python.org/pypi/borg.project`.

With this installed, an administrator can add new workspaces in any folder. These start out private, with access granted only to *team members*. Team members are explicitly assigned, either user-by-user or by referencing one or more groups. The administrator can also define which content types are addable inside the folder.

Inside the workspace, team members are automatically given a local role called *TeamMember*. There is a local workflow policy for project content, which takes this role into account.

Here is a screenshot of the form used to configure a new project workspace:

Advanced Member Management Options

These relatively simple additions and customizations meet all our requirements. As with other aspects of Plone, the less you need to deviate from the out-of-the-box configuration, the better. However, there are times when you need a bit more power.

The Pluggable Authentication Service

At the root of every Zope instance, there is a **user folder**, called `acl_users`. User folders provide functionality for authenticating, authorizing, finding, and inspecting users. The user folder in the Zope application root typically contains only the main administrator user. There is a more specific user folder inside each Plone site, also called `acl_users`, which manages regular users.

Since Plone 2.5, user folders are powered by **PAS**—the *Pluggable Authentication Service*. This is a very flexible kind of user folder, which delegates responsibility for managing numerous aspects of site membership to different plug-ins. Plug-ins can perform functions such as extracting user credentials from a request, authenticating these credentials, creating a user object for a particular user ID, providing user properties, assigning global or local roles, and enumerating a user's assigned groups.

This structure affords great flexibility. For example, it would be possible to have an extraction plug-in looking for a username in an HTTP cookie, an authenticating plug-in checking an LDAP directory, and a user property plug-in reading user data from an SQL database. Unfortunately, this flexibility means that PAS can be complex. The fact that the user interface in the `acl_users` folder in the ZMI is a little unwieldy does not help either.

You should rarely need to write custom PAS plug-ins, but it is an option if your needs are quite specific. There is a PAS reference guide at `http://plone.org/documentation/manual/pas-reference-manual`, which contains more detail on the different PAS interfaces, as well as examples of custom plug-ins.

Membrane and Remember

Membrane (`http://plone.org/products/membrane`) is a library that allows a developer to model users and groups as Archetypes content objects. This can sometimes make it easier to manage and browse users and groups. For example, a group could be a folderish content type, and users in that group could be objects inside the folder. The same users could be members of additional groups via references. Member properties are automatically extracted from the schemata of content types. A combination of marker interfaces and adapters are used to control various aspects of users and groups.

On its own, Membrane is purely a developer's tool. It is implemented as a series of PAS plug-ins which may or may not be used by a particular application. It makes no attempt at integrating with the standard member management user interface, such as the **Users and Groups** control panel. However, a product called Remember (`http://plone.org/products/remember`) is an attempt to fashion something close to Plone's standard member types using Membrane, in order to give developers a flexible base on which to build if they wish to have something similar to the standard behavior. This also enables support for Plone's standard member management user interface.

Membrane and Remember are beyond the scope of this book. However, with the skills you have learned in this and previous chapters, you should be fully equipped to use either of these tools. The examples and documentation that come with Membrane should get you going.

Summary

In this chapter, we have looked at:

- The user and group management features that Plone gives us out of the box
- How we may conceptualize a membership policy for the Optilux website
- How to add and use new user properties
- Options for more advanced member management

In the next chapter, we will look at how to improve the user experience with *KSS*—Plone's new AJAX framework.

14
Rich User Interfaces with KSS

As a platform for graphical user interfaces, the humble web browser is fairly limited. Web applications have exploded in popularity because they are easy to write and deploy, not because they offer a superior user experience compared to desktop applications. There are a limited number of standard controls, and the stateless nature of HTTP means frequent round trips to the server.

More recently, web developers have started to make use of high-level JavaScript libraries to provide richer user interfaces with more advanced client-side interaction patterns. This is often referred to as **AJAX**, which stands for "Asynchronous JavaScript And XML", referring to the technologies involved. In this chapter, we will learn about **KSS**, the AJAX framework used in Plone 3.

Understanding KSS

KSS, which stands for **Kinetic Style Sheets**, takes a non-invasive approach to AJAX programming.

 In fact, KSS used to stand for something else, which turned out to be an expletive in Norwegian.

Given Plone's attention to accessibility and graceful degradation in older browsers, it was never an option to make JavaScript functionality so integral that the system would not work in browsers without JavaScript support. Therefore, Plone's developers have adopted the following philosophy:

Build applications that work without JavaScript first, and add JavaScript only to enhance the user experience for those who are able to use it.

Secondly, most Plone programmers are more comfortable with Python than JavaScript. KSS takes the view that dynamic page logic should primarily be controlled from Python.

As users of KSS, we will typically:

- Add appropriate CSS classes and IDs to HTML tags in page templates, in order to allow KSS events to be bound to these elements.

- Write a *KSS style sheet* specifying which actions we want to take place. Actions are bound to specific events on specific elements, using a CSS-like syntax.

- Write the server-side logic to be invoked as KSS actions. These will typically send a number of commands back to the client-side action processor.

When Plone loads a KSS-enabled page, the following sequence of events occurs:

1. *KSS style sheets* may be included in the page using `<link />` tags, much in the same way as CSS style sheets are.

2. Each file is parsed by the KSS framework as soon as the page is loaded. This will cause *actions* specified in the KSS style sheets to be bound to client-side events, such as the clicking of a particular button or the triggering of a timer.

3. When a KSS-bound *event* occurs, the associated action will be invoked. This may simply be some client-side effect or behavior, but it usually involves an asynchronous request to the server. This does not cause the page to be reloaded.

4. The server-side action performs some application-specific operation or calculation.

5. The server-side action assembles a response consisting of one or more *commands*, and sends them back to the client. Commands are made available through plug-ins. Several plug-ins are included with Plone, covering primitive operations such as inserting or changing some text in the page, as well as higher-level constructs such as refreshing a portlet.

6. The client-side library executes the commands it was given.

This approach avoids the need to inject JavaScript directly into page templates. In fact, most AJAX-like tasks can be achieved without touching JavaScript at all.

It is also possible to extend the KSS command set and provide new client-side actions. This should rarely be necessary, though in some cases it may add convenience or facilitate performance optimizations. Writing new KSS plug-ins is beyond the scope of this book, but you can find out more from `http://kssproject.org`.

KSS-Enabling Film Ratings

In Chapter 11, we added the ability for users to rate films displayed on the Optilux website. We did so with a viewlet containing a form. This works fine without JavaScript, but it is cumbersome to require a full page reload only to update this one viewlet. Let us therefore look at how we can improve this user experience with KSS.

We will take the following approach:

- Bind a KSS server-side action to the rating buttons shown in the viewlet. This will be invoked via an asynchronous request.
- Ensure that the default button behavior (which would cause the form to be submitted and thus the page to be reloaded) is disabled when the KSS handler is in use.
- In the server-side action handler, rate the film the same way that we did in the `update()` function of the viewlet.
- Send back a command to refresh the viewlet, so that it takes the new rating into account.

None of this should compromise the existing functionality, which will still be there for users with JavaScript turned off.

The Kinetic Style Sheet

In the `optilux.cinemacontent` package, under the `browser/` directory, we have a file called `cinemacontent.kss`, containing:

```
#film-rating-box input:click {
    evt-click-preventdefault: true;
    action-server: rateFilm;
    rateFilm-vote: kssAttr('vote');
}
```

The first line is a CSS-like selector, in this case matching a *click* event on an `<input />` element inside the node with ID `film-rating-box`. We make sure that the browser will not submit the form as normal when this event is caught, by setting `evt-click-preventdefault` to `True`. Instead, we ask for the `rateFilm` server-side action to be invoked. This takes a `vote` parameter, which we set to the value of a variable encoded in the page. We will see how in a moment.

We register this file as a browser resource in `browser/configure.zcml`:

```
<browser:resource
    name="cinemacontent.kss"
    file="cinemacontent.kss"
    />
```

Our new KSS style sheet needs to be included in the page, with a tag such as:

```
<link rel="kinetic-stylesheet" type="text/css"
  href="http://localhost:8080/optilux/++resource++cinemacontent.kss" />
```

We could add something like this to our page templates, but it is often easier to use the KSS registry, managed by the `portal_kss` tool. This is similar to `portal_css`, which manages CSS style sheets, and `portal_javascripts`, which manages JavaScript files. By visiting this tool in the ZMI, you can enable or disable particular KSS files.

 In common with the `portal_css` and `portal_javascripts` tools, the `portal_kss` tool has a **Debug** mode. Enable this during development, to disable caching and merging of KSS resources. Turn it off when the site moves to production.

To add a new resource to the KSS registry during site setup, we can use a GenericSetup import step. In `profiles/default/kssregistry.xml`, we have:

```
<object name="portal_kss" meta_type="KSS Registry">
 <kineticstylesheet cacheable="True" compression="safe"
cookable="True"
    enabled="1" expression="" id="++resource++cinemacontent.kss"/>
</object>
```

If you run this import step from `portal_setup` or re-install the `optilux.cinemacontent` product, you should see a new entry in the `portal_kss` tool for `++resource++cinemacontent.kss`.

Page Template Markup

As is often the case during KSS development, we need to ensure that the rendered page contains enough context to unambiguously bind the action. Therefore, we will add an ID to the ratings viewlet, in `browser/ratings.pt`:

```
<dl id="film-rating-box"
    ...
                Did you like this film?
```

```
<input
    class="kssattr-vote-yes"
    type="submit"
    name="optilux.cinemacontent.ratings.VotePositive"
    value="Yes"
    i18n:attributes="value"
    i18n:name="yes_button"
    />
<input
    class="kssattr-vote-no"
    type="submit"
    name="optilux.cinemacontent.ratings.VoteNegative"
    value="No"
    i18n:attributes="value"
    i18n:name="no_button"
    />
    . . .

</dl>
```

This corresponds to the CSS selector in the `cinemacontent.kss` file. Also note the peculiar CSS classes assigned to two input buttons. These are not used for styling and have no effect if KSS is not being used. Instead, they encode some additional information, which is passed along to the server-side action in a parameter.

 This overloading of the `class` attribute is not ideal, but is the only approach that works with the XHTML 1.0 Transitional doctype that Plone uses. KSS also supports an XML namespace approach, so that we could have written `kss:vote="yes"`. However, since HTML allows any number of CSS classes to be applied to the same node, having extra attributes there is harmless and does not preclude you from using additional CSS classes for styling.

Recall the following line from the KSS style sheet:

```
rateFilm-vote: kssAttr('vote');
```

The `kssAttr('vote')` syntax will look for a class called `kssattr-vote-<value>` on the matched node, and extract the `<value>` part. It is also possible to fetch this parameter from any parent of the matched node, by passing `true` to the optional second parameter of `kssAttr()`, like:

```
kssAttr('someparameter', true);
```

Here, we have simply hard-coded the string values `"yes"` and `"no"` in the page template, but if necessary you can construct parameters dynamically using `tal:attributes`. You can also use several parameters at once, separating them by whitespace. Below is a more involved example, from `calendar.pt` in `plone.app.portlets`:

```
<a href="#" rel="nofollow"
        title="Previous month"
        tal:define="prevMonthMonth view/prevMonthMonth;
                    prevMonthYear view/prevMonthYear"
        tal:attributes="...
                    class string:kssCalendarChange \
                    kssattr-year-${prevMonthYear} \
                    kssattr-month-${prevMonthMonth} \
                    calendarPrevious;"
    ... >
```

The parameters `year` and `month` are dynamically calculated KSS attributes. `kssCalendarChange` and `calendarPrevious` are used for KSS selector matching and styling, respectively.

Server-Side Logic

Let us now look at the server-side action. This was referenced in the KSS style sheet with:

```
action-server: rateFilm;
rateFilm-vote: kssAttr('vote');
```

During invocation of an action, KSS will attempt to call `rateFilm` on the current context, passing the specified parameters. That is, it will send an HTTP POST request to a URL like `http://localhost:8080/optilux/films/some-film/rateFilm`, with a parameter named `vote`.

A server-side action is most commonly implemented as a view. In `browser/configure.zcml`, we have:

```
<browser:page
    for="optilux.cinemacontent.interfaces.IFilm"
    name="rateFilm"
    class=".ratings.DynamicRatings"
    attribute="rate_film"
    permission="zope2.View"
    />
```

The DynamicRatings class, in browser/ratings.py, looks like this:

```
from zope.interface import alsoProvides
from kss.core import kssaction
from plone.app.kss.plonekssview import PloneKSSView

from plone.app.layout.globals.interfaces import IViewView

from Acquisition import aq_inner
from Products.Five.browser import BrowserView

from optilux.cinemacontent.interfaces import IRatings

...

class DynamicRatings(PloneKSSView):

    @kssaction
    def rate_film(self, vote):
        vote = vote.lower()
        if vote not in ("yes", "no"):
            return

        portal_state = getMultiAdapter((self.context, self.request),
                                        name=u"plone_portal_state")
        if portal_state.anonymous():
            return

        ratings = IRatings(self.context)
        user_token = portal_state.member().getId()
        if user_token is None or not ratings.available(user_token):
            return

        ratings.rate(user_token, (vote == "yes"))
        # Now send the command back that we should refresh this viewlet
        # Because the viewlet is registered for IViewView, we need to
        # mark the KSS view (self) with this first.

        alsoProvides(self, IViewView)

        ksscore = self.getCommandSet('core')
        zopecommands = self.getCommandSet('zope')

        selector = ksscore.getHtmlIdSelector('film-rating-box')
        zopecommands.refreshViewlet(selector,
                                manager='plone.belowcontenttitle',
                                name='optilux.cinemacontent.ratings')
```

The first thing to note is that the view class inherits from `PloneKSSView`, which provides various utility methods and setup code. The rendering of the view is bound to a specific method – `rate_film()` – via the `attribute` parameter to `<browser: page />`. That is, this method is called when the view is rendered, rather than the more usual `__call__()`. The choice is arbitrary, although it makes it possible to share a single class (with a single constructor, and shared class variables and helper functions) among multiple views specified with different `attribute` parameters.

The `rate_film()` method expects the aforementioned `vote` request parameter, and is marked with the `@kssaction` decorator. This takes care of the rendering of KSS commands into XML, which is then returned to the waiting client-side handler. There is no need to provide an explicit return value.

The first half of the view contains the rating logic. It is very similar to the `update()` method for the ratings viewlet in the same file. There is nothing KSS-specific about this part. In a few instances, we abort and return nothing. These are essentially error conditions that should not happen. We could have raised an exception here as well, but it would only have shown up in the logs, not the browser window.

The second half of the view is concerned with sending KSS commands back to the client. KSS commands are collated in **command sets**, provided by various plug-ins and looked up by name. There are three main command sets that ship with Plone, called `core`, `zope`, and `plone`. We will cover these in more detail later in this chapter.

In this case, we want to tell KSS to refresh the ratings viewlet. Behind the scenes, this will look up and render the viewlet, returning it as a block of HTML with the instruction to replace the current viewlet with the updated version. The viewlet, from Chapter 11, was registered like this:

```
<browser:viewlet
    name="optilux.cinemacontent.ratings"
    for="optilux.cinemacontent.interfaces.IFilm"
    view="plone.app.layout.globals.interfaces.IViewView"
    manager="plone.app.layout.viewlets.interfaces.IBelowContentTitle"
    class=".ratings.RatingsViewlet"
    permission="zope2.View"
    />
```

Note that because the viewlet is registered for the `IViewView` marker interface, we need to apply this to the current view – that is, the KSS action view. Without doing so, we would get a component lookup error.

Recall from Chapter 11 that the IViewView marker interface is applied to the view instance during page rendering to denote the canonical *view* (i.e. the page under the **View** tab) of an object. It is not applied to the KSS view during an asynchronous request.

Like most KSS commands, the refreshViewlet() method from the zope command set expects a selector as its first parameter. This is needed so that the client-side logic knows what to refresh. Bear in mind that when a page is composed and returned to the browser, there is no longer any distinction between the HTML fragments that came from a particular viewlet and those that came from other parts of the page template.

It is possible to pass a string containing a CSS-like selector, but it is more efficient to use an HTML ID. Therefore, we use the getHtmlIdSelector() function from the core command set to obtain an object representing a particular node.

With this logic in place, you should now be able to test the new dynamic ratings portlet in the browser.

Debugging KSS

Debugging server-side KSS actions is no different from debugging regular views. For example, you can place the usual import pdb; pdb.set_trace() line in any action to drop into the debugger. Remember that while the debugger is halting execution, the KSS *spinner* will continue to be displayed in the browser, since KSS is waiting for a response. If you wait long enough (more than 4 seconds), KSS may give up and assume the connection to the server has been lost.

There is nothing to stop you from invoking the view that implements a server-side action directly and inspecting its response manually. For example, we could go to the URL http://localhost:8080/optilux/films/some-film/rateFilm?vote=yes, and look at the output in the browser's source view.

Firebug, that most essential of web developer tools, will display KSS log messages in its console.

Firebug is a plug-in to Firefox. You can get it from:
http://getfirebug.com

This can help you identify whether a particular KSS rule has been loaded, and identify any errors KSS may have caught. To see debug log output, turn the `portal_javascripts` tool to **Debug/Development mode** in the ZMI. Here is how it looks:

You can send debug messages to the log from your own KSS declarations. For example:

```
#my-node:click {
    action-client: log;
    log-message: 'About to try something tricky';
    ...
}
```

You can also use Firebug to inspect the exact nodes making up a page before and after a KSS command, or to watch the HTTP requests being sent by KSS.

Tests for KSS Commands

In Chapter 10, we described how to use `zope.testbrowser` for functional testing of the front end. Unfortunately, the test-browser is not JavaScript-aware. KSS itself uses Selenium (see `http://www.openqa.org/selenium`) for some of its tests. Selenium relies on browser automation, and is thus as JavaScript-capable as the browser. However, Selenium tests can be more cumbersome to set up and run.

Luckily, KSS affords us some abstractions, which make it easier to write tests for actions. We can assume that the core KSS functionality is adequately tested already, and it is not too much of a burden having to manually test that our specific KSS event handlers are bound properly on page load. It is more interesting to test the server-side logic, including both the functionality it provides and the commands it sends back.

The command payload is normally sent as XML. However, KSS comes with an alternative renderer that returns Python data structures — useless for the real world, of course, but very useful in tests. To set this up, we will use a custom test layer and base class for our KSS tests. These can be found in `tests/base.py`:

```python
from Products.Five import zcml
from Products.Five import fiveconfigure

from Testing import ZopeTestCase as ztc

from Products.PloneTestCase import PloneTestCase as ptc
from Products.PloneTestCase.layer import onsetup, PloneSite

from plone.app.controlpanel.tests import ControlPanelTestCase
from kss.core.tests.base import KSSLayer, KSSViewTestCase

@onsetup
def setup_optilux_cinemacontent():
    fiveconfigure.debug_mode = True
    import optilux.cinemacontent
    zcml.load_config('configure.zcml', optilux.cinemacontent)
    fiveconfigure.debug_mode = False

    ztc.installPackage('optilux.cinemacontent')

setup_optilux_cinemacontent()
ptc.setupPloneSite(products=['optilux.cinemacontent'])

...

class CinemaContentFunctionalTestCase(ptc.FunctionalTestCase):
    """Test case class used for functional (doc-)tests
    """

...

class CinemaContentKSSTestCase(CinemaContentFunctionalTestCase,
                                KSSViewTestCase):
    """Test case used for KSS tests
    """

    class layer(KSSLayer, PloneSite):
        pass
```

The new `CinemaContentKSSTestCase` base class mixes in the KSS test case class, which provides some additional test setup and utility methods. It also explicitly defines a **test layer** that includes both the KSS layer and the standard Plone layer we have been using implicitly up until now.

> A test layer is responsible for setup and tear-down of a collection of tests. For example, the Plone layer loads all of Plone's ZCML so that it does not need to be loaded for each and every test method. We could have used a test layer to load the `optilux.cinemacontent` ZCML files and install it as a product, but when we do not need to re-use the test setup in more than one package, it is easier to use the `@onsetup` decorator and deferred methods to hook into the `PloneSite` layer as we have done since Chapter 5. To see how the `PloneSite` layer works, look at `Products.PloneTestCase.layer`. To learn more about layers in general, take a look at the `testrunner-layers-api.txt` doctest in the `zope.testing` package.

We use the new test base class in `tests/test_doctests.py`:

```
import unittest
import doctest

from zope.testing import doctestunit
from zope.component import testing, eventtesting

from Testing import ZopeTestCase as ztc

from optilux.cinemacontent.tests import base

def test_suite():
    return unittest.TestSuite([

        ...

        # Test the KSS functionality for ratings
        ztc.ZopeDocFileSuite(
            'tests/dynamic_ratings.txt', package='optilux.
            cinemacontent',
            test_class=base.CinemaContentKSSTestCase,
            optionflags=doctest.REPORT_ONLY_FIRST_FAILURE |
                    doctest.NORMALIZE_WHITESPACE | doctest.ELLIPSIS),

        ...

        ])
```

The actual test is in `tests/dynamic_ratings.txt`, shown below, slightly abbreviated:

```
First, let us create a rateable film.
    >>> self.loginAsPortalOwner()
    >>> _ = self.portal.invokeFactory('Film Folder', 'films')
    >>> _ = self.portal.films.invokeFactory('Film', 'film')

    >>> from optilux.cinemacontent.interfaces import IRatings
    >>> film = self.portal.films.film
    >>> ratings = IRatings(film)

    >>> from Products.CMFCore.utils import getToolByName
    >>> portal_membership = getToolByName(self.portal,
        'portal_membership')

    >>> member = portal_membership.getAuthenticatedMember()
    >>> ratings.available(member.getId())
    True
    >>> ratings.score is None
    True
```

This command, from kss.core.tests.base, causes KSS commands returned from KSS actions to be rendered as dicts rather than an XML string. This makes them easier to introspect in tests.

```
    >>> self.setDebugRequest()
```

Let's say we liked this film. This should cause a change in the ratings, and return a command to render the ratings viewlet without the buttons.

```
    >>> view = film.restrictedTraverse('@@rateFilm')
    >>> result = view(vote="yes")
    >>> [(r['name'], r['selector']) for r in result]
    [('replaceHTML', 'film-rating-box')]
```

The 'replaceHTML' command has a parameter 'html' containing the HTML to be replaced.

```
    >>> print result[0]['params']['html']
    <dl id="film-rating-box" class="portalMessage info">...100%...
```

And let's check that the rating was indeed changed:

```
    >>> ratings.available(member.getId())
    False
    >>> ratings.score
    100
```

The call to `self.setDebugRequest()`, invoking a method from `KSSViewTestCase`, switches the command renderer. We traverse to the action view using `restrictedTraverse()`, and then call it as KSS would have done in an asynchronous request. The returned value is a list of commands, each represented by a dict. Take a look at the results in the debugger if you want to learn more about the KSS response.

A Brief KSS Reference

We will now take a closer look at the syntax of KSS style sheets and the most common commands used in client-side and server-side actions. For more details, please refer to `http://kssproject.org`.

Kinetic Style Sheet Syntax

We have already seen the general syntax for event handler declarations in KSS style sheets:

```
<CSS selector>:<eventname> {
    evt-<eventname>-<parameter>: <value>;

    action-[server|client]: <actionname>
    <actionnname>-<parameter1>: <value>;
    <actionnname>-<parameter2>: <value>;

    ... /* more action specifiers as necessary */
}
```

A KSS file can contain as many such declarations as are needed. The CSS selector follows CSS-like rules. Consult any good CSS reference for more details.

 Note that at the time of writing, you can only specify one CSS selector per action block. That is, you cannot add multiple alternative selectors separated by commas, as you can in CSS.

If the same selector is used in multiple declarations, their action specifiers will be merged according to CSS conventions. If a particular type of action is specified for one selector and then later specified again for an equivalent selector, the latter declaration will override the earlier one.

Sometimes, there are legitimate reasons to want to use the same actions for the same selector. In this case, you can specify a unique *instance* of the selector with a unique name in parentheses. Here is an example from some code that uses client-side actions to provide a toggle for showing or hiding *closed* items in a table listing:

```
/* Hide this button, remove the hiddenItem class from any closed
button */
#showClosedButton:click(show_button) {
    evt-click-preventdefault: true;

    action-client: toggleClass;
    toggleClass-classname: hiddenItem;

    action-client: removeClassName;
    removeClassName-kssSelector: css("#deliverablesTable tr.closed");
    removeClassName-name: hiddenItem;

    action-client: setStateVar;
    setStateVar-varname: showHidden;
    setStateVar-value: true;
}
/* At the same time, show the "show" button */
#showClosedButton:click(hide_button) {
    evt-click-preventdefault: true;

    action-client: toggleClass;
    toggleClass-kssSelector: htmlid(hideClosedButton);
    toggleClass-classname: hiddenItem;
}
```

When the #showClosedButton button is clicked, all rows in the #deliverablesTable table with the CSS class closed are made visible. They were previously hidden by having the hiddenItem class set. At the same time, the button #showClosedButton is hidden, and the previously hidden button #hideCloseButton is revealed, by toggling the hiddenItem class on both. The two uses of toggleClass are distinct and should not be merged. Therefore, we use two instances of the event selector: one called show_button and the other called hide_button.

Lastly, there is one special selector — document — which does not bind to a specific element, but to the HTML document itself. It will match exactly once when a page is loaded. This is normally combined with the load event:

```
document:load {
    action-client: log;
    log-message: 'Page loaded!';
}
```

Standard Events

Events are provided by client-side KSS plug-ins. The standard ones include:

Event name	Equivalent JS event	Trigger
click	onclick	The user clicks a button or link.
dblclick	ondblclick	The user double-clicks a button or link.
mousedown, mouseup, mousemove, mouseover, mouseout	onmousedown, onmouseup, onmousemove, onmouseover, onmouseout	Used to detect basic mouse operations. Note that these may be triggered concurrently with click and/or double-click events.
keypress	onkeypress	A key is pressed on the keyboard.
keyup, keydown	onkeyup, onkeydown	Basic key events. Again, these will be triggered concurrently with a keypress event.
focus	onfocus	The user moves focus to a particular form control.
blur	onblur	Focus leaves a particular form control.
change	onchange	The value of a form control is changed.
select	onselect	Text is selected in a text box.
submit	onsubmit	A form is submitted.
load	onload	The given element is loaded. Unlike the corresponding browser event, this can match any node, not only the entire document. It may also be triggered on content dynamically inserted into the page with a KSS action.
timeout	(N/A)	When a timeout event is bound, it will be associated with a new timer, and the given action will be executed each time the timer completes.

Unsurprisingly, the core set of KSS events correspond to the basic events available in JavaScript. Consult a JavaScript reference if you need to understand more about which types of events are triggered for which HTML elements, or how events behave in different browsers.

Inside the actions block, events can be configured using the evt- namespace. For example, here is how to set the delay for a timer:

```
#my-node:timeout {
    evt-timeout-delay: 2000;
    evt-timeout-repeat: True;
    ...
}
```

This sets the timeout to 2000 milliseconds, or 2 seconds. Other standard options include:

Event option	Used by	Effect
allowbubbling	All core events	Allow this event to "bubble" from child nodes. Use this if you want to have a selector on a parent node receive events occurring on child nodes. It is `false` by default.
preventbubbling	All core events	Prevent this event from "bubbling" to parent nodes. Use this if an event handler on a parent node should not be triggered if an event handler on a child node is invoked. It is `false` by default, but only has an effect if `allowbubling` is set to `true` on a parent node.
keycodes	Key events	Only react to the specified ANSI key codes. For example, key code 13 is **Enter**, and key code 27 is **Escape**.
preventdefault	click	Do not submit the form or follow the link that was clicked.
delay	timeout	Delay, in milliseconds, between timeout events.
repeat	timeout	If set to `false`, a timer will only run once.

Client-Side Actions

We have already seen how server-side actions (those named with `action-server`) refer to a view or other callable on the current context. There are also client-side actions, again provided by various plug-ins. For example:

```
#my-link:click {
    evt-click-preventdefault: True;
    action-client: log;
    log-message: "About to send a message";
    action-client: alert;
    alert-message: "I can't let you do that, Dave";
}
```

These execute without making a request to the server. The most common client-side actions include:

Action	Parameters	Effect
log	message	Send a message to the KSS log. You can view this with Firebug as well as other compatible log readers.
alert	message	Show an alert box for debug purposes.
replaceHTML, replaceInnerHTML	html, withKssSetup	Replace the matched node or the contents of the matched node with the given HTML string. If `withKssSetup` is set to `false`, no attempt is made at binding KSS events to any newly created nodes.
insertHTMLAfter, insertHTMLBefore, insertHTMLAsLastChild, inserTHTMLAsFirstChild	html, withKssSetup	Insert new HTML around or inside the matched node.
deleteNode, deleteNodeAfter, deleteNodeBefore	(none)	Delete the matched node, or the node immediately before or after it.
setAttribute	name, value	Set an attribute on the matched node.
setKssAttribute	name, value	Set a KSS attribute. This is equivalent to a class like `kssattr-<name>-<value>`.
setStyle	name, value	Set a CSS style on the matched node.
addClassName, removeClassName	name	Add or remove a particular CSS class on the matched node.
toggleClass	classname	Toggle (add or remove) the given CSS class on the matched node.
focus	(none)	Move the cursor to the matched node.
setStateVar	varname, value	Store an arbitrary name/value pair. This can be retrieved and passed to another command later.

By default, client-side actions operate on the node that was matched by the event selector. However, it is possible to specify an alternative selector by using the special -kssSelector parameter. In fact, we already saw this in the toggle button example earlier:

```
/* At the same time, show the "show" button */
#showClosedButton:click(hide_button) {
    evt-click-preventdefault: true;

    action-client: toggleClass;
    toggleClass-kssSelector: htmlid(hideClosedButton);
    toggleClass-classname: hiddenItem;
}
/* The reverse of the above two actions */
#hideClosedButton:click(hide_button) {
    evt-click-preventdefault: true;

    . . .

    action-client: addClassName;
    addClassName-kssSelector: css("#deliverablesTable tr.closed");
    addClassName-name: hiddenItem;

    . . .
}
```

Here, the first toggleClass action is told to operate on the element with HTML ID #hideClosedButton. The addClassName action is applied to every node matching the CSS query "#deliverablesTable tr.closed".

Note that an explicit selector is always specified when server-side actions return commands to the client.

Parameter Functions

There are a number of KSS functions that can be used when passing parameters to actions. For example:

```
input#my-textbox:change {
    action-server: spyOnChanges;
    spyOnChanges-value: currentFormVar('myfield');
    spyOnChanges-privacylevel: kssAttr('privacylevel', true);
}
```

The standard functions are:

Function	Description
formVar(<formname>, <varname>)	Send the current value of the given form variable (i.e. the field with a corresponding name attribute), from the form with the given name. It passes a raw string.
currentFormVar(<varname>)	Like formVar(), but only looks in the current form. The node matched by the event selector must be part of a form.
currentForm()	Used with the -kssSubmitForm parameter — see below.
nodeAttr(<attrname>, [recurse])	Get the value of the given attribute on the matched node. If the optional second parameter is true, recursively look at parent nodes to find the attribute.
kssAttr(<varname>, [recurse])	Get a KSS attribute. These are encoded in class attributes, with names like kssattr-<varname>-<value>, as described earlier. If the optional second parameter is true, recursively look at parent nodes to find the attribute.
nodeContent([includeChildren])	Get the textual content (CDATA) of the matched node. Newlines are converted to spaces. If the optional parameter is true, extract text from child nodes as well.
stateVar(<varname>)	Retrieve a value previously stored with the setStateVar client-side action.

Note that the formVar() and currentFormVar() functions can only be used to send simple string values. In particular, they are not aware of Zope form marshaling of multi-selection fields or defaults. For actions that need to process the form as if a *submit* button was pressed, you can use the special -kssSubmitForm parameter. Here is an example from CMFPlone's plone.kss:

```
#sharing-save-button:click {
  evt-click-preventdefault: true;
  action-server: updateSharingInfo;
  updateSharingInfo-kssSubmitForm: currentForm();
}
```

The line updateSharingInfo-kssSubmitForm: currentForm(); will cause the form that the #sharing-save-button element is in to be collated and sent to the server-side updateSharingInfo action. The form fields can be read from the request much as in a standard form handler as we saw in Chapter 11. If the element matched by the event selector is not inside the form to be submitted, you can pass the name of the form as a string instead of using the currentForm() function:

```
someAction-kssSubmitForm: 'some-form';
```

Server-Side Commands

As we have seen earlier in this chapter, server-side actions typically return a sequence of commands to the client-side KSS handler. These are provided in named command sets. So long as an action view class inherits from `PloneKSSView` and the action method is annotated with `@kssaction`, we can look up a command set, and then call a method on the returned object to queue up a command:

```
@kssaction
def some_view(self):
    core = self.getCommandSet('core')
    core.replaceHTML('.replaceable', '<b>Changed!</b>')
```

Most commands take a selector as their first parameter. As with client-side commands, the command will affect any nodes that are matched by its selector. If there are no matching nodes, this is not considered an error, but may be logged. In the example above, we use a string which is treated as a CSS selector. However, it is generally more efficient to use HTML IDs if possible.

The `core` command set also includes a few helper methods for obtaining appropriate selectors. These are:

Method	Selector type
`getSelector(type, selector)`	Get a selector of the given type—either `'htmlid'` or `'css'`.
`getCssSelector(selector)`	Shortcut to get a CSS-type selector.
`getHtmlIdSelector(selector)`	Shortcut to get an HTML id-type selector.

The 'core' Command Set

The `core` command set contains basic commands, which mostly correspond to the client-side actions outlined earlier.

Method	Effect
`replaceInnerHTML` `(selector, new_value,` `withKssSetup='True')`	Replace the contents of the selected node with the given string of HTML. If `withKssSetup` is set to `'False'`, no attempt is made at binding KSS events to any newly created nodes.
`replaceHTML(selector, new_value,` `withKssSetup='True')`	Replace the selected node and its contents with the given string of HTML.

Method	Effect
`insertHTMLAfter(selector, new_value, withKssSetup='True')`	Insert a string of HTML after the selected node. There are also `insertHTMLBefore()`, `insertHTMLAsFirstChild()`, and `insertHTMLAsLastChild()`, which accept the same parameters.
`setAttribute(selector, name, value)`	Set an HTML attribute on the selected node. Note that for cross-browser compatibility reasons, the `setStyle()` command should be used to manage the `style` attribute.
`setStyle(selector, name, value)`	Set a particular CSS style on the selected node.
`clearChildNodes(selector)`	Remove all child nodes for the selected node.
`deleteNode(selector)`	Delete the selected node. There are also `deleteNodeAfter()` and `deleteNodeBefore()`, which delete the node immediately after or before the selected node.
`copyChildNodesFrom(selector, id)`	Copy the child nodes of the node with the given ID, and make them the children of the selected node. The `copyChildNodesTo()` function takes the same parameters, but acts in reverse.
`moveNodeAfter(selector, id)`	Move the selected node immediately after the node with the given ID.
`setStateVar(varname, value)`	Set a client-side variable, which can later be retrieved with `stateVar()` in a KSS style sheet.
`toggleClass(selector, classname)`	Toggle (add or remove) the given CSS class on the selected node.
`focus(selector)`	Move focus to the selected node.

Please refer to `kss.core.plugins.core.interfaces` for more details.

The 'zope' Command Set

The `zope` command set contains higher-level functions relating to the composition of pages.

Method	Effect
`refreshProvider(selector, name)`	Refresh a named content provider—i.e. an element pulled into a page using the `provider:` TAL expression—located in the page at the node given by the selector. This can be used to refresh an entire viewlet manager, for example.
`refreshViewlet(selector, manager, name)`	Refresh the named viewlet found at the selected node. The `manager` parameter can either be the name of the viewlet's manager, or the actual viewlet manager instance.

Again, take a look at `plone.app.kss.commands.interfaces` for more details.

The 'plone' Command Set

Finally, the `plone` command set contains commands specific to Plone's user interface.

Method	Effect
`issuePortalMessage(message, msgtype='info')`	Show a standard information message box. In addition to `'info'`, the message type can be `'warn'` or `'error'`.
`refreshPortlet(portlethash, **kwargs)`	Refresh the given portlet. Look at `plone.portlets.utils` to find out how to calculate portlet hashes. Any keyword arguments will be passed to the renderer as if they were form parameters.
`refreshContentMenu()`	Refresh the content menu—the bar containing the **actions**, **state**, and **add item** drop-downs.

This command set is further described in `plone.app.kss.commands.interfaces`.

KSS-Enabling the "my cinema" Functionality

There is another piece of functionality that naturally lends itself to being KSS-enabled: the *my cinema* toggle button, shown on every cinema. Again, this is rendered by a viewlet. However, if the *my cinema* portlet is displayed, it may also need to be updated when the button is pressed.

The selector in `cinemacontent.kss` is simple:

```
#my-cinema-toggle input:click {
    evt-click-preventdefault: True;
    action-server: toggleMyCinema;
}
```

We have also added an ID, `my-cinema-toggle`, to the viewlet in `browser/mycinema.pt`.

The server-side action — the `toggleMyCinema` view — is again similar to the logic in the `update()` method of the corresponding viewlet. However, the KSS commands being sent back are a little more involved than they were for the film rating functionality. From `browser/mycinema.py`:

```
from zope.interface import alsoProvides
from zope.component import getMultiAdapter

from kss.core import kssaction
from plone.app.kss.plonekssview import PloneKSSView

from plone.app.layout.globals.interfaces import IViewView

from Acquisition import aq_inner
from Products.Five.browser import BrowserView
from Products.Five.browser.pagetemplatefile import \
    ViewPageTemplateFile
from Products.CMFCore.utils import getToolByName

from optilux.cinemacontent.interfaces import ICinema
from optilux.cinemacontent.browser.interfaces import IMyCinemasBox
from optilux.cinemacontent import CinemaMessageFactory as _

...

class DynamicMyCinema(PloneKSSView):
    implements(IMyCinemasBox)

    @kssaction
    def toggle(self):
        portal_state = getMultiAdapter((self.context, self.request),
            name=u"plone_portal_state")
```

```
if portal_state.anonymous():
    return

cinema = aq_inner(self.context)
member = portal_state.member()

cinema_code = cinema.cinema_code
home_cinemas = list(member.getProperty('home_cinemas', []))

enabled = True
if cinema_code in home_cinemas:
    home_cinemas.remove(cinema_code)
    enabled = False
else:
    home_cinemas.append(cinema_code)

member.setProperties(home_cinemas=home_cinemas)

# Refresh the viewlet with the toggle button

alsoProvides(self, IViewView)

ksscore = self.getCommandSet('core')
zopecommands = self.getCommandSet('zope')

selector = ksscore.getHtmlIdSelector('my-cinema-toggle')
zopecommands.refreshViewlet(selector,
                        manager='plone.belowcontentbody',
                        name='optilux.cinemacontent.mycinema')

plonecommands = self.getCommandSet('plone')

# Issue a status message that things have changed

if enabled:
    plonecommands.issuePortalMessage(
            _(u"This cinema is now a 'home' cinema."))
else:
    plonecommands.issuePortalMessage(
            _(u"This cinema is no longer a 'home' cinema."))

# Refresh any instances of the "my cinema" portlet. Here,
# we cheat
# and simply re-use the template from the mycinema portlet.

if not home_cinemas:
    # If there are no home cinemas, replace the portlet <dl />
    # with a blank <div /> with the same class. We do this so
    # that we can find the node again later if the user
    # toggles the cinema back on
```

```
                    ksscore.replaceHTML('.portletMyCinema',
                                    '<div class="portletMyCinema" />')
            else:
                # There are cinemas to display - render the portlet
                # template. This view will be the 'view' variable in the
                # template. This is okay, because we provide the
                # IMyCinemasBox interface, which the template is
                # expecting.

                self.home_cinemas = home_cinemas
                ksscore.replaceHTML('.portletMyCinema',
                self.portlet_template())
        portlet_template = ViewPageTemplateFile('../portlets/mycinema.pt')
        def cinemas(self):
            context = aq_inner(self.context)
            cinema_codes = self.home_cinemas
            catalog = getToolByName(context, 'portal_catalog')
            for brain in catalog(cinema_code = cinema_codes,
                            object_provides = ICinema.__identifier__):
                yield dict(title=brain.Title,
                        address=brain.Description,
                        url=brain.getURL())
```

In the KSS response, we first refresh the viewlet, much as we did for ratings. Then, we use the `issuePortalMessage()` function from the `plone` command set to present a standard Plone information box. Finally, we want to refresh the contents of the *my cinema* portlet, if it is displayed.

The `plone` command set includes a function for refreshing a portlet, based on a **portlet hash**. This is a string, which encodes certain information about a portlet. You will see portlet hashes around the portlets rendered in the standard columns. They are used to automatically refresh portlets in certain circumstances. However, it is difficult to predict the portlet hash for the *my cinema* portlet, because we cannot know how and where it may have been assigned by the site administrator — or whether it is even visible.

Instead, we cheat and update the block of HTML that is the portlet, using the low-level `replaceHTML()` command from the `core` command set. This will have no effect if the portlet is not displayed, since the selector will simply not match anything.

To avoid duplicating the rendering logic, we re-use the portlet's page template, but render it in the context of the `DynamicMyCinema` KSS view. The template only expects a method called `cinemas()` to be available on its view.

In order to make this requirement explicit, we have added a new interface called IMyCinemasBox, which is implemented by both the portlet renderer and the KSS view. To KSS of course, this is all immaterial. All it cares about is that it gets a string containing the HTML to replace, and a selector telling it what to replace.

Summary

In this chapter, we have learned:

- The philosophy behind KSS, Plone 3's new AJAX framework
- How to bind KSS actions to elements in the page, using a KSS style sheet
- How to write server-side actions
- How to construct sequences of KSS commands for the client to execute

The techniques covered here should suffice for most uses. To learn more about KSS, including how to create custom plug-ins, visit the KSS project's home page, at http://kssproject.org.

This is the last chapter in which we add new functionality to the Optilux Cinemas application. In the next chapter, we will outline how we might have taken the example even further, using what we have learned so far.

15
Next Steps

We have come far over the past fourteen chapters! The example application is now complete and sports a wide array of features, a powerful user interface, and integration with an external database system.

Hopefully, the pieces of the puzzle are now coming together, and you feel equipped to tackle your own needs. Feel free to borrow from the example code if it helps you achieve your own ends, and refer back to the preceding chapters if you need more clarification. If you are still stuck, take a look in Chapter 1 for some tips on how to get help from the Plone community. You may even find the author lurking in the chat room or on the mailing lists.

In this chapter, we will recap on the achievements to date, and suggest some avenues for further exploration.

Our Achievements So Far

Let us begin by revisiting the requirements from Chapter 2:

	Requirement	Status
1	The site should have a look and feel consistent with Optilux's corporate branding.	We built a custom theme in Chapter 8.
2	The site should show information about all of Optilux's cinemas.	This is accomplished using a combination of built-in, third-party, and custom content types.
3	Non-technical cinema staff should be able to update information about each cinema.	Plone's content type metaphors and standardized UI makes this possible.
4	The site should allow staff to highlight promotions and special events. These may apply to one or more cinemas.	There is a special **Promotion** content type, developed in Chapter 10 to support this, and a portlet to display relevant promotions.

	Requirement	Status
5	Cinema staff should be able to publish information about new films. It should be possible to update this information after publication.	The **Film** content type from Chapter 10 is used for this purpose.
6	Customers should be able to find out in which cinemas a particular film is showing, and which films are showing at a particular cinema. Note that the scheduling of films at cinemas is managed in an existing relational database.	In Chapter 12, we connected to an external *MySQL* database to find this information, and presented it using custom page templates and forms.
7	Only films that are currently showing or will be shown in the near future should be viewable.	This is achieved by setting "effective" and "expiration" dates on **Film** content.
8	Customers should be able to search and browse films by cinema, location, date/time or film name.	This is possible via the views of the various content types.
9	Customers should be able to reserve tickets online. Tickets will be picked up and payment taken at the cinema. Reservations must use Optilux's existing relational database based ticketing system.	We made this possible in Chapter 12, by providing a form to create new reservation records in the external database.
10	Cinema managers should be able to view reports on reservations and site usage.	We created a simple report in Chapter 11, but have not added more comprehensive reporting functions.
11	Customers should not need to log in to use the site, but a username and password should be required when they wish to reserve tickets.	The security and membership policy was defined in Chapters 6 and 13.
12	Logged-in customers should have easy access to their preferred cinema or cinemas, e.g. those in their area.	In Chapter 13, we added a new "home cinema" member property and a dedicated portlet for this purpose.
13	Customers should be able to email enquiries to the site manager if they have questions or feedback.	An enquiry form was created in Chapter 11.
14	Customers should be able to discuss and rate movies.	We added ratings in Chapter 11. Free-form discussion could be enabled using Plone's standard discussion functionality, or perhaps via a more powerful third-party product.

	Requirement	Status
15	The site should support cinema staff in developing future programming and promotions through a private collaborative workspace.	We incorporated such workspaces in Chapter 13, via a third-party product.

Of course, when the case study was designed, we picked requirements that we knew we could fulfill over the course of the book. However, if you are developing an application to sit on top of Plone, it is likely that many of your own requirements will reflect those listed in the table in general terms.

- The first thing customers ask for is usually custom branding. This was covered in Chapter 8.

- Customers also typically want to turn off a few of Plone's features, and change a few defaults. Although this can usually be done by a site administrator through the Web, we learned in Chapter 4 that customization is better done in a repeatable and testable manner, using file system code and GenericSetup profiles.

- There is a plethora of add-on products to be found at `http://plone.org/products` and elsewhere. In Chapter 7, we at looked how to integrate such components into a Plone deployment.

- Most non-trivial applications end up relying on custom content types to capture and manage domain-specific information. Schema-driven development with Archetypes makes it easy to define new content types. These can benefit from Plone's standard user interface paradigms. In Chapter 10, we looked at how to model requirements in terms of content objects, and then showed how to construct and install new content types.

- Also in Chapter 10, we learned how to create custom portlets. Portlets are useful for representing additional information, which is not tightly linked to the current content object.

- By relying on standard and generated forms to manage content objects in a consistent fashion, Plone applications tend to feature fewer custom forms and display templates than applications written for other platforms. Still, there is often a need for bespoke forms and views; we covered these in Chapter 11.

- Sometimes, we may want to create general components that augment existing Plone functionality. In Chapter 11, we saw how to use viewlets to hook into Plone's user interface. The film rating component developed there also demonstrated how to use adapters and annotations to attach additional information to existing content objects.

- Many organizations have existing relational databases, which they may need to integrate with Plone, and sometimes relational data models make more sense than Plone's content-centric approach. In Chapter 12, we looked at how to connect to external SQL databases.

- It is quite common to need to capture some additional information about users as part of an application. In Chapter 13, we saw how to manage additional member data.

- In Chapter 14, we learned how to make our user interface more responsive and dynamic using KSS, Plone's new AJAX framework.

Additional Functionality

Of course, there are still ways in which the example application could be improved. If it is useful to you, feel free to modify or extend it as you wish. We will suggest a few areas for improvement below.

Discussion and Participation

As a general trend, the Internet is becoming more collaborative and participative. It would be nice to give site members a few more tools to build communities around films and cinemas. Commenting on content objects can be enabled in `portal_types` and GenericSetup type profiles. However, this is rather rudimentary and not designed for hundreds of users engaging in lively discussion.

There are various discussion modules to be found at `http://plone.org/products`. One or more of these could likely work out of the box, though some additional integration with our custom content types and member properties may be desirable.

There are other forms of participative functionality that may be interesting, such as tagging or *sticky notes* for users to keep track of information about content. There are various implementations of such tools at `http://plone.org/products`. If a custom solution is required, it would likely depend on annotations for storing metadata and viewlets or portlets to provide a user interface, much as the ratings component from Chapter 11 did.

Additional Reporting

We created a report showing recent changes to films and cinemas in Chapter 11. There may be any number of additional reports that would be useful, but mostly they would work on the same principle: construct a catalog or database query and present the results in a page template.

For more comprehensive usage metrics, it may be better to look at general traffic analysis software, such as Google Analytics (see `http://www.google.com/analytics`) or AWStats (see `http://awstats.sourceforge.net`). In fact, Plone 3 has a control panel option for pasting in the type of tracking HTML and JavaScript code that these tools use. Furthermore Zope's `z2.log` file follows the Apache log file conventions and thus can be read by log analysis tools such as AWStats.

More Advanced Ticketing

The ticket reservations system we implemented in Chapter 12 is fairly rudimentary. There is no payment processing, and thus no way to ensure that customers do not reserve tickets that they never pick up.

For real-world usage, we would probably want to integrate with some kind of payment channel. There are various commercial services that can take payments on behalf of other websites, passing back a token to validate a transaction. Designing such a system is beyond the scope of this book, but after reading the preceding chapters, you should have the necessary knowledge to do so yourself. Most likely, a payments solution would involve requests to a remote service to authorize a payment, and one or more views to handle the responses this service would give.

There are existing e-commerce solutions at `http://plone.org/products`, which may provide the necessary infrastructure or be adaptable to a specific use case.

New Content Types

A lot of the functionality we have developed has been located in the `optilux.cinemacontent` package and centered around the **Cinema** and **Film** content types. It is very common for application-specific behavior to be tied to custom content types like this.

If we need to manage new types of information, we may well end up adding more content types to this package, or create a separate package providing functionality not directly related to *cinema content*.

Internationalization

Finally, if Optilux expands abroad, we may want to translate the application to different languages. We have been following good practices when defining user interface elements to allow for translation should we need it. However, since most bespoke web applications are monolingual (but not necessarily English!), we have not gone into the details of internationalization.

Translating Content

A truly multi-lingual website will offer its content in multiple languages. It is even possible to pick the right language automatically, because web browsers will send a *preferred* language as part of a request to the server.

Archetypes-based content types can be made translatable using a product called LinguaPlone (see http://plone.org/products/linguaplone). Using this would require some minor changes to the code in the optilux.cinemacontent package. Content authors would then be able to create translated versions of content items. Users would browse the site as normal, but only see content in their own language.

Please refer to the documentation that ships with LinguaPlone for more information.

Translating User Interface Strings

In addition to translating content, any text that is presented as part of the user interface would need to be translated. Zope and Plone rely on the popular GNU gettext (see http://www.gnu.org/software/gettext) system to manage **message catalogs**—lists of translated *messages*.

In fact, we have been marking strings bound for the user interface so that they can be translated throughout this book. Doing so is good practice. It introduces minimal overhead and makes life much easier should you need to translate some or all of your application in the future.

Internationalization tools can be used for more than just translating a system from English to Chinese. Sometimes, the differences between e.g. American and British English are significant enough to warrant translation. Other times, translation tools can be used to simplify or standardize the terminology used in a third-party component without having to customize its code directly.

For example, in page templates, we have used markup such as:

```
<a href="http://plone.org" title="The Plone home page"
   i18n:attributes="title title_plone_homepage;"
   i18n:translate="link_plone_homepage">Visit Plone's home page!</a>
```

The i18n:translate attribute specifies that the string inside the tag should be translated by looking up the link_plone_homepage **message ID**. i18n:attributes lists which attributes of the tag (in this case, only title) need to be translated and the associated message IDs. Multiple attribute-message ID pairs can be specified, separated by semicolons.

Message IDs are optional in both cases. If they are not specified, the full translated string is used. However, this can be more difficult for translators and is generally only useful for short, unambiguous strings of one or two words:

```
<a href="http://plone.org" title="Info"
   i18n:attributes="title"
   i18n:translate="">Info</a>
```

For strings originating from Python code, we have defined **message factories** and referenced them via the special name _():

```
from zope.i18nmessageid import MessageFactory
CinemaMessageFactory = MessageFactory('optilux.cinemacontent')

...

from optilux.cinemacontent import CinemaMessageFactory as _

...

title = schema.TextLine(title=_(u"Title"))
```

Translation extraction tools such as i18ndude (see http://plone.org/products/i18ndude) will be able to look for these strings in page templates and Python code, as well as in GenericSetup XML files and ZCML configuration files. From these, a **message catalog template** file is created with the extension .pot. Translation tools such as poEdit (see http://www.poedit.net), or indeed any text editor, can then be used to translate messages into .po files, which are placed in the i18n sub-directory of a product.

Again, the user's web browser will inform Plone which language is preferred. If possible, message strings rendered to page templates will be output in the preferred language, falling back on the default language if necessary.

To learn more about the tools of internationalization—or if you would like to help translate Plone itself—see http://plone.org/development/teams/i18n. The document at http://plone.org/documentation/how-to/i18n-for-developers is a useful reference for making sure page templates are translatable.

Summary

In this chapter, we have recapped on the progress to date and looked at a few improvements we could want to make to the example application in the future. We have also briefly touched on issues of internationalization.

This concludes Part 3 of the book. In Part 4, we will look at how to deploy the application to a production server and make sure it keeps running smoothly.

Part 4

Real-world Deployments

Server Management

Setting Up a Production Server

Authenticating with LDAP

Looking to the Future

16
Server Management

Up until now, we have been concerned mostly with developing code in a sandbox. We have loaded our development environment with development tools and turned on various debugging settings. Now it is time to move our code into a production environment, tighten up security, and configure Zope for maximum performance and stability.

Deployment Checklist

We should not expect to change any code to move from a development environment to live production. In brief, all we need to do is:

- Remove development and debugging tools from the environment
- Ensure that *debug mode* is turned off, both for Zope itself and for tools such as `portal_css`, `portal_javascripts`, and `portal_kss`, which have dedicated development mode settings
- Configure the Zope instance for performance and resilience, using Zope Enterprise Objects (ZEO)
- Ensure that Zope is started and stopped at appropriate times, for example during system startup
- To improve performance, set the `PYTHONOPTIMIZE` environment variable to 1 to ensure that Python is run as if with the -O option when Zope runs
- Schedule regular backups of Zope's database
- Set up log rotation and other regular maintenance

We would also normally configure another web server, such as Apache and/or a cache proxy, such as Squid or Varnish, in front of Zope. This will be covered in subsequent chapters.

Zope Enterprise Objects

During development, we have used a single instance of Zope, configured through our buildout environment. For live deployment, most sites will use **Zope Enterprise Objects** (**ZEO**). ZEO is a technology that allows multiple Zope instances (running on different ports) — known as **ZEO clients** — to access a shared instance of the ZODB, managed by the **ZEO server**. Using ZEO is a widely recognized best practice and has a number of advantages:

- The database (ZEO server) and application instances (ZEO clients) can reside on different machines for additional resilience and isolation.

- Even on a single machine, multiple ZEO clients will usually provide superior performance to a single instance configured with many threads. The usual rule of thumb when optimizing for performance is to use one ZEO client per processor core.

- Multiple ZEO clients can be load-balanced to improve performance. This requires a dedicated load balancing solution in front of Zope, since each ZEO client needs to run on a different address/port.

- Even if a single *primary* ZEO client is used to serve an application, having a secondary ZEO client on stand-by can be very useful for debugging and testing. For example, if the primary ZEO client instance hangs for some reason, the secondary instance can be used to salvage it (if you know what you are doing). This is the setup we will demonstrate in this chapter. However, you should find it relatively easy to configure ZEO in any of the scenarios above using what you will learn here.

Before adding ZEO to our buildout environment, let us look at how we can set up ZEO manually.

First, we must create a ZEO server instance. This can be done using the `mkzeoinstance.py` script, which is found in the `utilities` directory of a standard Zope installation (or possibly a `bin` directory, depending on how Zope was installed).

```
$ /path/to/zope/utilities/mkzeoinstance.py zeoserver
```

This creates a directory, which has, among other files, a configuration file `etc/zeo.conf`. Here is what it might look like:

```
%define INSTANCE /path/to/zeoserver

<zeo>
  address 8100
  read-only false
  invalidation-queue-size 100
```

```
</zeo>
<filestorage 1>
  path $INSTANCE/var/Data.fs
</filestorage>
<eventlog>
  level info
  <logfile>
    path $INSTANCE/log/zeo.log
  </logfile>
</eventlog>
<runner>
  program $INSTANCE/bin/runzeo
  socket-name $INSTANCE/etc/zeo.zdsock
  daemon true
  forever false
  backoff-limit 10
  exit-codes 0, 2
  directory $INSTANCE
  default-to-interactive true
  # user zope
  python /usr/bin/python2.4
  zdrun /path/to/zope/lib/python/zdaemon/zdrun.py
  logfile $INSTANCE/log/zeo.log
</runner>
```

This configures a single ZODB storage in var/Data.fs. Zope instances can then be configured to act as ZEO clients rather than defining their own file storage.

We described how to set up a Zope instance manually in Chapter 3. To configure such an instance for ZEO, edit the instance's etc/zope.conf and replace the <zodb_db main> section with:

```
<zodb_db main>
  mount-point /
  cache-size 5000
  <zeoclient>
    server localhost:8100
    storage 1
    name zeostorage
    var /path/to/instance/var
    cache-size 300MB
  </zeoclient>
</zodb_db>
```

Here, we assume that the ZEO server is running on the same machine as the instance and is configured to listen on the default port, 8100. Multiple client instances can be configured in this way, connecting to the same ZEO server, but they must each listen to a different port and/or IP address.

 Apart from the database configuration, the instance configuration under ZEO remains the same. In particular, each instance should hold a copy of (or reference to) the set of products and packages used in the application. The ZEO server does not manage application code.

To start Zope when ZEO is in use, we must first start the ZEO server, and then each instance. The ZEO server can be started using:

```
$ ./bin/zeoctl start
```

It can be stopped with:

```
$./bin/zeoctl stop
```

The ZEO client instances are still managed using `zopectl`. Each client must be started individually.

A Deployment Buildout

For the purposes of the Optilux application, we will continue to use our buildout environment to manage server configuration. In order to keep development and deployment separate, we will create a new `deployment.cfg` file, next to `buildout.cfg`. It looks like this:

```
[buildout]
extends =
    buildout.cfg

parts =
    plone
    zope2
    productdistros
    zeoserver
    primary
    secondary
[productdistros]
recipe = plone.recipe.distros
urls =
  http://plone.org/products/richdocument/releases/3.0/RichDocument-
3.0.tar.gz
```

```
nested-packages =
version-suffix-packages =
[zeoserver]
recipe = plone.recipe.zope2zeoserver
zope2-location = ${zope2:location}
zeo-address = 8100
[primary]
recipe = plone.recipe.zope2instance
zope2-location = ${zope2:location}
zeo-client = true
zeo-address = 8100
zodb-cache-size = 5000
zeo-client-cache-size = 300MB
user = admin:admin
http-address = 8080
debug-mode = off
verbose-security = off
eggs =
    ${plone:eggs}
    ${buildout:eggs}
zcml =
    optilux.policy
products =
    ${buildout:directory}/products
    ${productdistros:location}
    ${plone:products}
[secondary]
recipe = plone.recipe.zope2instance
zope2-location = ${zope2:location}
zeo-client = true
zeo-address = 8100
zodb-cache-size = 5000
zeo-client-cache-size = 300MB
user = ${primary:user}
http-address = 8081
debug-mode = on
verbose-security = on
eggs = ${primary:eggs}
zcml = ${primary:zcml}
products = ${primary:products}
zope-conf-additional =
    zserver-threads 1
```

First, notice that that this buildout configuration `extends` the default configuration, which means that buildout will treat values in that file as defaults for sections in this file with the same name. This allows us to keep the listing of eggs and other standard options in one place. We specify the parts `plone` and `zope2`, but their actual definitions are taken from the default `buildout.cfg`, as are the `eggs` and `develop` options from the main `buildout` section. Second, notice that we are not including any development tools, such as DocFinderTab, here.

> In fact, DocFinderTab is pretty harmless, and Clouseau, our other development tool, will be deactivated if Zope is not running in debug mode. Still, this configuration demonstrates a point, and it never hurt to be a little paranoid around production servers.

The `zeoserver` section uses the `plone.recipe.zope2zeoserver` recipe to set up a ZEO server in `parts/zeoserver`.

> See `http://cheeseshop.python.org/pypi/plone.recipe.zope2zeoserver` for more information about the options it supports.

The most important options are `zope2-location`, which we point to the Zope installation created by the `zope2` part, and the `zeo-adddress`.

Following this, we define two instances, `primary` and `secondary`, both using the `plone.recipe.zope2instance` recipe.

> See `http://cheeseshop.python.org/pypi/plone.recipe.zope2instance` for the full list of supported options.

By setting `zeo-client = true`, we turn them into proper ZEO clients, referencing the ZEO server at the given `zeo-address`. We also specify that the client should aim to cache up to 5000 objects from the ZODB in memory, and keep 300Mb free for a client-side ZEO cache. These settings should suffice for most production cases, but you may wish to tweak them. The **Database** section in the ZMI **Control_Panel** contains some statistics that may help you do so.

In this case, we want to use the primary instance to serve the site, and keep the secondary instance around for debugging purposes. Therefore, we turn debug mode and verbose security off for the publicly accessible instance, and leave them on for the secondary instance. We also add an additional line to the configuration file via the free-form `zope-conf-additional` option, reducing the number of threads for the secondary instance to one (the default is four). This can make debugging and maintenance easier, since there will only ever be one request going through that Zope instance at a time.

For the other options—user, eggs, zcml, and products—we make the settings in the primary section, and reference them for the secondary instance. This ensures that the two always stay in sync.

Moving the Code and Database to a Live Server

We can now move the buildout environment to the live server or a staging environment and re-build it using this new configuration file by using:

```
./bin/buildout -c deployment.cfg
```

Note that without specifying the configuration file explicitly, buildout would use the default buildout.cfg file instead, building us another development environment.

To start the ZEO server and the two clients, we can do:

```
$ ./bin/zeoserver start
```

```
$ ./bin/primary start
```

```
$ ./bin/secondary start
```

After a short delay, Zope should come up on ports 8080 and 8081. If something goes wrong during startup, you can use fg in place of start to run Zope in the foreground and inspect error messages. You can also check the log files in var/log/primary.log, var/log/secondary.log, and var/log/zeoserver.log.

When moving the buildout from development onto a server, the minimum you need to move is:

- The bootstrap.py script. Run this again on the server to re-build the buildout structure, including the bin/buildout script.
- The two configuration files, buildout.cfg and deployment.cfg.
- The full contents of the src/ and products/ directories, which contain the custom source code for this project.

If you use a version control system such as Subversion to manage your code, you could check these files into a repository, and tag a release when you are ready to move into staging or production. You can then check out the tag directly on the server.

Recall that the contents of the ZODB are stored in a file called `Data.fs`. During development, you will likely have created and deleted lots of objects here. Hopefully, you will also have followed the advice from Chapter 4 and made sure that site-specific configuration settings are made using a GenericSetup profile or Python code and are covered by unit tests. This should mean that you can set up the production site by creating a new Plone site in an empty ZODB and installing the *policy product* for your application.

Of course, in practice you may have an instance of the Zope site in your development or staging environment with data that you wish to move into the live environment. The easiest way of doing so is to copy the `Data.fs` file from one environment into another. When using buildout, this should live in `var/filestorage/Data.fs` (you do not need to copy the other files there; they will be re-created for you). To save space, you may want to pack the ZODB from the **Database** section of the **Control_ Panel** in the root of the ZMI first.

If you do not want to move the entire `Data.fs` file, you can use Zope's export/ import mechanism. In the root of the ZMI, find the Plone site and click **Import/ Export**. If you leave the default options and click **Export**, it will create a new file in `parts/instance/var/` (assuming this is the home of the development instance as created by buildout) with an extension of `.zexp`. Move this to `parts/primary/ import` on the production server, and click **Import/Export** in the root of the ZMI there. You should be able to select the file in the **Import file name** list there, and click **Import**.

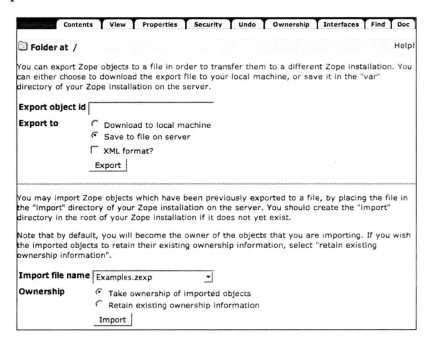

Zope's export/import mechanism can only be relied upon if the instance where an object was exported has exactly the same products and packages—including the same versions—as the instance where the file is to be imported.

Of course, this process only works once. As soon as the live environment diverges from the development environment, you cannot easily synchronize the two. That is why it is so important to keep content (in the ZODB) and configuration (in GenericSetup profiles) separate.

It is also a good idea to periodically test any new code on a snapshot of the live database. In this case, you can copy the `Data.fs` file from the live environment into the development environment using the steps described earlier.

Zope as a Service

For production servers, you probably want each ZEO client and the ZEO server to be started when the system is booted. The exact procedure will vary depending on the operating system, but in general a startup script should run `bin/zeoserver start` and the equivalent commands for the ZEO clients to start these in daemon mode.

On Windows, each Zope instance can be installed as a Windows service, managed from the **Services** control panel. For example, this will install the primary instance as a service that is automatically started:

```
> bin\primary --startup=auto install
```

Note that the ZEO server still needs to be started as a standalone process.

For security reasons, you can let Zope assume the identity of a particular user when it runs. A common setup involves creating a new user called `zope` and installing the deployment buildout to the home directory of this dummy user. The `effective-user` directive in `zope.conf` can be used to set the user name to assume. In the buildout configuration, this can be set as follows:

```
[zeoserver]
...
effective-user = zope
...
[primary]
...
effective-user = zope
...
```

You may also wish to set up log rotation for the various files in `var/log`, using whatever log rotation solution is available for your operating system. Without this, the logs can grow without bounds. You can use the `event-log` and `z-log` options for the instance sections, and the `zeo-log` option for the ZEO server section to give an alternative path for the log files.

Backups and Database Maintenance

The `Data.fs` file that contains the ZODB when using the default FileStorage back-end is append-only. This means that the file will not shrink, even as objects are deleted, until it is *packed*. This brings some performance benefits, and also makes it possible to roll the database back to a previous version via the **Undo** tab in the ZMI—at least if there have not been too many complex changes.

The ZODB can be packed in the **Control_Panel** in the ZMI. This functionality is also exposed in the **Maintenance** control panel under **Site Setup** in Plone. When packing, you can give a number of days of revision history to keep. Setting this to 0 recovers the most space, but makes it impossible to go back if something goes wrong. Note that when the database is packed from the ZMI, a single backup copy of the database prior to packing is stored as `Data.fs.old`. You will need to remove this to realize any space savings.

When using ZEO, we can automate the packing of the database with the `zeopack` script. This is found under `utilities/ZODBTools/zeopack.py` where Zope is installed. Because it depends on the ZODB code, it will only run if the Zope `SOFTWARE_HOME` is in the `PYTHONPATH`.

 In practice, this means that to run this script directly, you need to set the environment variable `PYTHONPATH` to include `/path/to/zope/lib/python`. See Chapter 3 to learn more about the `SOFTWARE_HOME`.

However, the `plone.recipe.zope2zeoserver` buildout recipe places an appropriate wrapper for this script in `bin/zeopack` in the buildout environment. If ZEO is running on port 8100, we can thus pack the database using:

```
$ ./bin/zeopack -p 8100 -d 7
```

Here, we keep 7 days of revision history. Note that with a large database, this can take a long time and impact on server performance. `zeopack` will *not* create a backup `Data.fs.old` file.

When using FileStorage, the easiest way of backing up the database is to take a copy of `Data.fs`. This is safe so long as the ZEO server is shut down first. A more robust solution, however, is to use the `repozo.py` script, found alongside `zeopack.py`. This can back up the database while Zope is running, and is capable of making incremental backups from the revision history. Repozo is thus the preferred tool for backing up a Zope database.

The `plone.recipe.zope2instance` recipe creates a wrapper for `repozo.py` as `bin/repozo` inside the buildout. Run this without arguments to see the various options available. Here is how to create incremental backups of the `Data.fs` file in the `backups` directory (which we must create):

```
$ mkdir backups
$ ./bin/repozo -BvzQ -r backups -f var/filestorage/Data.fs
```

Should you need to restore a backup, you can create a new `Data.fs` file by using:

```
$ ./bin/repozo -Rv -r backups -o Data.fs
```

You should shut down Zope before attempting to restore a backup, and it is probably a good idea to make an extra copy of the possibly-corrupted `Data.fs` file before attempting to restore a backup over it. Of course, since the `Data.fs` file is completely self-contained, you can just as easily move it into your development environment for analysis and testing.

As always, you should schedule regular backups. `repozo` is efficient enough to be run daily or even more frequently. If you also schedule packing of the database with `zeopack`, you should be aware that every time the database is packed, `repozo` will need to take a full backup. It is therefore generally a good idea to have very frequent backups, and to pack the database less frequently.

Summary

In this chapter, we have covered:

- How a *live* server should be configured differently from a development instance
- What ZEO is, and how it is essential for serious deployments
- How to turn our development buildout into a deployment one
- How to move code and data between development, staging, and live environments
- Some tips for treating Zope as an operating-system level service
- Instructions on how to regularly pack and back up the ZODB

In the next chapter, we will look at how to configure Zope behind Apache and Varnish for improved resilience and performance.

17
Setting Up a Production Server

In the previous chapter, we learned how to configure Zope for a production environment, with ZEO enabled and all the development-mode and debug-mode settings turned off. Now it is time to make our site accessible to the outside world.

In this chapter, we will explain the concept of **virtual hosting**, making a Plone Site object inside the Zope root appear directly under a particular domain. We will also cover how to set up Apache, for added stability and control, as well as Varnish, a caching *reverse proxy*, in front of Zope.

Virtual Hosting

Up until now, we have accessed the Plone instance in our development environment with a URL such as `http://localhost:8080/optilux`. When we deploy this to a production server, we would like to make it available under a publicly accessible URL such as `http://optilux-cinemas.com`.

To achieve this, we must first configure the name servers handling the `optilux-cinemas.com` domain to point this at whichever IP address the server is running on. Contact your network administrator or domain name registrar if you are unsure how to do this.

We must then configure Zope (and later, Apache) to watch out for this domain name in requests coming from users' browsers and forward them to the appropriate *local* URL where the Plone site is found. Using this approach, it is even possible to have multiple Plone sites (or indeed any kind of web server) running on the same physical machine and being served up on different domains.

Using Zope Only

Zope supports virtual hosting via its **Virtual Host Monster** (**VHM**) feature. In modern Zope installations, a VHM object called `virtual_hosting` is automatically added to the Zope application root. In fact, the name of the VHM does not matter. So long as there is a VHM in the application root, Zope will be able to respond to virtual host requests. Click on the VHM in the ZMI to see its documentation.

The VHM is responsible for **rewriting** URLs. If the object at `http://localhost:8080/optilux/front-page` is accessed via an appropriately configured virtual host, its URL can seamlessly appear as `http://optilux-cinemas.com/front-page`. This affects various variables in the request, such as `ACTUAL_URL` and `URL1`, as well as the return value of objects' `absolute_url()` method.

The easiest way to enable virtual hosting is to add a host mapping directly in Zope. Click on the **Mappings** tab of the `virtual_hosting` object, and you should see a text box like the following:

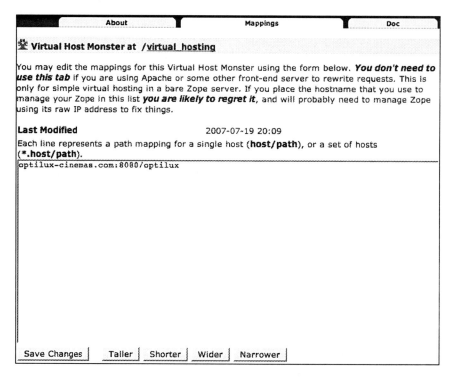

Here, we have added the line `optilux-cinemas.com:8080/optilux`. This means that if Zope receives a request to the domain `optilux-cinemas.com`, on port `8080`, it will map this to the `optilux` sub-object—in this case, our Plone site.

With this mapping enabled, you will not be able to access the ZMI on the mapped domain. In this case, you may need to use the raw IP address to gain access to the ZMI.

This presumes that the `optilux-cinemas.com` domain points to an IP address where Zope is listening. For testing, it can be useful to add a fake domain to `/etc/hosts` (`C:\Windows\System32\Drivers\etc\hosts` on Windows). For example, to make `optilux-cinemas.com` an alias for `localhost`, amend the hosts specifier for `127.0.0.1` as follows:

```
127.0.0.1          localhost optilux-cinemas.com
```

If you now try to access `optilux-cinemas.com`, it should resolve to your local machine.

If you start Zope as root, you should be able to change the HTTP port in `zope.conf` (e.g. via `buildout.cfg`, as shown in the previous chapter) to `80`, the standard web traffic port. Presuming you have no other web server running, this will mean that the site appears directly under `http://optilux-cinemas.com`, without the need to specify a port. If you do this, you will need to specify port `80`, not `8080`, in the VHM mapping.

Zope behind Apache

Configuring virtual hosts in Zope can be useful for simple sites, but most installations will place Zope behind another web server, such as Apache. While Zope is an excellent application server, its built-in web server cannot compete with Apache for resilience and features.

 If you followed the instructions in the previous section and added a virtual host mapping in Zope, remove it again before configuring Zope behind Apache.

The Apache web server is available for all modern operating systems. It comes pre-installed on most Linux servers, and there is a GUI installer for Windows. At the time of writing, Mac OS X ships with Apache 1.3 by default. However, you can use MacPorts (`http://macports.org`) to install Apache 2.2 in parallel.

 Make sure you turn off the **Personal Web Sharing** service in the **Sharing** preferences pane if you are running a separate Apache installation under Mac OS X.

For the remainder of this chapter, we will assume that Apache 2.2 or later is configured as the standard web server listening on port 80 for the IP address of your server. We will not cover Apache configuration in detail, showing only the parts specific to Zope integration. Please refer to http://httpd.apache.org for extensive documentation and examples.

Configuring Virtual Hosting and RewriteRules in Apache

Apache supports URL rewriting via the mod_rewrite module. We will use this to forward requests to Zope, and provide hints to the Zope VHM about the external URL for our site.

In Apache's httpd.conf (or an appropriate file included from this file), make sure that the mod_rewrite module and its dependencies are loaded:

```
LoadModule alias_module modules/mod_alias.so
LoadModule proxy_module modules/mod_proxy.so
LoadModule rewrite_module modules/mod_rewrite.so
```

The exact path to the modules may differ in your installation. Typically, these will either be enabled already or listed, but commented out with a leading #, in which case you should remove the comment markers from the appropriate lines. There will be numerous other modules loaded as well. Leave them as they are unless you know what you are doing.

Next, add the following near the bottom of httpd.conf, or in an appropriate included file.

```
NameVirtualHost 123.123.123.123:80

<VirtualHost 123.123.123.123:80>
        ServerName      optilux-cinemas.com
        RewriteEngine   on
        RewriteRule     ^(.*)   http://localhost:8080/VirtualHostBase/
http/optilux-cinemas.com:80/optilux/VirtualHostRoot/$1 [L,P]
</VirtualHost>
```

This defines a virtual host for the domain optilux-cinemas.com when requests come in to this IP address on port 80. Here, we assume the IP address of the server is 123.123.123.123. This should match the address specified in the Listen directive earlier in the configuration file:

```
Listen 123.123.123.123:80
```

Next, we turn on the rewrite engine, and add a single rule. This uses a regular expression matching any incoming URL and maps this to `http://localhost:8080/VirtualHostBase/http/optilux-cinemas.com:80/optilux/VirtualHostRoot/$1`. Here, `$1` is a wildcard representing the part of the incoming URL following `http://optilux-cinemas.com`.

The long internal URL is in fact valid and will be parsed by the VHM to determine how to treat the virtual host. Let us examine each slash-separated part in turn:

- First, `http://localhost:8080` refers to the Zope server we are forwarding to.

- Then, `VirtualHostBase` informs the VHM about the protocol and the host to rewrite to. In this case, the protocol is `http`, and the host is `optilux-cinemas.com:80`.

- Next, we specify the path to the object which is to act as the site root. Here, it is the `optilux` object under the Zope application root—our Plone site. The `VirtualHostRoot` item terminates the specification of the virtual host configuration.

- Subsequent parts to the URL will now represent objects inside the Optilux site. We tell Apache to take the matched portion of the URL from the preceding regular expression, and append it here. Thus, if the user entered `http://optilux-cinemas.com/front-page`, Zope will see `http://localhost:8080/VirtualHostBase/http/optilux-cinemas.com:80/optilux/VirtualHostRoot/front-page` and will adjust the URLs it generates appropriately so that links output from Plone appear within the domain `http://optilux-cinemas.com`.

Finally, `[L, P]` passes two flags to the rewrite rule. `L` will cause Apache to stop trying to match rewrite rules after this one has matched, which is usually a good idea should you have more than one rule in effect. `P` invokes `mod_proxy`, which performs the mapping of incoming URLs from the external domain (`http://optilux-cinemas.com`) to Zope's domain (`http://localhost:8080`).

With this configuration in place, you should be able to restart Apache and access the site on `http://optilux-cinemas.com`, assuming Zope is running and that a Plone site exists at `/optilux` inside the Zope application root.

 You will not be able to access the root of the ZMI from the virtual host. For that, you should connect to port 8080 (or whichever port Zope is running on) directly.

We have only scratched the surface of what you can do with *virtual hosts* and *rewrite rules*. For example, it is possible to serve certain parts of a site from disk using Apache, or to automatically redirect certain URLs to an SSL connection. Please consult the Apache documentation for more information.

Caching

Web traffic is difficult to predict. Many sites suffer great peaks and troughs in load over a day or a year. However, a large number of users will essentially view identical pages. Having Plone re-compose an identical page time and again is not a very good use of server resources.

Given the amount of work Plone has to do to build each page, it can typically only handle 6-10 requests per second on average hardware. Simple web servers, which do not dynamically construct each response, can be much, much quicker, often managing hundreds of requests per second on equivalent hardware. For this reason, most production sites will use some form of caching. By avoiding constantly re-calculating expensive pages, this can dramatically boost performance.

Plone sites typically use three main types of caching:

- Direct caching of expensive calculations in an application. This is purely a developer task and is, by definition, application-specific.

- Caching of pages (or parts of pages) in RAM. This can be configured from within Zope.

- Caching of pages and other resources in a separate caching reverse proxy such as Squid or Varnish.

Caching is a complex topic. Cache too little, and performance suffers. Cache too much, and users may see out-of-date or inconsistent content. Sometimes we can afford to show slightly outdated content to anonymous users, but require up-to-the-minute information for logged-in users. Luckily, Plone comes with an optional extra called **CacheFu**, which takes care of the most common settings.

Setting Up CacheFu

CacheFu is a collection of old-style products. You can obtain it from `http://plone.org/products/cachefu`. Make sure you download the appropriate version for your version of Plone. You can add the download URL to the deployment buildout as we have done for other dependencies in previous chapters. Or, if you wish to keep the cache configuration on the live server only, you can just as easily extract it into the `products` directory.

The example code for this chapter includes CacheFu 1.1 and sets up a simple Varnish 1.0 configuration, as explained below.

You can install **CacheSetup** from the **Add-on products** control panel under **Site Setup** in Plone. Once it is installed, you should see a new **Cache Configuration** control panel. This offers detailed control over the caching policy, but aims to provide you with sensible defaults.

On the **Main** tab, you can enable and disable CacheFu as a whole, and choose which caching policy to use. A **caching policy** is a collection of caching rules optimized for a particular scenario. The default policy will suffice for most users. You can also create your own policies.

You should then choose your overall server configuration: Zope on its own, Zope behind Apache, or Zope behind Squid/Varnish behind Apache using virtual hosting. This informs CacheFu whether and how it should tell the caching proxy to purge cached pages when they change in Plone. You should also enter all the domains through which the site can be accessed. For example, you could enter `http://optilux-cinemas.com:80` and `http://www.optilux-cinemas.com:80`, if these were both valid domains for the site. If you have Squid or Varnish configured, enter the URL and port of the cache proxy as well.

The **Policy** tab is used to manage the various caching policies installed, and to create new policies if necessary. The policy to edit is chosen in drop-down boxes on the **Headers** and **Rules** tabs. Note that it is possible to edit one policy while another is active. The active policy is chosen from the **Main** tab.

The **Headers** tab contains the configuration of various HTTP **header sets** that may be sent out by CacheFu. These are used to inform the browser and any caching proxies what can and cannot be cached, and for how long. The standard sets will usually suffice unless you know what you are doing.

Header sets are invoked by various **caching rules**, configured under the **Rules** tab. The order here matters—the first matching rule will be used. Again, the defaults are probably sensible, but you should configure application-specific content types and templates to optimize performance.

In the future, CacheFu may allow third-party products to register themselves more easily with the cache policy using GenericSetup. Even now, it is possible to change the policy from Python code executed during product installation. However, some manual tweaking will usually be necessary for non-trivial setups.

Caching the Optilux Content Types and Views

Let us now configure the Optilux content types and custom views in CacheFu. First, click on the **Content** entry under the **Rules** tab. This sets cache headers on standard, non-folderish content items. Here, we can select *Attached file*, *Attached image* (these are used by the RichDocument product), *Film*, *Web page*, and *Promotion* in addition to the default selection.

By default, these will be cached in the proxy for up to one hour for anonymous users. This means that content can be at most one hour out of date, which is probably an acceptable trade-off for non-logged in users.

For logged-in users, content is cached with an **ETag** that includes various data, such as the member ID and the time the object was last changed. An ETag is a cache key, which is sent to the browser to help it decide whether to show a cached copy of the page or fetch it again. This should ensure that logged-in members see a cached version if the content item is not changed. However, different users do not share the same cached copy, making it possible to cache personalized pages. The ETag is set to be valid for an hour (3600 seconds), after which the object will be re-fetched anyway.

For folderish content types, we need to be a little less aggressive, because views of folders are impacted by children being added, removed, or changed. This makes it harder to ensure that a copy of a page held in the cache proxy is consistent with other pages the user may see. In the **Containers** entry, select *Cinema*, *Cinema Folder*, and *Film Folder*. With these settings, even anonymous users see content cached in memory in Zope only.

There are many more configuration options, and you can create your own policies, rules, and header sets to carefully control caching. Doing so may require a deeper understanding of web caching concepts than we have space for here, but there are plenty of good references online. You should also consult the documentation that comes with CacheFu.

Using Varnish as a Caching Reverse Proxy

Even without a caching proxy between Zope and the browser, CacheFu can produce significant performance gains by caching pages in memory and giving browsers useful hints about caching items locally. For the greatest performance gains, however, you should use a caching **reverse proxy**.

 Reverse here refers to the fact that the cache proxy sits immediately before the web server caching *outgoing* content. By contrast, a *forward proxy* sits near the browser and caches *incoming* content.

Traditionally, Squid (`http://www.squid-cache.org`) has been the cache proxy of choice. It is a very mature, very powerful application. Unfortunately, it can also be tricky to set up and fully understand. Therefore, we will describe a more recent, purpose-built reverse proxy called Varnish instead. You will find plenty of information on setting up Squid on its official website and elsewhere online.

 When using Squid or Varnish with Apache, make sure to configure CacheFu for a "Squid/Varnish in behind Apache" scenario, and enter the host and port of the caching proxy on the **Main** tab of the CacheFu configuration screen.

Varnish works best on Linux and other UNIX-like operating systems. It is not available for Windows.

 If you are in a Windows environment, consider the commercial product Enfold Proxy. See `http://enfoldsystems.com`.

At the time of writing, Varnish 1.1.1 had just been released. However, various reports indicated stability problems when using this release with Plone. Therefore, we will describe a Varnish 1.0 configuration here. This version is more mature, but please note that it lacks some features, notably support for multilingual content (via the so-called "Vary" header) and Mac OS X.

See the Varnish home page at `http://varnish-cache.org` for installation instructions. Once you have Varnish installed, you will need to create an appropriate configuration file for Plone. There is one called `plone.vcl` included with this book, which should suffice for the most common cases. It looks like this:

```
backend default {
    set backend.host = "127.0.0.1";
    set backend.port = "8080";
}
acl purge {
    "localhost";
}
sub vcl_recv {
    if (req.request != "GET" && req.request != "HEAD") {
        if (req.request == "PURGE") {
            if (!client.ip ~ purge) {
                error 405 "Not allowed.";
            }
            lookup;
```

```
            }
            pipe;
        }
        if (req.http.Expect) {
            pipe;
        }
        /* Do not cache other authorised content */
        if (req.http.Authenticate || req.http.Authorization) {
            pass;
        }
        /* We only care about the "__ac.*" cookies, used for
           authentication */
        if (req.http.Cookie && req.http.Cookie ~ "__ac(_(name|password|per
           sistent))?=") {
            pass;
        }
        if (req.http.Cookie && req.http.Cookie ~ "_ZopeId") {
            pass;
        }
        lookup;
    }
    sub vcl_hit {
        if (req.request == "PURGE") {
                set obj.ttl = 0s;
                error 200 "Purged";
        }
        deliver;
    }
    sub vcl_miss {
        if (req.request == "PURGE") {
                error 404 "Not in cache";
        }
        fetch;
    }

    sub vcl_fetch {
        if (!obj.valid) {
            error;
        }
        if (!obj.cacheable) {
            pass;
        }
        if (resp.http.Set-Cookie) {
            pass;
        }
        insert;
    }
```

At run-time, Varnish translates this to C code, compiles it as a dynamic library, and links it to the running Varnish daemon process, making it very efficient. Please refer to the VCL manual (run `man varnish` in a terminal) for full details on the **Varnish Configuration Language** (**VCL**). Briefly, this file:

- Specifies that the default *backend* (Varnish-speak for the server being cached) is running on localhost, port 8080
- Passes requests for other content through to Zope if the user is logged in, either via HTTP Basic authentication, or using cookie-based authentication

To start Varnish on port 8082 with this configuration file, keeping its cache in a 1Gb file called `cache-storage`, run:

```
$ varnishd -a localhost:8082 -f plone.vcl -s file,cache-storage,1G
```

You may want to start this as a service in the same way that Apache and Zope are started for your operating system.

Adjusting the Apache Configuration

Varnish will proxy Zope directly—any request that can be made to `localhost:8080` can be made equally to `localhost:8082` where it may or may not result in a cached response. To make sure that the virtual host uses the cache, we must adjust the `RewriteRule` we added to the Apache configuration earlier in this chapter:

```
RewriteRule    ^(.*)   http://localhost:8082/VirtualHostBase/http/
optilux-cinemas.com:80/optilux/VirtualHostRoot/$1 [L,P]
```

Only the port is changed. Requests to `http://optilux-cinemas.com` should now be cached.

Varnish via Buildout

If Varnish is not available as a package for your operating system, or if you want to tie the configuration of Varnish into your deployment buildout, you can employ the `plone.recipe.varnish` buildout recipe to download, compile, and configure Varnish.

To use it, add the following to your `buildout.cfg` or `deployment.cfg`:

```
[buildout]
parts =
    ...
    varnish-build
    varnish-instance
```

```
...

[varnish-build]
recipe = plone.recipe.varnish:build
url = http://puzzle.dl.sourceforge.net/sourceforge/varnish/varnish-
1.0.4.tar.gz

[varnish-instance]
recipe = plone.recipe.varnish:instance
bind = 127.0.0.1:8082
cache-size = 1G
config = ${buildout:directory}/plone.vcl
```

 The URL here is used to download Varnish and points to the latest "known good" version at the time of writing, but check `http://varnish-cache.org` to see if there is a later version and adjust the URL accordingly.

With this buildout configuration, the Varnish daemon would bind to port `8082` on 1ocalhost, using the specified configuration file. The recipe will generate wrapper scripts for all the Varnish binaries. To start Varnish, run:

```
$ ./bin/varnish-instance
```

The recipe can also generate suitable configuration files for Varnish 1.1 and later. To learn more about the options available, see the `plone.recipe.varnish` page in the Cheese Shop, at `http://cheeseshop.python.org/pypi/plone.recipe.varnish`.

Benchmarking

Tuning cache configuration can be difficult. Careful testing is usually needed, both to watch out for overly stale content, and to find out where the performance suffers. There are numerous tools to help benchmark performance and spot problems. We will not cover any in great depth here, but **ApacheBench** is a useful, simple tool for quick-and-dirty performance testing. It comes installed with Apache and can be run like this:

```
$ ab -n 100 -c 3 http://127.0.0.1:8080/optilux/front-page
```

This will run 100 requests, at most 3 concurrently, fetching the front page of the `optilux` Plone instance. If you have followed the examples in this chapter, try that command first on a Plone site without CacheFu installed, then on a site with CacheFu configured, and finally on a URL where Varnish is doing its magic, for example via:

```
$ ab -n 100 -c 3 http://127.0.0.1:8081/optilux/front-page
```

You may be surprised to see the difference in the key measures, such as requests-per-second.

To find out more about the types of options supported by ApacheBench, run:

```
$ ab -h
```

ApacheBench only downloads the URL you give it, not style sheets, images, or other resources that the browser would normally download. Naturally, it also does not have a local cache as web browsers do. Therefore, it is mostly useful for investigating comparative performance.

Additionally, it can be very instructive to use the Firebug plug-in to Firefox (http://getfirebug.com) to observe the traffic going between the browser and the web server:

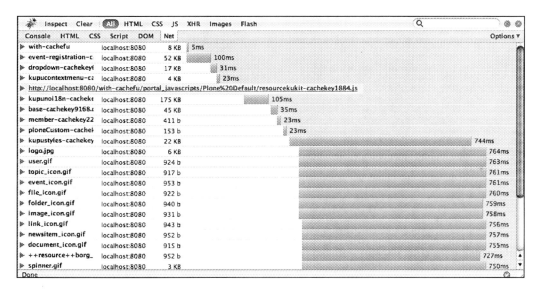

Here, we can see the time taken to fetch the entire page, broken down into each request made. Looking at the response headers for a particular item, we can see that various cache headers have been set. This can be invaluable in diagnosing problems with items being cached either too aggressively or not at all.

Finally, if you are using Varnish, you can use the `varnishstat` program to see live cache statistics, including cache hits and misses. This can help you diagnose suboptimal performance or stale content caused by under-caching or over-caching.

Summary

In this chapter, we have covered:

- How to configure virtual hosting in Zope only, to get a Plone site to appear directly under a particular domain
- How to use RewriteRules to perform virtual hosting with Apache in front of Zope
- How to install and configure CacheFu to set up a suitable caching policy for a Plone site
- How to configure a reverse caching proxy — Varnish — in front of Zope to dramatically improve performance

In the next chapter, we will look at how to connect Plone to an LDAP repository for user authentication.

18
Authenticating with LDAP

Up until now, we have stored users and groups in the ZODB, using Plone's built-in member management functionality. This works great for standalone sites, but many organizations have centralized user databases, which are often held in LDAP or Microsoft Active Directory repositories. Using an external user database means that site members do not have to be explicitly created in Plone, and that users can keep the same username and password across multiple systems.

In this chapter, we will look at how to connect Plone to LDAP and Active Directory. We will also briefly look at how to manually configure and prioritize plug-ins for PAS, Zope's Pluggable Authentication Service.

LDAP and Active Directory

LDAP is not black-magic voodoo, even if it can feel that way sometimes. It is in fact very logical, but it uses unfamiliar terminology and relies on precise specifications of how things are stored and searched. Luckily, it is not very difficult to connect to an existing repository for authentication in Plone, provided its configuration is not too esoteric, and you know a few key details about its configuration. The administrator for your organization's LDAP repository should be able to provide this information.

 The tools described in this chapter support both standard LDAP and Active Directory. However, creating users and groups from Plone is only supported with standard LDAP.

A detailed guide to LDAP is beyond the scope of this book. To learn more, please consult a good LDAP reference or the documentation that comes with OpenLDAP or Active Directory. Before we dive in, however, let us define a few key terms.

LDAP term	Meaning
LDAP	Lightweight Directory Access Protocol. We will focus on LDAP v3, which is the current version.
OpenLDAP	A popular open-source LDAP server implementation.
Active Directory	Microsoft's directory tool, which exposes an LDAP interface.
LDAP entry	A record in the LDAP directory, for example representing a user or a group.
LDIF	LDAP Data Interchange Format. LDAP entries can be imported and exported as plain-text files in this format.
Schema	Defines the object classes and permitted attributes for LDAP entries. It is possible to define your own schema, but most implementations will use one of the standard schemata, such as **core** or **cosine**.
Attribute	A piece of information about an LDAP entry, such as a line of a user's address, a photo, or a telephone number.
Object class	Declares optional and mandatory attributes for an LDAP entry. Each entry has one or more object classes, much as an object in Python is instantiated from a class that may have additional base classes.
Structural object class	The primary (or "core") object class of an entry in the repository. An entry must have exactly one structural object class, but may have additional classes defining secondary attributes.
DN (distinguished name)	A unique, canonical reference to an LDAP entry, e.g. a unique specifier for a particular user. A distinguished name consists of several attribute-value pairs. For example, the DN "*cn=Manager,dc=optilux-cinemas,dc=com*" means "the object with the common name *Manager*, under the domain *optilux-cinemas.com*".
CN (common name)	The common (full) name of a person or group. Can be configured as the login name or user ID, but is most often used as the "full name" property in Plone.
UID (user ID)	A unique ID for a user. Can be configured as the login name or user ID.
DC (domain component)	Part of a domain name, used to specify the domain of a particular resource. For example, the domain `optilux-cinemas.com` would be expressed as "dc=optilux-cinemas, dc=com".

LDAP term	Meaning
OU (organizational unit)	An organizational unit logically groups entries. In the simple schema we will use later, all users are in an OU called "people" and all groups are in an OU called "groups". Organizational units may be nested.
Root DN	In OpenLDAP, this is the DN of a user that has overall administrative control.
Relative DN	A single attribute-value pair as used in a DN. When creating new users through Plone, a relative DN is used to construct a proper DN for the new user.

Setting up a Test Environment

To demonstrate LDAP connectivity, we will create a simple LDAP repository with OpenLDAP. If you already have an LDAP server configured or you are using Active Directory, you can skip this section.

OpenLDAP can be downloaded from `http://openldap.org`. Many operating systems will also have OpenLDAP pre-installed or available as a pre-configured package.

OpenLDAP is configured with a configuration file normally found in `/etc/openldap/slapd.conf`. On the author's test system, it looks like this:

```
include        /etc/openldap/schema/core.schema
include        /etc/openldap/schema/cosine.schema
pidfile        /var/run/slapd.pid
argsfile /var/run/slapd.args
database   bdb
suffix     "dc=optilux-cinemas,dc=com"
rootdn     "cn=Manager,dc=optilux-cinemas,dc=com"
rootpw     secret
directory /var/openldap-data
index  objectClass    eq
```

There are many more configuration options, and the settings above are not necessarily appropriate for a production system. See the man page for `slapd.conf` for more details.

Authenticating with LDAP

This example configuration includes the *core* and *cosine* schemata, which means that we can use object classes and attributes defined in these files. The *cosine* schema is quite extensive, and includes a lot of commonly useful attributes. Next, we define some runtime files, and then choose a Berkley DB back-end storage. Entries here will be suffixed with the domain components for the `optilux-cinemas.com` domain. The root DN is set to "*cn=Manager,dc=optilux-cinemas,dc=com*", with a clear-text password "*secret*".

For production systems, you should not use a clear-text password! See the *man page* of `slapd.conf` and the `ldappassword` command for information about how to encrypt the password, and otherwise configure access rights to the LDAP repository. Also, the `slapd.conf` file should *not* be world-readable.

We should also create some entries in the repository. The file `optilux.ldif` found in the `extra` directory in the book's accompanying source code contains a bare-bones repository with one user and one group. It looks like this:

```
version: 1
# Top level - the organization
dn: dc=optilux-cinemas,dc=com
dc: optilux-cinemas
description: Optilux Corporation
objectClass: dcObject
objectClass: organization
o: Optilux Corporation

# Top level - manager
dn: cn=Manager,dc=optilux-cinemas,dc=com
objectclass: organizationalRole
cn: Manager

# Second level - organizational units
dn: ou=people, dc=optilux-cinemas,dc=com
ou: people
description: All people in the organization
objectclass: organizationalunit

dn: ou=groups, dc=optilux-cinemas,dc=com
ou: groups
description: All groups in the organization
objectclass: organizationalunit

# Third level - people
dn: uid=ssmith,ou=people,dc=optilux-cinemas,dc=com
objectClass: pilotPerson
objectClass: uidObject
```

```
uid: ssmith
cn: Susan Smith
sn: Smith
userPassword:: e1NIQX01ZW42RzZNZXpScm9UM1hLcWtkUE9tWS9CZlE9
mail: ssmith@optilux-cinemas.com
# Third level - groups
dn: cn=Staff,ou=groups,dc=optilux-cinemas,dc=com
objectClass: top
objectClass: groupOfUniqueNames
cn: Staff
uniqueMember: uid=ssmith,ou=people,dc=optilux-cinemas,dc=com
```

Here, we define an organization called *Optilux Corporation* corresponding to the domain component *optilux-cinemas* under the domain optilux-cinemas. com. This contains two **organizational units**: *people* and *groups*. We then add one user—*ssmith*—to the *people* OU, and one group—*Staff*—to the *groups* OU. The userPassword property is an SHA1 hash (as indicated by the double colons) of the user's password, which happens to also be the string *secret*.

 In Chapter 6, we added code to the setuphandlers.py file of the optilux.policy product to create a *Staff* group in Plone itself. If the group is coming from LDAP instead, as it is above, we should remove this setup step so that we do not end up with two groups with the same name.

To import the LDIF file, run the following command after starting slapd, the LDAP daemon.

```
$ ldapadd -xWD 'cn=Manager,dc=optilux-cinemas,dc=com' -f optilux.ldif
```

You can use the ldapsearch command to query the repository. However, it may be easier to use a graphical browser such as the LDAP Browser/Editor, available from http://www-unix.mcs.anl.gov/~gawor/ldap.

Connecting Plone to an LDAP Repository

To use LDAP from Python, we must first install the python-ldap module. This can be downloaded from http://python-ldap.sourceforge.net, or installed using your operating system's package management tools if applicable.

To use LDAP in Plone, we will need few add-on products. First, get the appropriate version of the PloneLDAP bundle from http://plone.org/products/ploneldap. This contains three Zope 2 products: PloneLDAP, LDAPUserFolder, and LDAPMultiPlugins. As before, you can either add the relevant download URL to the [productdistros] section of a buildout.cfg file, or extract the products to the products/ directory of your buildout or instance.

Secondly, we must install the `simplon.plone.ldap` egg, either by adding it to the `eggs` list in `buildout.cfg` or by listing it as a dependency in the `setup.py` file of another package. It has a ZCML file, which needs to be loaded, so we should either add a ZCML slug (by listing the package under the `zcml` option of the `[instance]` section in `buildout.cfg`), or explicitly include it from the `configure.zcml` file of the policy product as we did with `borg.project`, for example.

With these products installed, re-start Zope and install **LDAP Support** from Plone's **Add-on products** control panel.

You should *not* install the **LDAPUserFolder CMF Tools** product. This is a relic of the LDAPUserFolder dependency and will not work properly with Plone.

With LDAP support in place, you should see a new **LDAP Connection** control panel under **Site Setup**. It looks like this:

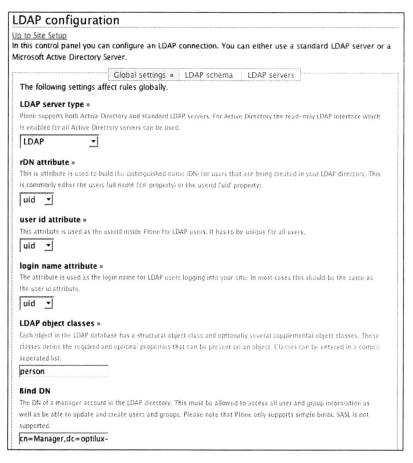

Let us go through the settings we would enter for the example repository we set up earlier, starting with the **Global settings** tab:

- The **LDAP server type** can be LDAP or Active Directory. We use the former.

- The **rDN attribute** (relative distinguished name) is used as the first part of the DN for users being created through Plone. It is most commonly the same as the attribute used for the user ID. We will opt for the *uid* attribute here.

- The **User ID attribute** gives the attribute used for user IDs in Plone. We will use the *uid* here as well.

- The **Login name attribute** is used during authentication. It will normally be the same as the user ID attribute. Again, we will use the *uid*.

> With Active Directory, you can use either *userPrincipalName* or *sAMAccountName* as the user ID and login name (the *objectGUID* property will not work, since Plone does not support binary user IDs). The difference between the two is that *userPrincipalName* includes the full domain, while *sAMAccountName* contains the plain user name only. The *sAMAccountName* attribute is the best choice if your Active Directory is configured for a single domain only, but may not be unique if you are using multiple domains.

- The **LDAP object classes** field gives the structural object class, and any additional object classes (separated by commas) applied to new users created via Plone. We use *pilotPerson,uidObject*, which means that we get a simple user object with a UID.

- The **Bind DN** is the DN used by Plone to access the LDAP repository. We will use the root DN, *cn=Manager,dc=optilux-cinemas,dc=com*.

- The **Bind password** is the password for the user listed under the **Bind DN**. We set this to the string *secret* in `slapd.conf`.

- The **Base DN for users** gives the location of users in the repository. Recall that we created users under the organizational unit *people*. Thus, we enter *ou=people,dc=optilux-cinemas,dc=com* here.

- The **Search scope for users** option defines whether users are found directly under the base OU only, or in sub-units as well. For our example, there is only one level anyway, so it does not matter what we choose, but *subtree* is the more common option.

- The **Base DN for groups** tells Plone where in the repository to find groups. Here, we will enter *ou=groups,dc=optilux-cinemas,dc=com*.

- The **Search scope for groups** option is akin to **Search scope for users**. Again, we choose *subtree*, although it does not make much difference to our example.

Do not forget to save the form before moving on to the other tabs.

On the **LDAP schema** tab, you can map LDAP attributes to Plone member properties. Member properties were described in Chapter 13.

By default, the *uid* attribute is defined but not mapped to any Plone properties. This makes it available as a possible user ID, login name, or relative DN under the **Global settings** tab. Similarly, the *sn* (surname) property is entered, but not mapped to a Plone property. We will not use this for anything, but having it here means that it will be entered in the directory with a dummy value when users are created through Plone. This is necessary since the *sn* property is mandatory for the *pilotPerson* structural object class we are using.

The *mail* attribute is mapped to the *email* property and the *cn* attribute is mapped to the *fullname* property. These last two properties are used frequently in the Plone user interface, and should always be mapped.

It is possible to mix standard Plone properties and LDAP-based properties for the same user. When searching for a property value, PAS will look at the available *property sheets* one by one, stopping at the first sheet it finds with the required property. With LDAP support installed, the LDAP-backed property sheet comes first, followed by the standard Plone property sheet.

To map a new property, click **Add property** and fill in the required details.

Finally, we must configure one or more servers on the **LDAP servers** tab. If multiple servers are defined, they will be tried in the order they are listed when attempting to access the repository. Click the **Add LDAP server** button, and enter the host name, connection type, and other options as requested.

If you have followed the examples and are using the example repository from this chapter, you can now test the configuration by logging in as user *ssmith* with password *secret*. You should also be able to create users and groups in Plone, and have them appear in the LDAP repository.

Configuring PAS Plug-ins Manually

Under the hood, the LDAP configuration is just a PAS plug-in, which is configured to work through a number of **PAS interfaces**. With LDAP installed and configured, take a look at the `ldap` object inside `acl_users` in the root of your Plone site in the ZMI:

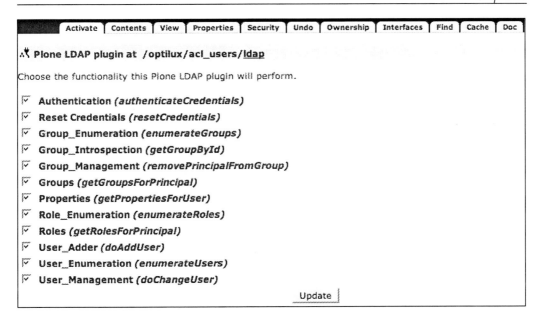

These interfaces perform various functions as part of the user management process. To disable an interface completely, uncheck the corresponding box and click **Update**.

To learn more about the role played by each PAS interface, look at the `plugins` object inside `acl_users`.

If you click on an interface, you will be able to configure the active plug-ins used to perform the relevant task. For example, click on **Properties**, and you will see the following screen:

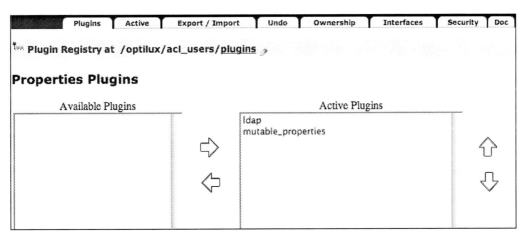

This means that when searching for user properties, PAS will first try the `ldap` plug-in, and then fall back on the `mutable_properties` plug-in (the standard properties plug-in used by Plone), before giving up. Select a plug-in, and use the up/down arrows to the change the priority order.

For the purposes of the Optilux application, we may want to let staff members come from the LDAP repository, but have external users that sign up to the site themselves be created in Plone only. In this case, we need to change the priority for the `User_Adder` interface. Click on **User_Adder Plugins** under `plugins` in `acl_users`, and then move the `source_users` plug-in to the top, above the `ldap` plug-in:

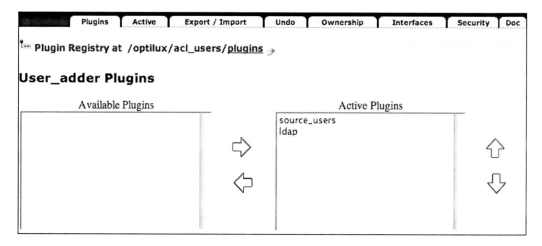

Now, the `ldap` plug-in will only be used if the `source_users` plug-in fails. If you wish to disable LDAP user creation entirely, move the `ldap` plug-in to the **Available plugins** list by selecting it and clicking the left arrow.

To learn more about the various PAS interfaces and plug-ins, you should consult the PAS reference guide at `http://plone.org/documentation/manual/pas-reference-manual`.

Summary

In this chapter, we have covered:

- A brief introduction to LDAP and its terminology
- How to set up a minimal LDAP repository for testing
- The Plone add-on products that enable LDAP connectivity
- How to configure LDAP for authentication and map LDAP attributes to Plone member properties
- How to configure the PAS interfaces exposed by the LDAP plug-ins in detail manually

In the next chapter, we will look at how to manage future upgrades and releases.

19
Looking to the Future

We are nearly at an end. Over the past eighteen chapters, we have learned how to build and deploy robust Plone 3 applications. We have seen key principles and professional development practices illustrated through a realistic case study. And hopefully, you now feel equipped to apply these principles and practices to your own Plone development projects.

In this chapter, we will briefly look at how to manage future releases and migrations, before recapping on our achievements to date and offering a few pointers to additional resources.

Making Future Releases

As any seasoned developer will know, it is much easier (or at least more fun) to build an application from scratch than to extend and maintain an existing one. Plone-based systems are no exception, but there are a few tips that can make life a little easier when the time comes to update or patch an application that is already live.

- In Chapter 4, we discussed the dangers of relying on settings changed manually through the Web. It becomes very difficult to manage multiple versions of a code base if you cannot reliably and automatically set up a blank instance of the site in a test environment. Use a *policy product*, and a GenericSetup base or extension profile to formalize your application configuration as we have done throughout this book. Resist the temptation to make a configuration change on a live server without making sure that this change is represented in developers' sandboxes.

- In Chapter 16, we described the flow of code from a development environment to a live server. Code travels *forwards*, and should only be changed in a development sandbox. When it has been properly tested, it can be moved to staging and live environments. Data travels *backwards*. The ZODB `Data.fs` file on the live server can be copied to a staging or development environment for testing and analysis, but should never be overwritten by data from another environment. You will be in trouble if you start to make code changes on a production server or overwrite live data with older data from another server.

- Test. Test again. Then test some more. There is absolutely no excuse for not having automated unit and integration tests for your code. The author would never pay money for code that was not covered by automated tests. At the same time, you must perform manual testing and sanity checks on the final functionality. This is doubly true when managing multiple versions of code across multiple environments and dealing with migration code.

- When a new code release is ready, set up a test server with a snapshot of the `Data.fs` file from the live environment. If you have written migration scripts, run them and make sure that they work as expected. If things to awry, return to the development environment, and attempt to reproduce the problem in a unit test. Then fix the problem and try again.

- Use version control. Even if you are the only developer on a project, not having source code version control is bordering on being reckless. It is essential to be able to roll back to previous versions of the code, and tag a *known good* collection of packages for a release.

- Keep good backups. This goes without saying.

In other words: prevention is the best medicine when it comes to managing multiple versions of code.

The extensive use of unit and integration tests for the code in this book was not only done to demonstrate good practices. It was the only way the author could have any confidence in the code, given the many versions of the code that had to be maintained in parallel.

When writing the example code for this book, the author used a local Subversion repository and checked in code for each chapter, with sensible log messages and in logically related change sets, just as he does when working on Plone itself. Each chapter essentially had its own *branch* of the code base. This made it much easier to track and merge changes when errors or omissions were found in one chapter and needed to be propagated to different versions of the code.

Managing Migrations

If you have deployed an application and subsequently made a change to its code, you may need a migration script if any of the following are true:

- Have you changed the GenericSetup profile or installation script for your product? Does the new code depend on settings made with the new installation routine? Often, it will be sufficient for users to re-install the product, but this can sometimes undo configuration settings that the user may have changed.

- Have you changed variables and data structures that are stored as part of content objects the ZODB? If so, you may need to migrate existing objects.

- Have you fixed a bug that caused existing data to be persisted in an incorrect state? You may need to migrate old data that is still affected by the defect.

In all cases, the process is the same: write and run a script or function that configures the portal and updates persistent objects appropriately.

If you used an extension profile to install a product, you can use GenericSetup's **upgrade step** support to manage migration scripts and make them available in the `portal_setup` tool. When using this, it is important to keep track of which version is in fact the current one. GenericSetup can either read this from a `version.txt` file in the root of your product, or from a `metadata.xml` file that is part of your product's installation profile.

For example, we could have the following in `profiles/default/metadata.xml` in a fictitious `guitar.shop` product:

```
<?xml version="1.0"?>
<metadata>
  <description>Guitar Shop</description>
  <version>1.3</version>
</metadata>
```

When making a new release that requires migration, make sure that you bump the version number appropriately.

Upgrade steps are written as Python functions and are registered with ZCML. For example:

```
<configure
    xmlns="http://namespaces.zope.org/zope"
    xmlns:genericsetup="http://namespaces.zope.org/genericsetup"
    i18n_domain="guitar.shop">

  <!-- Installation profile -->
```

```
    <genericsetup:registerProfile
        name="default"
        title="Guitar Shop"
        directory="profiles/default"
        description="Extension profile for the Guitar Shop product."
        provides="Products.GenericSetup.interfaces.EXTENSION"
        for="Products.CMFPlone.interfaces.IPloneSiteRoot"
        />
    <!-- Upgrade step for the migration -->
    <genericsetup:upgradeStep
        sortkey="1"
        source="1.0"
        destination="1.1"
        title="Upgrade from 1.0 to 1.1"
        description="Fixes the front page title"
        profile="guitar.shop:default"
        handler=".upgrades.v1_0_to_v1_1"
        />

    <!-- Here is another upgrade, from 1.1 to 1.2. This one has two
    steps -->
    <genericsetup:upgradeSteps
        sortkey="2"
        source="1.1"
        destination="1.2"
        profile="guitar.shop: default"
        >
        <genericsetup:upgradeStep
            title="Upgrade titles"
            description="Fix all other titles"
            handler=".upgrades.v1_1_to_v1_2a"
            />
        <genericsetup:upgradeStep
            title="Upgrade site title"
            description="Fixes a typo with the portal title"
            handler=".upgrades.v1_1_to_v1_2b"
            />
    </genericsetup:upgradeSteps>
    ...
</configure>
```

Here, we define two upgrade paths: upgrading from version 1.0 to 1.1 will call the function `v1_0_to_v1_1()` in `upgrades.py`. The upgrade from 1.1 to 1.2 is split into two parts, calling `v1_1_to_v1_2a()` and then `v1_1_to_v1_2b()`.

Notice how the upgrade step directive specifies the source and destination version for the upgrade step, as well as a sort key. Sort keys ensure that steps are run in the correct order when upgrading across multiple versions. Also note how the upgrade step explicitly references the extension profile that is being upgraded.

All upgrade step handler functions are passed the `portal_setup` tool as an argument. Since this is stored inside the Plone site root, it can be used as a base from which to acquire other tools or obtain the site root. Here are a few (frivolous) examples of the types of things an upgrade step may do:

```python
from Products.CMFCore.utils import getToolByName
def v1_0_to_v1_1(portal_setup):
    """This is a migration step, referenced from configure.zcml

    Here, we "fix" the portal front page.
    """
    portal_url = getToolByName(portal_setup, 'portal_url')
    portal = portal_url.getPortalObject()
    front_page = portal['front-page']
    front_page.setTitle('Welcome to the Guitar Shop')
def v1_1_to_v1_2a(portal_setup):
    """Here is another upgrade step, this one part of a two-step upgrade
    """
    portal_catalog = getToolByName(portal_setup, 'portal_catalog')
    for brain in portal_catalog(portal_type = 'Document'):
        brain.getObject().setTitle('All your base are belong to us!')
def v1_1_to_v1_2b(portal_setup):
    """This is the second step
    """
    portal_url = getToolByName(portal_setup, 'portal_url')
    portal = portal_url.getPortalObject()

    # typo in properties.xml - we should fix that one too!
    portal.manage_changeProperties(title="Guitar Shop")
```

Here is how this looks on the **Upgrades** tab of `portal_setup`:

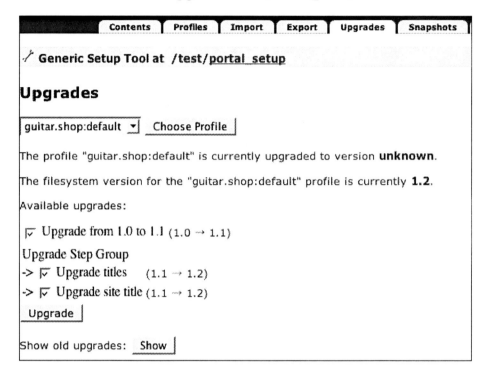

To run one or more upgrade steps, simply ensure that the relevant boxes are ticked, and click **Upgrade**. If you need to re-run upgrade steps that have already been run, you can find them by clicking the **Show** button.

Of course, the hard part is to actually write the migration code. Migration code can often be tricky, because it can be difficult to predict what state the live site may be in. Be defensive, and make no assumptions.

Migration Profiles

If you need to manage a large number of migrations, you may want to consider making a special extension profile for each version upgrade and invoking that migration profile as part of a migration step. Plone does this for many of its version migrations, for example:

```
<genericsetup:registerProfile
    name="1.2_to_1.3"
    title="Migration profile for Guitar Shop 1.2 to 1.3"
    description=""
```

```
           directory="profiles/migrations/v1_2_to_v1_3"
           for="Products.CMFPlone.interfaces.IMigratingPloneSiteRoot"
           provides="Products.GenericSetup.interfaces.EXTENSION"
           />
     <genericsetup:upgradeStep
          sortkey="3"
          source="1.2"
          destination="1.3"
          title="Upgrade from 1.2 to 1.3"
          description="Runs a migration profile"
          profile="guitar.shop:default"
          handler=".upgrades.v1_2_to_v1_3"
          />
```

First, we register an extension profile that will be used to change the site configuration during migration. Then we register an upgrade step that will invoke this profile. Notice how the extension profile is registered for the interface IMigratingPloneSiteRoot. This ensures that this profile does not show up during site creation or in Plone's **Add-on products** control panel.

We can now add XML files to the directory profiles/migrations/v1_2_to_v1_3 just as we would for a regular extension profile. For example, we could have the following in properties.xml:

```
<?xml version="1.0"?>
<site>
 <property name="title">The All New Guitar Shop</property>
</site>
```

The upgrade handler method is now as simple as:

```
def v1_2_to_v1_3(portal_setup):
    """This example invokes an extension profile which in turn
    performs a migration.
    """
    portal_setup.runAllImportStepsFromProfile(
                'profile-guitar.shop:1.2_to_1.3', purge_old=False)
```

We could add more setup code here if required. Specifically, *import-various* type import steps like the one in setuphandlers.py in the optilux.policy product from Chapter 6 are unnecessary. It is easier to perform any additional imperative configuration straight in the upgrade step handler function than to register a new import step.

Our Achievements

Finally, let us quickly summarize our achievements to date.

- In Chapter 1, we discussed Plone's history and community. The Plone community should always be the first place you turn to if you are stuck or want to get in touch with other developers.

- In Chapter 2, we introduced the Optilux Cinemas case study, setting the scene for the rest of the book.

- In Chapter 3, we learned how to set up a development environment, using zc.buildout to orchestrate various dependencies such as the Zope application server and Plone itself.

- In Chapter 4, we took a look at the various ways in which Plone can be customized and issued a few warnings about the perils of relying too much on persistent through-the-web settings that are difficult to reproduce across environments.

- In Chapter 5, we created a *policy product* to manage site policy decisions and configuration settings related to the case study application. We expanded this with new policies in nearly every subsequent chapter. We also emphasized the importance of automated unit and integration tests.

- In Chapter 6, we explored Plone's security model, and made the case for using workflow as the primary tool for implementing a security policy by showing how to install a custom workflow using GenericSetup.

- In Chapter 7, we demonstrated how to safely test, install, and customize Plone add-on products.

- In Chapter 8, we re-branded our growing application with a custom theme. This illustrated how to customize style sheets, templates, browser views, viewlets, and portlets—all without modifying the source code of Plone itself.

- In Chapter 9, we took a break from the example application to look deeper at nine core concepts underpinning Zope and Plone development. If you found that chapter a little fast-paced at first, you may want to go back to it now that you have had more time to see these techniques in practice.

- In Chapter 10, we dove into the most important skill Plone developers need: building custom content types with the Archetypes framework. We also created a custom portlet, using Plone 3's new portlets infrastructure.

- In Chapter 11, we looked in more detail at forms and other types of browser views. We used `zope.formlib` to generate forms with minimal configuration in Python. We also looked at ways of managing page flow, including the older CMFFormController product, and created viewlets—snippets that can be *plugged in* to the standard user interface at various points.

- In Chapter 12, we connected our application to an external relational database, using the SQLAlchemy library and a little bit of Zope glue. We also used some advanced features of the `zope.formlib` library to create a ticket reservations form and a Plone control panel to configure database connections.

- In Chapter 13, we looked at how to manage personalized information, building a form and a portlet to track a user's *preferred* cinema.

- In Chapter 14, we improved the user experience of a few of the application's features by using KSS, the new AJAX framework adopted in Plone 3.

- In Chapter 15, we considered ways in which the example application could be taken further and briefly looked at issues of internationalization.

- In Chapter 16, we showed how to move the example application from a development environment to a production server using ZEO (Zope Enterprise Objects) for improved scalability and resilience.

- In Chapter 17, we configured Apache, the popular web server, and Varnish, a caching *reverse proxy*, in front of Zope, in order to improve performance, stability, and fault-tolerance.

- In Chapter 18, we connected Plone to an LDAP repository providing authentication services and user properties.

- Finally, in this chapter, we provided some tips on managing releases of a live application, and performing migrations.

Where to Go Next

Undoubtedly, you will have more questions after reading this book. Here are some places to turn to for answers:

- The Plone mailing lists, in particular the *plone-users* list, as well as the *#plone* IRC chat room on `irc.freenode.net`, are the natural places to ask questions and get in touch with the Plone community. See `http://plone.org/support`.

- The Plone website also contains a wealth of other information, such as the documentation at `http://plone.org/documentation`.

- Before attempting to solve a problem yourself by writing a new product, why not find out if others have already done the hard work for you? Make a habit of browsing `http://plone.org/products` or the Collective subversion repository at `http://svn.plone.org/svn/collective`. Even if you cannot find something that fits the bill perfectly, you will often find solutions to build on or learn from, or other developers with whom you can collaborate.

- Finally, should you need professional help, go to `http://plone.net` and look for a Plone consultant, developer, or trainer.

Summary

In this chapter, we have:

- Offered some tips about managing multiple versions of an application
- Demonstrated how to use the new GenericSetup upgrade-step functionality to invoke migration scripts
- Recapped on the key lessons from this book
- Provided a few pointers to additional resources

And that, as they say, is it.

I hope you have enjoyed this book, and that it has helped you become a better Plone developer. I have certainly enjoyed writing it. Developing with Plone can be a lot of fun—at least sometimes.

Most of all, however, I hope to see you on a Plone mailing list, in the Plone chat room or, better yet, at a Plone sprint or conference.

Index

Thank you for buying
Professional Plone Development

Packt Open Source Project Royalties

When we sell a book written on an Open Source project, we pay a royalty directly to that project. Therefore by purchasing Professional Plone Development, Packt will have given some of the money received to the Plone project.

In the long term, we see ourselves and you—customers and readers of our books—as part of the Open Source ecosystem, providing sustainable revenue for the projects we publish on. Our aim at Packt is to establish publishing royalties as an essential part of the service and support a business model that sustains Open Source.

If you're working with an Open Source project that you would like us to publish on, and subsequently pay royalties to, please get in touch with us.

Writing for Packt

We welcome all inquiries from people who are interested in authoring. Book proposals should be sent to authors@packtpub.com. If your book idea is still at an early stage and you would like to discuss it first before writing a formal book proposal, contact us; one of our commissioning editors will get in touch with you.

We're not just looking for published authors; if you have strong technical skills but no writing experience, our experienced editors can help you develop a writing career, or simply get some additional reward for your expertise.

About Packt Publishing

Packt, pronounced 'packed', published its first book "Mastering phpMyAdmin for Effective MySQL Management" in April 2004 and subsequently continued to specialize in publishing highly focused books on specific technologies and solutions.

Our books and publications share the experiences of your fellow IT professionals in adapting and customizing today's systems, applications, and frameworks. Our solution-based books give you the knowledge and power to customize the software and technologies you're using to get the job done. Packt books are more specific and less general than the IT books you have seen in the past. Our unique business model allows us to bring you more focused information, giving you more of what you need to know, and less of what you don't.

Packt is a modern, yet unique publishing company, which focuses on producing quality, cutting-edge books for communities of developers, administrators, and newbies alike. For more information, please visit our website: www.PacktPub.com.

Building Websites with Joomla! 1.5 Beta 1

ISBN: 978-1-847192-38-7   Paperback: 380 pages

The bestselling Joomla tutorial guide updated for the latest download release

1. Install and configure Joomla! 1.5 beta 1

2. Customize and extend your Joomla! site

3. Create your own template and extensions

4. **Free eBook upgrades up to 1.5 Final Release**

5. Also available covering Joomla v1

Alfresco Enterprise Content Management Implementation

ISBN: 1-904811-11-6   Paperback: 350 pages

How to Install, use, and customize this powerful, free, Open Source Java-based Enterprise CMS

1. **Manage your business documents:** version control, library services, content organization, and search

2. **Workflows and business rules:** move and manipulate content automatically when events occur

3. **Maintain, extend, and customize Alfresco:** backups and other admin tasks, customizing and extending the content model, creating your own look and feel

Please visit **www.PacktPub.com** for information on our titles

CherryPy Essentials

ISBN: 978-1-904811-84-8   Paperback: 272 pages

Design, develop, test, and deploy your Python web applications easily

1.   Walks through building a complete Python web application using CherryPy 3

2.   The CherryPy HTTP:Python interface

3.   Use CherryPy with other Python libraries

4.   Design, security, testing, and deployment

Building Websites with TYPO3

ISBN: 978-1-847191-11-3   Paperback: 250 pages

A practical guide to getting your TYPO3 website up and running fast

1.   A practical step-by-step tutorial to creating your TYPO3 website

2.   Install and configure TYPO3

3.   Master all the important aspects of TYPO3, including the backend, the frontend, content management, and templates

4.   Gain hands-on experience by developing an example site through the book

Please visit **www.PacktPub.com** for information on our titles

CPSIA information can be obtained at www.ICGtesting.com
Printed in the USA
243751LV00006B/2/A

9 781847 191984